W9-AAD-963

Algebra

AUTHOR
James T. Shea

CONSULTANT
Susan L. Beutel
Consulting/Resource Teacher
Lamoille North Supervisory Union, VT

ACKNOWLEDGMENTS

Executive Editor: Wendy Whitnah

Senior Math Editor: Donna Rodgers

Design Coordinator: John Harrison

Project Design
and Development: The Wheetley Company

Cover Design and
Electronic Production: John Harrison , Adolph Gonzalez and
Chuck Joseph

WORKING WITH NUMBERS SERIES:

Level A	Level D	Consumer Math
Level B	Level E	Refresher
Level C	Level F	Algebra

ISBN: 0-8114-5222-0

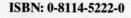

STECK-VAUGHN
C O M P A N Y
ELEMENTARY • SECONDARY • ADULT • LIBRARY

TABLE OF CONTENTS

You can think of algebra as a language of mathematics. Once you know this language, you will find that mathematical concepts and applications will be easier to understand. You also will find that many everyday-life problems will be easier to solve.

This book contains a number of features that will help you master the concepts and skills of algebra. Among these features are the following.

A Pretest and a Mastery Test

At the beginning of the book, the Pretest will tell you what material you may know already and what material you have not yet mastered.

At the end of the book, the Mastery Test will tell you what material you have learned and what you may need to review further.

Unit and Cumulative Reviews

Each unit concludes with a Unit Review that provides you with an opportunity to demonstrate your understanding of the skills and concepts presented in that particular unit.

Beginning with Unit 2, each unit also has a Cumulative Review that provides you with an opportunity to demonstrate your understanding of all the skills you have learned up to that point in the book.

Problem-Solving Strategies

A problem-solving strategy is an effective plan for solving a problem. There are two lessons in each unit on problem-solving strategies. Thus, by the time you finish the book, you will have learned fourteen different strategies for solving problems.

Answers and Some Solutions

The answers to all of the problems are provided in the back of the book. This allows you to check your work after it is completed. Solutions, or step-by-step explanations, are provided for selected problems. These take you through the steps used to solve the problems.

PRETEST

Write an algebraic expression for each verbal expression.

a	*b*
1. y multiplied by 6 _____	t increased by 2 _____

Evaluate each expression if $a = 8$, $b = 4$, and $c = 2$.

a	*b*	*c*	*d*
2. $ac + b =$	$\dfrac{a + b}{c} =$	$3b - 2c =$	$a + b - c =$

Solve.

a	*b*	*c*	*d*
3. $n = 4(3 + 2)$	$2s = 10$	$x = 3(2) + 4(1)$	$6 + y = 18$

Write the opposite of each integer.

a	*b*	*c*	*d*
4. -6	4	-31	56

Simplify.

a	*b*	*c*	*d*
5. $8 + (-15) =$	$-2 + (-6) =$	$9 - 15 =$	$6 - (-4) =$
6. $3(-5) =$	$(-2)(-6) =$	$\dfrac{-16}{-4} =$	$\dfrac{-18}{6} =$
7. $-3x + x + (-7x) =$	$27xy - 15xy =$	$3(1.5x) =$	$\dfrac{4.8t}{-6} =$
8. $5x + 2 + (x - 4) =$	$2y + 4 - (y + 6) =$	$\frac{1}{2}(18a - 10) =$	$3b - 4(b + 6) =$

Name _____ Date _____

Solve.

9. In the formula $A = lw$, find A when l is 5 inches and w is 25 inches.	**10.** In the formula $A = lw$, find w when A is 36 square meters and l is 9 meters.
11. In the formula $A = \pi r^2$, find A when r is 49 centimeters.	**12.** In the formula $V = lwh$, find w when V is 120 cubic inches, l is 8 inches, and h is 5 inches.
13. In the formula $I = prt$, find p when I is \$300, r is 4%, and t is 1 year.	**14.** In the formula $I = prt$, find I when p is \$800, r is 7%, and t is 3 years.
15. In the formula $C = (F - 32)\frac{5}{9}$, find C when F is 59°.	**16.** In the formula $F = (C \cdot \frac{9}{5}) + 32$, find F when C is 45°.

Solve.

	a	b	c	d
17.	$12x = 360$	$0.5y = 15$	$a + 6 = -10$	$b - 5 = 24$
18.	$\frac{n}{4} = 6$	$\frac{3x}{4} = -6$	$2n - 5 = 17$	$3s - 4s = -6$
19.	$8a - 5 = 3a + 15$	$2b + 6 = b - 4$	$3x - 2 = 2(x + 3)$	$4y - (2y + 6) = 10$
20.	$\frac{x}{3} + 5 = \frac{x}{6} + 2$	$\frac{a}{2} + 3 = \frac{2a}{8}$	$\frac{9}{t} = \frac{3}{5}$	$\frac{s}{4} = \frac{6}{8}$

Name _____   Date _____

Write an equation. Solve.

21. Lakesha is 3 times as old as Jerry. The sum of their ages is 72. How old is each?

Answer _____

22. Marcy has 16 coins. She has 3 times as many nickels as pennies and 12 times as many dimes as pennies. How many pennies does Marcy have?

Answer _____

23. Three times a number increased by 15 is equal to 30. What is the number?

Answer _____

24. The length of a rectangle is 3 times the width. The perimeter is 36 inches. Find the length and width.

Answer _____

Simplify.

	a	*b*	*c*
25.	$(-3)^2(2)^3 =$	$2ab^2(3c) =$	$(2x^2y)(-3xy^3) =$
26.	$(ab^2)^3 =$	$\dfrac{2x^3}{x^2} =$	$\dfrac{8a^3b}{-4ab^3} =$
27.	$(3a - 3b) + (-a + 5b) =$	$(4a + 2b) - (a + 3b) =$	$4a^2 - 5b^3 + 3a^2 =$
28.	$\dfrac{x}{3y} = \dfrac{3y}{x} =$	$\dfrac{a}{b^2} \div \dfrac{a}{b} =$	$\dfrac{8ab + 10a^2b}{2ab} =$
29.	$3(2x - y) =$	$(x + y)(2x + y) =$	$2a(a^2 - 3b) =$

Make a table of solutions. Graph the equation.

a

30. $3x - 5y = 15$

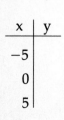

x	y
-5	
0	
5	

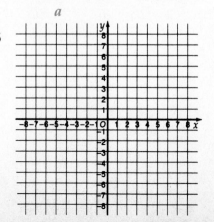

b

$2x + 3y = 6$

x	y

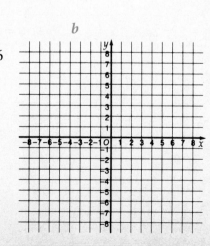

Solve each system of equations.

	a	*b*	*c*

31.

a

$x + y = 6$

$x - y = 4$

b

$3x + 2y = 26$

$3x - 2y = 10$

c

$2x + 3y = 9$

$x - 2y = 1$

Ordered pair _____   Ordered pair _____   Ordered pair _____

32. $5x - 2y = 3$

$2x + 5y = 7$

$a + 4b = 12$

$2a - b = 6$

$\frac{1}{2}x + y = 6$

$\frac{1}{2}x - y = 2$

Ordered pair _____   Ordered pair _____   Ordered pair _____

Simplify.

a   *b*   *c*

33. $\sqrt{81} =$ $\sqrt{16x^2y^4} =$ $\sqrt[3]{8x^3} =$

34. $(x + y)^2 =$ $(x + 2)(2x + 3) =$ $(x + y)(2x - 3y) =$

Solve.

a   *b*   *c*

35. $4x \leq 28$ $b + 2 > 12$ $2x - 6 < 4$

36. $-12 \geq 4 + s$ $\frac{a}{2} \leq -6$ $3y + 2 > 8$

Solve each proportion.

	a	*b*	*c*
37.	$\dfrac{x}{4} = \dfrac{6}{12}$	$\dfrac{2}{x} = \dfrac{6}{9}$	$\dfrac{4}{5} = \dfrac{x}{20}$

Solve.

38. The ratio of the length of a rectangle to the width is 2 to 3. The area of the rectangle is 96 square inches. Find the dimensions.

Answer _____

39. Maria earns $16 for working 2 hours. Suppose she works 30 hours a week. How much does she earn in a week?

Answer _____

Factor each polynomial.

	a	*b*	*c*
40.	$x^2 + 2xy + y^2 =$	$25x^2 - 9 =$	$2x^2 + 7x - 4 =$
41.	$x^2 - 6x + 9 =$	$9x^2 + 12xy + 4y^2 =$	$9 + 6y + y^2 =$

Solve.

	a	*b*	*c*
42.	$x^2 + 16 = -8x$	$2x^2 + 5x + 2 = 0$	$x^2 - 7x + 6 = 0$

Solve.

43. The length of a rectangle is 4 inches more than the width. The area of the rectangle is 45 square inches. Find the length and width.

Answer _____

44. The product of two consecutive whole numbers is 600. What are the numbers?

Answer _____

WHERE TO GO FOR HELP

The table below lists the problems in the Pretest and the pages of the book on which the corresponding skills and concepts are taught and practiced. For each problem that you could not answer or answered incorrectly, you can use the table to find the page number or numbers where that skill or concept is taught.

PROBLEMS	PAGES	PROBLEMS	PAGES	PROBLEMS	PAGES	PROBLEMS	PAGES
1a	13–14	8c	51	23	72–73	34a	146
1b	13–14	8d	50	24	72–73	34b	158
2a	15	9	20	25a	79	34c	158
2b	15	10	21	25b	82	35a	128
2c	15	11	29	25c	82	35b	127
2d	15	12	23	26a	83	35c	128
3a	16	13	25	26b	84–85	36a	127
3b	17	14	24	26c	86	36b	128
3c	16	15	31	27a	87	36c	128
3d	17	16	31	27b	88	37a	139
4a	36	17a	58	27c	89	37b	139
4b	36	17b	58	28a	90	37c	139
4c	36	17c	56	28b	91	38	140
4d	36	17d	57	28c	93	39	140
5a	38	18a	59	29a	92	40a	148
5b	37	18b	61	29b	97	40b	154
5c	39	18c	65	29c	92	40c	159
5d	39	18d	62	30a	104	41a	149
6a	40	19a	68	30b	105	41b	148
6b	40	19b	68	31a	108–109	41c	148
6c	41	19c	71	31b	110	42a	163
6d	41	19d	71	31c	111–112	42b	163
7a	45–47	20a	69	32a	113	42c	166–167
7b	45–47	20b	69	32b	115–116	43	170
7c	48	20c	70	32c	120	44	170
7d	49	20d	70	33a	132		
8a	50	21	72–73	33b	132		
8b	50	22	72–73	33c	133		

What is Algebra?

Study the following number sentences. Do you see a pattern?

$$1 \times 3 = 3 \qquad 1 \times 5.7 = 5.7 \qquad 1 \times 12 = 12$$

You can write a general statement about the three number sentences. *If a number is multiplied by 1, the product is the number.* Here is a way to describe the pattern using a variable.

$$1 \times n = n$$

Variables are letters or symbols used to represent numbers. **Algebra** is the study of variables and the operations of arithmetic with variables. Sometimes more than one variable is needed to describe a pattern.

EXAMPLE 1

> **Study the three number sentences. Describe the pattern using two variables, a and b.**
>
> $$22 + 8 = 8 + 22$$
> $$3 + 5 = 5 + 3$$
> $$10 + 2 = 2 + 10$$
>
> The pattern is $a + b = b + a$.

EXAMPLE 2

> **Write three number sentences that fit the pattern $\frac{d}{d} = 1$.**
>
> Choose any number for d. Here are three possible number sentences.
>
> $$\frac{4}{4} = 1 \qquad \frac{1.2}{1.2} = 1 \qquad \frac{99}{99} = 1$$

PRACTICE

Describe the pattern using one or two variables.

a	b	c	d
1. $5 \times 6 = 6 \times 5$	$3 - 3 = 0$	$6 + 6 = 2 \times 6$	$0 \times 7 = 0$
$7 \times 10 = 10 \times 7$	$8 - 8 = 0$	$10 + 10 = 2 \times 10$	$0 \times 10 = 0$
$4 \times 8 = 8 \times 4$	$99 - 99 = 0$	$3 + 3 = 2 \times 3$	$0 \times 25 = 0$
_____	_____	_____	_____

Write three number sentences that fit the pattern.

a

2. $n + 0 = n$

_____

_____

_____

b

$3 \times a = a + a + a$

_____

_____

_____

3. $r + 2 = s$

_____

_____

_____

$4 \times m = n$

_____

_____

_____

Writing Expressions

An **algebraic expression** consists of one or more numbers and variables, along with arithmetic operations. Here are some examples of algebraic expressions.

$$c - rs \qquad 8 \cdot 3x \qquad 9a(5b) \qquad \frac{a}{f} - 5$$

A dot or parentheses may be used instead of $\times$ to show multiplication. This is to avoid confusion between the variable x and the multiplication sign $\times$. Also, a number or variable can be written directly before another variable to indicate multiplication, as in the expressions rs or $3x$. To show the product of r and s you can write rs, $r \cdot s$, or $r(s)$. A fraction bar is often used to show division. So $\frac{a}{f}$ means $a \div f$.

To solve verbal problems in algebra, you often need to translate verbal expressions into algebraic expressions. Study the following examples. When no variable is indicated, the letter n is used.

Verbal Expression	Algebraic Expression
the product of 7 and y	$7y$
9 more than a	$a + 9$
a number decreased by y	$n - y$
a number divided by 5	$\dfrac{n}{5}$

PRACTICE

Write an algebraic expression for each verbal expression. Use the variable n when no variable is indicated.

a   *b*

1. y multiplied by z yz the difference between e and f $e - f$

2. the sum of p and q $p + q$ the quotient of b and 7 $\dfrac{b}{7}$

3. 2 more than r $r + 2$ a decreased by 6 $a - 6$

4. 12 divided by a number $\dfrac{12}{n}$ the product of 3 and a number $3n$

5. 8 less than a number $n - 8$ a number increased by 1 $n + 1$

6. a number times 100 $100n$ a number subtracted from 20 $20 - n$

EXPRESSIONS AND FORMULAS
Evaluating Expressions

To **evaluate** an expression means to find a single value for it. If you were asked to evaluate $8 + 2 \cdot 3$, would your answer be 30 or 14? Since an expression has a unique value, a specific order of operations must be followed. This order is described at the right.

ORDER OF OPERATIONS
1. Do operations within parentheses.
2. Do all multiplications and divisions from left to right.
3. Do all additions and subtractions from left to right.

The correct value of $8 + 2 \cdot 3$ is 14 because multiplication should be done before addition. To change the expression so that it has a value of 30, write $(8 + 2) \cdot 3$. The operation within the parentheses must be done first. Study the following examples. Notice in Example 3 that the numerator and denominator of a fractional expression should be evaluated separately.

EXAMPLE 1

Evaluate:
$12 - 2 \cdot 5$
$12 - 10 = 2$

EXAMPLE 2

Evaluate:
$9(12 + 8)$
$9(20) = 180$

EXAMPLE 3

Evaluate: $\dfrac{3 + 6}{1 + 2}$
$\dfrac{9}{3} = 3$

EXAMPLE 4

Evaluate:
$\frac{1}{2}(3 + 11)$
$\frac{1}{2}(14) = 7$

PRACTICE

Evaluate each expression.

	a	b	c	d
1.	$5 \cdot 2 + 1$	$5(2 + 1)$	$(4 + 6)(8)$	$4 + 6 \cdot 8$
	$10 + 1 = 11$	$5 \cdot 3 = 15$	$10 \cdot 8 - 80$	$4 + 48 = 52$
2.	$2(9 + 3)$	$2 \cdot 9 + 3$	$18 - (3 \cdot 6)$	$(18 - 3)(6)$
	$2 \cdot 12 = 24$	$18 + 3 = 21$	$18 - 18 = 0$	$15 \times 6 = 90$
3.	$8 \cdot 5 - 1$	$8(5 - 1)$	$2 \cdot 10 - 7$	$2(10 - 7)$
	$40 - 1 = 39$	$8 \cdot 4 = 32$	$20 - 7 = 13$	$2 \cdot 3 = 6$
4.	$\dfrac{4 + 8}{3}$ $\dfrac{12}{3}$	$\dfrac{7 + 9}{4}$ $\dfrac{16}{4}$	$\dfrac{11(2) + 18}{8}$ $\dfrac{22 + 18}{18}$ $\dfrac{40}{}$	$\dfrac{10 - 2(3)}{2}$ $8 \cdot 3 = \dfrac{24}{2}$
	$12 \div 3 = 4$	$16 \div 4 = 4$	$40 \div 8 = 5$	$24 \div 2 = 12$
5.	$\dfrac{6 + 10}{2 + 2}$ $\dfrac{16}{4}$	$\dfrac{6}{2} + \dfrac{10}{2}$	$\dfrac{12}{4} + \dfrac{21}{7}$	$\dfrac{12 + 21}{4 + 7}$
	$16 \div 4 = 4$			
6.	$\frac{1}{2}(6 + 26)$	$\frac{1}{2}(6) + \frac{1}{2}(26)$	$\frac{2}{3}(18) + 9$	$\frac{2}{3}(18 + 9)$

Evaluating Expressions with Variables

If you are given the value of each variable in an expression, you can evaluate the expression using the methods on the previous page. You must substitute the value for each variable first. Then perform the indicated operations.

EXAMPLE 1

> **Evaluate:** $r(r - 2)$ if $r = 6$.
> $$6(6 - 2) = 6(4)$$
> $$= 24$$

EXAMPLE 2

> **Evaluate:** $7p - \dfrac{1}{2}q$ if $p = 4$ and $q = 2$.
> $$7(4) - \dfrac{1}{2}(2) = 28 - 1$$
> $$= 27$$

PRACTICE

Evaluate each expression if $a = 9$, $b = 3$, and $c = 7$.

	a	b	c	d
1.	$4a + 7$	$c(c + 3)$	$7b + 2b$	$(7 + 2)b$
2.	$2bc$	$ab + ac$	$a(b + c)$	$ab + c$
3.	$c(a - b)$	$ca - cb$	$ca - b$	$cb - a$
4.	$\dfrac{a + b}{2}$	$\dfrac{2a + 2b}{4}$	$\dfrac{a}{b} + 9$	$\dfrac{a + 9}{b}$

Evaluate each expression if $x = 10$, $y = 25$, and $z = 20$.

	a	b	c	d
5.	$x + y$	$2y - 3x$	$3xy$	$3yx$
6.	$z + 5x$	$y - 2x$	$(y - z)(z - x)$	$x(x + 2)$
7.	$\dfrac{2}{3}(y - x)$	$\dfrac{2(y - x)}{3}$	$\dfrac{x}{2(y - z)}$	$\dfrac{x}{2}(y - z)$

Solutions to Equations

If two numbers or expressions are equal, you can write an **equation.** The equation $14 - x = 4 + x$ indicates that the expression $14 - x$ has the same value as $4 + x$. A **solution** to an equation is a number that, when substituted for the variable, makes the left and right sides of the equation have the same value. For example, 5 is a solution to $14 - x = 4 + x$ since both $14 - 5$ and $4 + 5$ are equal to 9. However, 7 is not a solution since $14 - 7$ is 7, while $4 + 7$ is 11. To show that 7 is not equal to 11, write $7 \neq 11$. See Example 1.

Solutions to equations that have the variable isolated on one side are easy to find, as shown in Example 2.

EXAMPLE 1

Is 14 a solution to $y - 7 = 0$?

Substitute 14 for y.

$$y - 7 = 0$$
$$14 - 7 = 0$$
$$7 \neq 0$$

7 does not equal zero. 14 is not a solution.

EXAMPLE 2

Find the solution: $\dfrac{2 + 8}{1 + 1} = y$

$$\dfrac{10}{2} = y$$
$$5 = y \qquad \text{The solution is 5.}$$

PRACTICE ————————————————————————————

Answer each question. Write *yes* or *no*.

	a	*b*
1.	Is 10 a solution to $2n = 40$? _____	Is 20 a solution to $2n = 40$? _____
2.	Is 2 a solution to $6 = 3n$? _____	Is 3 a solution to $6 = 3n$? _____
3.	Is 9 a solution to $\dfrac{36}{n} = 4$? _____	Is 15 a solution to $3 = \dfrac{n}{5}$? _____
4.	Is 8 a solution to $24 = n + 3$? _____	Is 100 a solution to $n - 9 = 91$? _____

Find each solution.

a	*b*	*c*	*d*
5. $7 + 2 = w$	$32 - 12 = c$	$t = 8(2 + 3)$	$p = 5(8) + 3(9)$
Solution _____	Solution _____	Solution _____	Solution _____
6. $3(8 - 6) = t$	$m = 88 + 3(5)$	$z = 44 + 22$	$k = 75 - 15$
Solution _____	Solution _____	Solution _____	Solution _____
7. $\dfrac{8 + 5}{4 - 3} = n$	$b = \dfrac{2(5) + 6}{2}$	$\dfrac{3}{4}(6 \cdot 7 + 2) = a$	$\dfrac{90 - 2(5)}{8} = z$
Solution _____	Solution _____	Solution _____	Solution _____

EXPRESSIONS AND FORMULAS
Missing Addends and Missing Factors

To **solve** an equation means to find the number that is a solution to the equation. The equations on this page involve missing addends or missing factors. These are solved by using the inverse operation to isolate the variable on one side of the equal sign. That is, solve for a missing addend by subtracting the same number from both sides of the equation, as in Example 1. In Example 2, solve for a missing factor by dividing. Check the solution by substituting the value for the variable in the equation.

EXAMPLE 1

Solve: $r + 9 = 21$

$$r + 9 = 21$$
$$r + 9 - 9 = 21 - 9$$
$$r = 12$$

The solution is 12.   **Check:** $12 + 9 = 21$

EXAMPLE 2

Solve: $9n = 99$

$$9n = 99$$
$$\frac{9}{9}n = \frac{99}{9}$$
$$n = 11$$

The solution is 11.   **Check:** $9(11) = 99$

PRACTICE
Solve. Check.

a	*b*	*c*	*d*
1. $b + 9 = 17$	$10 + a = 40$	$8y = 40$	$12n = 48$
Solution _____	Solution _____	Solution _____	Solution _____
2. $2a = 8$	$5b = 35$	$n + 14 = 30$	$4x = 100$
Solution _____	Solution _____	Solution _____	Solution _____
3. $p + 33 = 333$	$7r = 77$	$b \cdot 6 = 90$	$17 + m = 83$
Solution _____	Solution _____	Solution _____	Solution _____
4. $d \cdot 20 = 180$	$9 + n = 9$	$4y = 4$	$f + 12 = 24$
Solution _____	Solution _____	Solution _____	Solution _____
5. $7x = 1$	$0 + k = 44$	$5z = 400$	$s + 50 = 555$
Solution _____	Solution _____	Solution _____	Solution _____
6. $6r = 3$	$7 + a = 8\frac{1}{2}$	$c + \frac{2}{3} = 5$	$2x = 6$
Solution _____	Solution _____	Solution _____	Solution _____

Write a Number Sentence

A number sentence shows how numbers are related to each other. If one of the numbers is not known, write a variable instead of a number. To solve the number sentence, you may need to find a missing addend or missing factor.

Read the problem.

Sally bought a sweater for $13.99. With sales tax, the total cost was $14.83. What was the amount of sales tax?

Write a number sentence.

In the number sentence, t is used as the variable for the unknown amount of tax.

Sweater price	Sales tax	Total cost
$13.99 $+$	t $=$	$14.83

Solve the problem.

To find t, the missing addend, subtract $13.99 from $14.83.

$$t = \$14.83 - \$13.99 = \$0.84$$

Since $13.99 + $0.84 = $14.83, the amount of sales tax was $0.84.

Write a number sentence. Use the number sentence to solve the problem.

---

1. Randy Anderson got a raise of 73¢ per hour. He now earns $8.45 per hour. What was his hourly rate before his raise?

Number sentence _____

Answer _____

2. A school has 475 students. If 228 girls attend the school, how many boys attend the school?

Number sentence _____

Answer _____

---

3. A carton weighs 66 kilograms. It weighs 3 times as much as a smaller carton. How much does the smaller carton weigh?

Number sentence _____

Answer _____

4. One evening, a ticket booth sold five times as many adult tickets as student tickets. The number of adult tickets sold was 145. How many student tickets were sold?

Number sentence _____

Answer _____

Write a number sentence. Use the number sentence to solve the problem.

5. Carla asked 100 people whether they preferred orange juice or grape juice. If 78 people preferred orange juice, how many preferred grape juice?

Number sentence _____

Answer _____

6. Audrey walks each morning for exercise. In two days, she walked a total of 4.5 miles. She walked 1.8 miles the first day. How far did she walk the second day?

Number sentence _____

Answer _____

7. A delivery truck follows the same route each day. In 5 days it travels a total of 240 kilometers. What is the length of the delivery route?

Number sentence _____

Answer _____

8. Nancy paid $2.72 sales tax on a purchase. If the total with tax was $36.79, what was the price without tax?

Number sentence _____

Answer _____

9. One-eighth of the students in Mrs. Perlman's class had perfect attendance. If 4 students had perfect attendance, how many students are in the class?

Number sentence _____

Answer _____

10. The length of a picture frame is 1.2 times the width. If the length is 27 cm, what is the width?

Number sentence _____

Answer _____

11. Christine is paid the same amount for each hour of work. If the total pay for 7 hours is $44.10, what is the hourly rate?

Number sentence _____

Answer _____

12. The Ingersoll family drove 624 miles in two days. If they drove 310 miles the second day, how far did they drive the first day?

Number sentence _____

Answer _____

The Area Formula

Area is measured in square units. A square inch measures 1 inch by 1 inch. The area of a rectangle is found by multiplying the length by the width. This verbal sentence can be written as the formula $A = lw$. To find A, substitute values for l and w into the formula and solve.

> The formula for the area of a rectangle is
> $$A = lw,$$
> where A = area, l = length, and w = width.

EXAMPLE

> **Jim's bedroom is 12 feet wide and 14 feet long. How many square feet of carpet will be needed to cover the bedroom floor?**
> Since both measurements are in feet, the area will be in square feet.
> $$A = lw$$
> $$A = 12(14)$$
> $$A = 168$$
> So, 168 square feet of carpet will be needed.

Solve. Use the formula for area of a rectangle.

1. How many square feet of linoleum are needed to cover a floor measuring 25 feet by 22 feet?

   Answer _____

2. The school's playground measures 30 meters by 50 meters. How many square meters of surface are there in the playground?

   Answer _____

3. A den measures 20 feet by 12 feet. How many square feet are there in the den?

   Answer _____

4. A kitchen measures 12 feet by 16 feet. How many square feet are there in the kitchen?

   Answer _____

5. Find A, when l is 15 feet and w is 8 feet.

   Answer _____

6. Find A, when l is 18 meters and w is 20 meters.

   Answer _____

7. When $l = 30$ inches and $w = 12\frac{1}{2}$ inches, find A.

   Answer _____

8. When w is 6.8 meters and l is 8.4 meters, find A.

   Answer _____

Missing Factors in the Area Formula

You can use the area formula to find the length or width if you know the area and the other dimension. Substitute the known values and solve for the unknown value by thinking of missing factors. Notice in the example that the expression on the left side of the equals sign can be traded with the expression on the right side.

EXAMPLE

What is the length of the rectangle whose area is 4200 square feet and whose width is 60 feet?

$$A = lw$$
$$4200 = 60l$$
$$60l = 4200$$
$$l = 4200 \div 60$$
$$l = 70$$

The length is 70 feet.

PRACTICE

Solve. Use the formula for area of a rectangle.

a	*b*	*c*
1. Find *l* when *A* is 1000 square feet and *w* is 20 feet.	Find *l* when *A* is 750 square meters and *w* is 25 meters.	Find *l* when *A* is 1800 square centimeters and *w* is 30 centimeters.
2. Find *l* when *A* is 7500 square yards and *w* is 75 yards.	What is the width of the rectangle that has an area of 1200 square feet and a length of 40 feet?	Find *w* when *A* is 300 square feet and *l* is 15 feet.
3. Find *w* when *A* is 1800 square feet and *l* is 60 feet.	Find *w* when *A* is 17.5 square meters and *l* is 5 meters.	Find *w* when *A* is 18 square miles and *l* is 4.5 miles.

The Volume Formula

Volume is measured in cubic units. A cubic inch measures 1 inch by 1 inch by 1 inch. The volume of a rectangular prism is found by multiplying the length by the width by the height. This verbal sentence can be written as the formula $V = lwh$. This formula is easy to remember if you think of finding the area of the base, lw, then multiplying by the height, h.

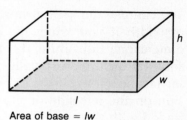

Area of base = lw

EXAMPLE

What is the volume of a tank that measures 6 m by 5 m by 0.5 m?

$V = lwh$
$V = (6)(5)(0.5)$
$V = 15$

So, the volume is 15 cubic meters.

The formula for the volume of a rectangular prism is
$$V = lwh,$$
where V = volume, l = length, w = width, and h = height.

Solve. Use the formula for volume of a rectangular prism.

1. In building a new house, Al excavated for a basement measuring 30 feet by 32 feet by 9 feet. How many cubic feet of dirt had to be removed?

    Answer _____

2. The floor of a railroad boxcar measures 6 feet by 36 feet. The car has been filled to a depth of 6 feet with grain. How many cubic feet of grain are in this carload?

    Answer _____

3. A ditch 2 m wide, 3 m deep, and 150 m long was dug. How many cubic meters of water will the ditch hold?

    Answer _____

4. The gas tank on Tina's car is shaped like a rectangular prism. It measures 42 inches by 11 inches by 10 inches. How many cubic inches does the gas tank hold?

    Answer _____

5. Firewood is usually sold by the cord. A stack of wood 8 feet long, 4 feet wide, and 4 feet high is a cord. How many cubic feet are there in a cord?

    Answer _____

6. What is the volume in cubic feet of a box whose inside dimensions are 42 inches by 3 feet by 4 feet? (Since the volume is to be in cubic feet, change 42 inches to 3.5 feet.)

    Answer _____

EXPRESSIONS AND FORMULAS

Missing Factors in the Volume Formula

If you know the volume of a rectangular prism and two of the dimensions, you can use the formula $V = lwh$ to solve for the other dimension. Substitute the known values and solve for the unknown value by thinking of missing factors.

A rectangular prism has a volume of 1800 cubic centimeters. If the length is 30 cm and the height is 6 cm, what is the width?

$$V = lwh$$
$$1800 = 30 \cdot w \cdot 6$$
$$1800 = 180w$$
$$w = 1800 \div 180$$
$$w = 10 \qquad \text{The width is 10 cm.}$$

PRACTICE

Solve. Use the formula for volume of a rectangular prism.

	a	b	c
1.	Find h when V is 1800 cubic meters, l is 30 meters, and w is 6 meters.	Find h when V is 960 cubic feet, l is 20 feet, and w is 8 feet.	Find h when V is 1500 cubic yards, l is 25 yards, and w is 10 yards.
2.	Find l when V is 252 cubic meters, w is 7 meters, and h is 4 meters.	Find l when V is 480 cubic feet, w is 4 feet, and h is 12 feet.	Find l when V is 900 cubic inches, w is 25 inches, and h is 6 inches.
3.	Find w when V is 480 cubic feet, l is 20 feet, and h is 6 feet.	Find w when V is 1080 cubic meters, l is 18 meters, and h is 6 meters.	Find w when V is 800 cubic yards, l is 40 yards, and h is 4 yards.

The Simple Interest Formula

When a customer deposits money in a savings account, the bank pays the customer for the use of the money. This payment is called **interest**. Likewise, a customer who borrows money must pay interest to the bank. The formula $I = prt$ is used to find *simple interest*, or interest on a specific amount at a fixed rate.

The formula for simple interest is
$$I = prt,$$
where I = interest, p = principal, r = rate, and t = time.

The rate and time must have corresponding units. That is, if the rate is given per year, the time must be in years. When using the formula, express the rate, r, as a decimal. For example, express 4.5% as 0.045.

EXAMPLE

The principal is $1200, the rate is 7% per year, and the time is 6 months. What is the amount of interest?

Change 6 months to $\frac{1}{2}$ or 0.5 year. Also, write 7% as 0.07.

$$I = prt$$
$$I = (\$1200)(0.07)(0.5)$$
$$I = \$42$$

The interest is $42.

PRACTICE

Find the amount of interest. Assume the interest rate is yearly.

	a	b	c
1.	$200 at 5% for 1 year	$225 at 4% for 1 year	$2500 at $6\frac{1}{2}$% for 2 years
2.	$300 at 6% for 1 year	$300 at 5% for 2 years	$1000 at $5\frac{1}{2}$% for 1 year
3.	$500 at 5% for 6 months	$350 at 9% for 9 months	$225 at 8% for 3 months
4.	$150 at 5% for 2 years and 6 months	$1000 at $6\frac{1}{2}$% for 1 year and 3 months	$450 at $10\frac{1}{4}$% for 3 years and 9 months

Missing Factors in the Simple Interest Formula

If you know the value for 3 of the variables in the formula $I = prt$, you can solve for the unknown value. Find the missing factor.

Remember, when using the formula, write r as a decimal.

When $p = \$500$, $I = \$25$, and $t = 1$ year, find r.

$$I = prt$$
$$25 = 500(r)(1)$$
$$25 = 500r$$
$$r = \frac{25}{500} = 0.05 = 5\%$$

The interest rate is 5%.

PRACTICE

Solve. Use the formula for interest.

a	b	c
1. Find the principal when the interest is $432, the rate is $6\frac{1}{4}\%$, and the time is 3 years.	Find the principal when the interest for one year amounts to $20 at 5%.	Find the principal when the rate is 5%, the time is 2 years, and the interest is $120.
2. Find the rate when the interest is $300, the time is 3 years, and the principal is $2000.	Find the rate when the principal is $420, the time is 6 months, and the interest is $12.60. (Hint: $t = \frac{1}{2}$.)	Find the rate when the interest is $24, the time is 2 years, and the principal is $200.
3. When $p = \$250$, $I = \$45$, and $r = 6\%$, find t.	Find t when $I = \$17.50$, $r = 7\%$, and $p = \$50$.	Find the time when the principal is $250, the rate is 4%, and the interest is $20.

EXPRESSIONS AND FORMULAS

The Distance Formula

If a person walks at a rate of 3 miles per hour for 4 hours, the total distance walked is 3×4 or 12 miles. The formula for distance is $D = rt$. The rate and time must have corresponding units. If r is *miles per hour*, then t must be in *hours*.

> The formula for distance is
> $$D = rt,$$
> where D = distance, r = rate, and t = time.

EXAMPLE

> **When Sue walks to school, she walks at a rate of 4 miles per hour. She walks for 30 minutes. How far does she walk?**
>
> (Hint: Change 30 minutes to 0.5 hours.)
> $D = rt$
> $D = 4 \times 0.5 = 2$
>
> Sue walks two miles.

Solve. Use the formula for distance.

1. A mail plane left Los Angeles at 2:00 P.M. and arrived in Seattle at 6:00 P.M. During the trip, the average speed was 320 miles per hour. What was the *air distance* of this trip?

   Answer _____

2. A certain plane flies at a speed of 600 miles per hour. If it requires 4 hours at this rate of speed to make the trip from Kiska to Tokyo, what is the distance?

   Answer _____

3. A plane flew from Seattle to Dutch Harbor in 4 hours, maintaining a speed of 500 miles per hour. What is the air distance between Seattle and Dutch Harbor?

4. *Tail winds* push the plane along much faster. A plane traveling at the rate of 300 miles per hour and having a tail wind of 40 miles per hour actually makes a speed of 340 miles per hour.

   How far is it from Newfoundland to Iceland, if the trip was made in 4 hours and the plane had an average speed of 500 miles per hour with a tail wind of 30 miles per hour?

   Answer _____

   Answer _____

5. A *head wind* slows the speed of a plane. A plane making a speed of 300 miles per hour and encountering a head wind of 50 miles per hour is slowed down to 250 miles per hour.

   What is the distance from Pernambuco to Dakar, if the trip requires 4 hours and the normal speed of the plane would have been 450 miles per hour, if it were not for a 50-mile-per-hour head wind?

   Answer _____

6. Encountering a head wind of 30 miles per hour, it took a plane, whose speed would have been 450 miles per hour, 6 hours to fly from San Diego to Honolulu. What was the distance between these two points?

   Answer _____

Missing Factors in the Distance Formula

If you know the distance and either the rate or time, you can solve for the unknown value. Use the formula $D = rt$ and substitute the known values. Then find the missing factor as you have done before.

EXAMPLE

Find r when $D = 25$ mi and $t = 1$ hr.
$$D = rt$$
$$25 = r(1)$$
$$r = 25$$
The rate is 25 miles per hour.

Solve. Use the distance formula.

1. A plane was sighted over two different observation posts that were 650 miles apart. The plane passed over the first post at 4:00 A.M. and over the second post at 6:30 A.M. At what speed was the plane traveling?

Answer _____

2. If it took a plane 6 hours to fly from Tampa to Los Angeles, a distance of 2496 miles, at what rate of speed was the flight made?

Answer _____

3. Find r when $D = 1400$ mi and $t = 3\frac{1}{2}$ hr.

Answer _____

4. Find r when $D = 1500$ mi and $t = 3$ hr.

Answer _____

5. Find t when $D = 1750$ km and $r = 350$ km per hr.

Answer _____

6. Find t when $D = 180$ km and $r = 45$ km per hr.

Answer _____

7. Find t when $D = 420$ m and $r = 70$ m per sec.

Answer _____

8. Find t when $D = 113.5$ ft and $r = 45.4$ ft per sec.

Answer _____

9. Find r when $D = 2150$ miles and $t = 5$ hours.

Answer _____

10. Find r when $D = 247.5$ miles and $t = 4.5$ hours.

Answer _____

The Circumference Formula

The perimeter of a circle has a special name, **circumference (C)**. You can compute the circumference of a circle if you know the length of the radius or diameter. Recall that the **diameter (d)** is the distance across a circle. The **radius (r)** is the distance from the center to a point on the circle.

Notice that $d = 2r$ and $r = \frac{1}{2}d$.

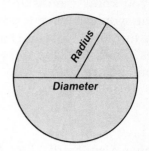

Suppose you draw any circle, then measure to find C and d. You will notice that the C is about $3d$. Mathematicians use the Greek letter π (pi) to represent the exact value, a nonrepeating decimal that is about 3.14.

> The formula for circumference is
> $$C = \pi d,$$
> where C = circumference, d = diameter, and π is about 3.14.

EXAMPLE 1

Find the circumference of a circle if the radius is 6 cm.

First find the diameter by doubling the radius. $d = 2r$, $d = 6 \cdot 2 = 12$

$C = \pi d$
$C = 3.14(12)$
$C = 37.68$ cm

The circumference is about 37.7 cm.

EXAMPLE 2

Find the circumference of a circle if the diameter is 8.2 m.

$C = \pi d$
$C = 3.14(8.2)$
$C = 25.748$

The circumference is about 25.7 meters.

Find the circumference of a circle that has the given radius or diameter. Let $\pi = 3.14$.

1. If the diameter of a circle is 24 feet, what is the radius?

Answer _____

2. If the radius of a circle is 15 centimeters, what is the diameter?

Answer _____

3. A botanical garden has a circular flower bed that is 21 feet in diameter. How many feet of fence is needed to enclose it?

Answer _____

4. A zoo has a circular pool for its polar bears. The pool's diameter is 28 feet. How many feet of fence will be needed to enclose the pool?

Answer _____

5. What is the circumference of a circle with a diameter of 7 feet?

Answer _____

6. What is the circumference of a circle with a radius of 7 inches?

Answer _____

EXPRESSIONS AND FORMULAS

The Circle Area Formula

The diagram at the right shows a circle with radius r, and a square with area r^2. The expression r^2 is read r *squared* and means $r \cdot r$. The area of the circle seems to be about 3 times the area of the square. So, it makes sense to find the area of a circle by multiplying 3.14 by r^2.

Remember, $r = \frac{1}{2}d$.

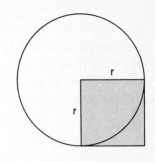

> The formula for the area of a circle is
> $$A = \pi r^2,$$
> where A = area, r = radius, and π is about 3.14.

EXAMPLE 1

Find the area of a circle that has a radius of 7 inches. Let $\pi = 3.14$.

$A = \pi r^2$
$A = 3.14(7^2)$
$A = 3.14(49)$
$A = 153.86$ sq in.

EXAMPLE 2

Find A when $d = 7$ in.

First find r by dividing d by 2.
$r = 7 \div 2 = 3.5$
$\quad A = \pi r^2$
$\quad A = 3.14(3.5)^2$
$\quad A = 3.14(12.25)$
$\quad A = 38.465$ sq in.

PRACTICE

Find the area of a circle that has the given radius or diameter. Let $\pi = 3.14$.

a	*b*
1. $r = 4.5$ cm	$d = 9$ cm
2. $r = 6$ inches	$d = 12$ inches

Solve.

3. The canvas net used by firefighters is a circular shape and has a diameter of 14 feet. How many square feet of canvas are in the net?

4. A bandstand in the shape of a circle is to be 8 meters across. How many square feet of flooring will be required? (The 8 meters represents what part of the circle?)

Answer _____

Answer _____

Volume of a Cylinder Formula

The figure below is called a **cylinder**. A cylinder has two circular bases that are parallel and congruent (same size). Since it is a three dimensional object, the volume is measured in cubic units. Recall that the area of a circular base is πr^2. Multiply the area of the base by the height to find the volume of the cylinder. Use 3.14 for π.

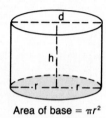

Area of base = πr^2

The formula for volume of a cylinder is
$$V = \pi r^2 h,$$
where V = volume, r = radius, and h = height.

EXAMPLE

A cylinder 10 inches high has a base with a radius of 5 inches. How many cubic inches of sand will it hold?

$V = \pi r^2 h$
$V = 3.14(5^2)(10)$
$V = 3.14(25)(10)$
$V = 3.14(250) = 785$

The cylinder will hold 785 cubic inches of sand.

Solve. Use the formula for the volume of a cylinder.

1. A water standpipe is 60 feet high and has a diameter of 14 feet. What is the volume of the standpipe (in cubic feet)?

Answer _____

2. A tank in the shape of a cylinder is 6 meters wide (diameter) and 14 meters high. What is the volume of the tank in cubic meters?

Answer _____

3. A city water tank has a diameter of 35 feet and a depth (altitude or height) of 60 feet. How many cubic feet of water will the tank hold?

Answer _____

4. Two cylinders have the same height—20 cm. One has a 7-cm radius; the other has a radius of 14 cm. The volume of the second cylinder is how many times that of the first?

Answer _____

5. A water tank in the shape of a cylinder has a diameter of 15 feet and is 35 feet high. How many cubic feet of water will it hold?

Answer _____

6. A shortening can, such as you buy in a grocery store, has a diameter of 6 inches and a depth of 7 inches. How many cubic inches will it hold?

Answer _____

Temperature Formulas

There are two commonly used temperature scales, *Fahrenheit* and *Celsius*. Each can be converted to the other by means of a formula.

To convert Fahrenheit (°F) to Celsius (°C), use the formula $C = (F - 32) \cdot \frac{5}{9}$.	To convert Celsius (°C) to Fahrenheit (°F), use the formula $F = \left(C \cdot \frac{9}{5}\right) + 32$.

EXAMPLE 1

Use a formula from above to find the freezing point on the Celsius scale. Water freezes at 32°F.

$C = (32 - 32) \cdot \frac{5}{9}$

$C = 0$

The freezing point is 0°C.

EXAMPLE 2

The boiling point on the Celsius scale is 100°C. Find the boiling point on the Fahrenheit scale.

$F = \left(100 \cdot \frac{9}{5}\right) + 32$

$F = 180 + 32$

$F = 212$

The boiling point is 212°F.

Solve.

1. When a Fahrenheit temperature is 95°, what is the equivalent Celsius temperature?

Answer _____

2. When a Celsius temperature is 45°, what is the equivalent Fahrenheit temperature?

Answer _____

3. Find C when F = 68°.

Answer _____

4. Find F when C = 15°.

Answer _____

5. Find C when F = 86°.

Answer _____

6. Find F when C = 30°.

Answer _____

7. Find C when F = 113°.

Answer _____

8. Find F when C = 75°.

Answer _____

9. Find C when F = 77°.

Answer _____

10. Find F when C = 60°.

Answer _____

Identify Extra Information

Some problems contain information that is not needed to solve the problem. When you read a problem, it may be helpful to cross out the extra facts.

Read the problem.

> Margie borrowed $500 to buy a bedroom set costing $849. The loan was for 6 months and the interest rate was 10% per year. What was the total amount of interest that Margie paid?

Decide which facts are needed.

> The problem asks for amount of interest. To use the interest formula, $I = prt$, you need to know the principal ($500), rate (10%), and time (6 months).

Decide which facts are extra.

> You do not need to know that the bedroom set costs $849.

Solve the problem.

> Use the formula $I = prt$.
> First change the rate to a decimal and write the time in years.
> The rate is 10% so $r = 0.1$. The time is 6 months so $t = \frac{1}{2}$ or 0.5.
>
> $I = prt$
> $I = \$500(0.1)(0.5)$
> $I = \$25$
>
> Margie paid $25 interest.

In each problem, cross out the extra facts. Then solve the problem.

1. The length of each side of a square is 4.2 centimeters, and the length of the diagonal is 5.9 centimeters. What is the area of the square to the nearest square centimeter?

2. Brad measured a juice box. It was 3.9 cm by 6.3 cm by 10.5 cm and contained 10% apple juice. What was the volume of the box? Round the answer to the nearest whole number.

Answer _____

Answer _____

In each problem, cross out the extra facts. Then solve the problem.

3. Jackie paid $180 for a train ticket. The train traveled a distance of 240 miles, at an average speed of 60 miles per hour. Without counting stops, how long did the trip take?

Answer _____

4. The radius of a circle is 5 inches and the circumference is 31 inches. What is the area of the circle? Round the answer to the nearest whole number.

Answer _____

5. The high temperature on Monday was 59°F at 4:00 P.M. What was the equivalent Celsius temperature?

Answer _____

6. The distance from Bob's house to the ocean is 350 miles. The distance from his house to Chicago is 440 miles. Suppose Bob drives to the ocean at an average speed of 50 miles per hour. Without counting stops, how long will the trip take?

Answer _____

7. Philip carried meals for 8 people on a circular serving tray. If the diameter of the tray was 72 cm, what was the circumference?

Answer _____

8. Kasia drove 165 miles in 3 hours and 15 minutes. Altogether, how many minutes was she driving?

Answer _____

9. A gardener planted 40 flower bulbs in a rectangular flower bed. The flower bed is 2 feet wide and $6\frac{1}{2}$ feet long. What is the area of the flower bed?

Answer _____

10. Pat is reading a recipe for making 24 blueberry muffins. The recipe calls for an oven temperature of 185°C. What is the equivalent Fahrenheit temperature?

Answer _____

Unit 1 Review

Write an algebraic expression for each verbal expression.

a b

1. 9 more than b _____ x decreased by 10 _____

2. the product of 9 and k _____ r divided by 2 _____

3. 10 less than c _____   the sum of p and q _____

Write three number sentences that fit the pattern.

a	b	c	d
4. $n \div n = 1$	$x + y = y + x$	$x - 5 = y$	$7 + a = b$

_____   _____   _____   _____

_____   _____   _____   _____

_____   _____   _____   _____

Evaluate each expression.

a	b	c	d
5. $(5 + 2)12$	$2 \cdot 12 + 11$	$\dfrac{20 - 3(4)}{2}$	$\dfrac{16 + 47}{4 + 5}$

Evaluate each expression if $a = 6$, $b = 10$, and $c = 3$.

a	b	c	d
6. $a + b$	ab	$(c + 2)b$	$\dfrac{7c - 1}{2b}$

Solve.

a	b	c	d
7. $11(9) = w$	$a = \dfrac{1}{2}(15 + 3)$	$f = 4(4) + 3(10)$	$\dfrac{15 + 6}{12 - 5} = b$
Solution _____	Solution _____	Solution _____	Solution _____
8. $8k = 40$	$x + 23 = 79$	$19 + m = 100$	$4x = 10$
Solution _____	Solution _____	Solution _____	Solution _____

Solve.

9. In the formula $A = lw$, find l when A is 48 square feet and w is 8 feet.

Answer _____

10. In the formula $A = lw$, find w when A is 5.2 square meters and l is 4 meters.

Answer _____

11. In the formula $C = \pi d$, find C when d is 30 inches. Use 3.14 for π.

Answer _____

12. In the formula $C = \pi d$, find C when d is 17 yards.

Answer _____

13. In the formula $V = lwh$, find V when l is 15 meters, w is 12 meters, and h is 10 meters.

Answer _____

14. In the formula $V = lwh$, find h when V is 2400 cubic feet, l is 48 feet, and w is 10 feet.

Answer _____

15. In the formula $A = \pi r^2$, find A when r is 22 feet.

Answer _____

16. In the formula $V = \pi r^2 h$, find V when r is 7 centimeters and h is 20 centimeters.

Answer _____

17. In the formula $I = prt$, find I when p is $350, r is $5\frac{1}{2}\%$, and t is 3 years.

Answer _____

18. In the formula $I = prt$, find t when I is $36, p is $1200, and r is 6%.

Answer _____

19. In the same formula, find r when I is $37.50, p is $250, and t is $2\frac{1}{2}$ years.

Answer _____

20. In the formula $C = (F - 32) \cdot \frac{5}{9}$, find C when F is 113°.

Answer _____

Integers and Opposites

The **integers** are a set of numbers that can be shown on a number line. **Positive integers** are greater than zero. **Negative integers** are less than zero. The arrows show that the numbers continue indefinitely in both directions.

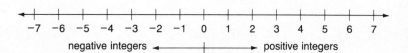

The integer −5 is read *negative five*. The integer 5 can also be written as +5, or *positive five*. These two integers, 5 and −5, are **opposites**. You can write the opposite of any integer by changing its sign. For example, the opposite of −7 is 7 and the opposite of 2 is −2.

Positive and negative numbers are used in many everyday situations.

10° below zero	−10
loss of $7	−7
gain of 12 yards	+12 or 12
profit of $100	+100 or 100

PRACTICE

Write the opposite of each integer.

	a	b	c	d
1.	4	−7	−21	45
2.	−19	33	−66	0

Write an integer to describe each situation.

	a	b	c
3.	33° above zero	8° below zero	deposit of $150
4.	loss of 10 yards	gain of 6 yards	profit of $88
5.	3500 ft above sea level	50 ft below sea level	up 7 floors
6.	down 4 floors	debt of $30	9 units to the left of 0

Adding Integers with the Same Sign

To add positive integers, think of whole numbers. So the sum of $+2$ and $+5$ is $+7$ because $2 + 5 = 7$. To add negative integers, think of moving in the negative direction (left) on the number line. This number line shows the sum of -2 and -5.

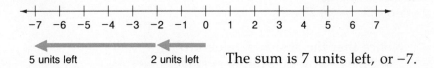

5 units left   2 units left   The sum is 7 units left, or -7.

In order to understand the rules for adding integers, you need to know the meaning of **absolute value**. The absolute value of an integer is its distance from zero on the number line. Distance always has a positive value. For example, both 2 and -2 have an absolute value of 2.

> **RULE:** To add integers with the same sign, add the absolute values and give the sum the same sign as the addends.

EXAMPLE 1

Add: $-8 + (-4)$
The sum will be negative. Add the absolute values.
$-(8 + 4) = -12$

EXAMPLE 2

Add: $9 + 8$
The sum will be positive. Add the absolute values.
$+(9 + 8) = 17$

EXAMPLE 3

Add: $-5 + 0$
Adding zero to a number gives the number.
$-5 + 0 = -5$

PRACTICE

Add.

	a	b	c	d
1.	$3 + 1 =$	$-2 + (-4) =$	$5 + 4 =$	$-1 + (-5) =$
2.	$-3 + (-6) =$	$0 + (-7) =$	$-12 + 0 =$	$-9 + (-1) =$
3.	$4 + 7 =$	$-6 + (-4) =$	$-9 + (-5) =$	$-8 + (-9)$
4.	$12 + 7 =$	$-10 + (-5) =$	$-4 + (-23) =$	$7 + 17 =$
5.	$-14 + (-16) =$	$25 + 64 =$	$-31 + (-45) =$	$-57 + (-39) =$
6.	$6 + 8 + 4 =$	$0 + (-5) + (-8) =$	$-7 + 0 + (-8) =$	$-12 + (-4) + (-5) =$
7.	$21 + 10 + 65 =$	$-19 + (-11) + (-55) =$	$0 + (-350) + (-240) =$	$-808 + (-80) + 0 =$

Adding Integers with Different Signs

To add integers with different signs, think of the number line. This number line shows the sum of −4 and 7.

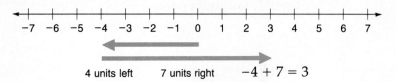

4 units left   7 units right   −4 + 7 = 3

The sum is 3 units right, or +3. Notice that the absolute value of 7 is greater than the absolute value of −4. This is why the sum is positive.

RULE: To add two integers with the different signs, subtract the absolute values. Give the result the same sign as the addend with the greater absolute value.

EXAMPLE 1

Add: −9 + 3
Subtract the absolute values.
  −(9 − 3) = −6
The sum will be negative.

EXAMPLE 2

Add: 7 + (−2)
Subtract the absolute values.
  +(7 − 2) = 5
The sum will be positive.

EXAMPLE 3

Add: −2 + 4 + (−5) + 9
First combine the integers with the same signs.
= −(2 + 5) + (4 + 9)
= −7 + 13
= 13 − 7 = 6

PRACTICE

Add.

	a	b	c	d
1.	6 + (−3) =	5 + (−9) =	−4 + 3 =	−2 + 7 =
2.	8 + (−1) =	−4 + 11 =	7 + (−6) =	−8 + 8 =
3.	−9 + 1 =	1 + (−7) =	−12 + 7 =	8 + (−15) =
4.	11 + (−9) =	−4 + 16 =	−18 + 7 =	−19 + 6 =
5.	14 + (−14) =	−7 + 13 =	14 + (−8) =	−17 + 9 =
6.	13 + (−17) =	9 + (−12) =	27 + (−13) =	−39 + 25 =
7.	−3 + (−4) + 6 =	−2 + 0 + 9 + (−4) =	−10 + 7 + 3 =	8 + (−1) + (−9) + 6 =
8.	7 + (−6) + (−5) =	1 + (−1) + 0 + 99 =	−8 + 7 + (−6) =	100 + (−20) + (−5) =

Subtracting Integers

Recall that each integer has an opposite. The opposite of an integer is used when subtracting the integer. Remember the following rule.

> **RULE:** To subtract an integer, add its opposite.

Thus, subtracting −2 is the same as adding 2 as in Example 1. Each subtraction expression can be written as addition, then simplified using the methods from the previous lessons. Study the following examples.

EXAMPLE 1

Subtract: 6 − (−2)
The opposite of −2 is 2.
$$6 - (-2) = 6 + 2$$
$$= 8$$

EXAMPLE 2

Subtract: −2 − 1
The opposite of 1 is −1.
$$-2 - 1 = -2 + (-1)$$
$$= -(2 + 1)$$
$$= -3$$

EXAMPLE 3

Subtract: −8 − (−9)
The opposite of −9 is 9.
$$-8 - (-9) = -8 + 9$$
$$= 9 - 8$$
$$= 1$$

PRACTICE

Subtract.

	a	b	c	d
1.	5 − (−2) =	−4 − 3 =	1 − 7 =	9 − 3 =
2.	−7 − (−4) =	−5 − 4 =	4 − (−9) =	11 − (−5) =
3.	8 − 17 =	−14 − (−9) =	−9 − 12 =	−17 − 8 =
4.	−13 − (−3) =	−15 − 7 =	4 − (−14) =	16 − 9 =
5.	7 − 17 =	5 − (−14) =	10 − 18 =	−15 − (−9) =
6.	13 − 23 =	−18 − 25 =	−29 − 19 =	11 − (−29) =
7.	18 − (−18) =	25 − (−17) =	−14 − 28 =	35 − 29 =
8.	−43 − (−29) =	47 − 53 =	−37 − (−45) =	−54 − 54 =

Multiplying Integers

Recall that one way to multiply is to add repeatedly. For example, you can find 3 times -6 by adding $(-6) + (-6) + (-6)$. So, $3(-6) = -18$. This example leads to the following rule.

RULE: The product of two integers with different signs is negative.

If you multiply two positive integers the product is positive. But what if you multiply two negative integers? You can think of $-3(-6)$ as the opposite of $3(-6)$. Then $-3(-6)$ is the opposite of -18, which is 18. Again, the product is positive. This example leads to the following rule.

RULE: The product of two integers with the same sign is positive.

EXAMPLE 1

Multiply: $-1(92)$
$-(1 \cdot 92) = -92$

EXAMPLE 2

Multiply: $-8(-5)$
$+(8 \cdot 5) = 40$

EXAMPLE 3

Multiply: $7(-2)(6)$
$= 7(6)(-2)$
$= 42(-2) = -84$

In Example 1, notice that multiplying a number by -1 yielded the opposite of the number. So, a negative integer can be written as the product of -1 and a positive integer. Study this method for finding $-8(-5)$ in Example 2.

$$-8(-5) = (-1)(8)(-1)(5)$$

$\quad = (-1)(-1)(8)(5)$ Rearrange the factors.

$\quad = 1(40)$ Notice that $(-1)(-1) = 1$.

$\quad = 40$ The answer is the same as in Example 2.

PRACTICE

Multiply.

	a	b	c	d
1.	$2(5) =$	$-3(-6) =$	$5(-1) =$	$-2(-3) =$
2.	$8(4) =$	$-9(5) =$	$3(-8) =$	$-4(-9) =$
3.	$-5(-7) =$	$-6(8) =$	$-9(-7) =$	$8(-9) =$
4.	$-4(-12) =$	$-13(-7) =$	$-5(23) =$	$-4(16) =$
5.	$2(-1)(3) =$	$3(-2)(-2) =$	$-2(-4)(-3) =$	$-4(-1)(4) =$
6.	$-5(-7)(-3) =$	$4(-9)(-6) =$	$-2(-13)(5) =$	$-8(-3)(-9) =$

Dividing Integers

Recall that division and multiplication are inverse operations. You can use what you know about multiplying integers to find out about dividing integers. Consider the multiplication sentence $2(-3) = -6$. You can write two related division sentences; $-6 \div (-3) = 2$ and $-6 \div 2 = -3$. Compare the signs of the dividend, divisor, and product. Notice that the rules for dividing integers are similar to the rules for multiplying integers.

RULES: The quotient of two integers with different signs is negative.
The quotient of two integers with the same sign is positive.

EXAMPLE 1

Divide: $-30 \div 10$

$-(30 \div 10) = -3$

EXAMPLE 2

Divide: $-45 \div -9$

$+(45 \div 9) = 5$

EXAMPLE 3

Divide: $\dfrac{48}{-6}$

$-(48 \div 6) = -8$

PRACTICE

Divide.

	a	b	c	d
1.	$8 \div (-4) =$	$-14 \div 2 =$	$-16 \div (-4) =$	$15 \div 3 =$
2.	$-45 \div (-9) =$	$28 \div (-4) =$	$-48 \div (-8) =$	$36 \div (-6) =$
3.	$-63 \div (-9) =$	$-20 \div 2 =$	$-55 \div (-5) =$	$54 \div 3 =$
4.	$104 \div (-4) =$	$-72 \div (-3) =$	$-84 \div (-7) =$	$120 \div (-12) =$
5.	$-126 \div 9 =$	$234 \div (-13) =$	$-240 \div (-15) =$	$483 \div (-21) =$
6.	$\dfrac{-18}{6} =$	$\dfrac{24}{-8} =$	$\dfrac{-40}{-5} =$	$\dfrac{81}{-9} =$
7.	$\dfrac{70}{-5} =$	$\dfrac{-66}{3} =$	$\dfrac{-108}{-6} =$	$\dfrac{153}{-9} =$
8.	$\dfrac{198}{-11} =$	$\dfrac{-350}{-14} =$	$\dfrac{312}{13} =$	$\dfrac{-450}{-18} =$

PROBLEM-SOLVING STRATEGY

Choose an Operation

You can solve many problems by simply adding, subtracting, multiplying, or dividing. However, in problems involving integers the operation may not be obvious. Writing a number sentence or equation may help you see how the important facts are related.

Read the problem.

> The temperature one morning at dawn was −6°F. By noon the temperature had risen to 20°F. What was the change in temperature?

Identify important facts.

> Dawn temperature −6°
>
> Noon temperature 20°

Choose an operation.

> You need to find the change in temperature. Use the variable c for the amount of change. The number sentence is $-6 + c = 20$. So, subtract to find the value of c.

Solve the problem.

> $$c = 20 - (-6) = 20 + 6$$
> $$= 26$$
> The change in temperature was 26 degrees.

Solve.

1. A submarine descended to a depth of 53 meters below sea level. A second submarine was 15 meters higher. At what depth was the second submarine?

Answer _____

2. A stock's value decreased the same amount each day for 4 days. If the total change in value was −2, what was the change each day?

Answer _____

3. Shares of stock in Company XYZ were listed at $72\frac{1}{2}$ per share. The next day the stocks lost $3\frac{1}{4}$. What was the new listing?

Answer _____

4. On a certain day, the high temperature in the United States was 90°F and the low temperature was −12°F. Find the difference in these two temperatures.

Answer _____

Solve.

5. Roberta and Helen were exploring a cave. They descended to a depth 74 feet from the entrance, and discovered a large cavern. The ceiling of the cavern was 17 feet above them. At what depth below the cave entrance was the cavern ceiling?

Answer _____

6. The total change in value of a certain stock for Monday and Tuesday was $+5\frac{3}{8}$. The value of the stock changed $+6\frac{3}{4}$ on Tuesday. What was the change in value on Monday?

Answer _____

7. The temperature one cold evening at 8:00 P.M. was 0°C. Between then and midnight the temperature dropped 3°C each hour. What was the temperature at midnight?

Answer _____

8. Two divers were collecting coral samples. Diver A was 23 feet below sea level, and 18 feet above Diver B. How far below sea level was Diver B?

Answer _____

9. Here are the changes in the value of Company QRS stock for three days.

Monday	Tuesday	Wednesday
$+3\frac{7}{8}$	$-2\frac{1}{8}$	$+4\frac{3}{4}$

What was the change in the stock's value from the beginning to the end of the three-day period?

Answer _____

10. Death Valley is the lowest point in the United States, −280 feet below sea level. Denver is often called the Mile High City because it is 5,280 feet, or 1 mile above sea level. How much greater is the elevation of Denver than Death Valley?

Answer _____

11. One day the difference between the high and low temperature was 35°F. The high temperature was 27°F. What was the low temperature?

Answer _____

12. One morning, the temperature rose 15 degrees Fahrenheit between sunrise and 9:00 A.M. If the temperature at 9:00 A.M. was 60°F, what was the temperature at sunrise?

Answer _____

43

Terms, Coefficients, and Monomials

Earlier in this book you learned to evaluate expressions when the value of each variable was known. Next you will learn procedures for simplifying algebraic expressions. In order to understand these procedures, it is important to learn several vocabulary words.

A **term** is a number, or a variable, or a *product* or *quotient* of numbers and variables.

EXAMPLES OF TERMS

$$\frac{a}{b} \qquad -6x^2 \qquad 5 \qquad a \qquad 8mn$$

An **expression** consists of one or more terms separated by addition or subtraction.

EXAMPLES OF EXPRESSIONS

$$4 + b \qquad ab - c \qquad x + \frac{b}{t}$$

Constants are terms that do not contain variables.

EXAMPLES OF CONSTANTS

$$-7 \qquad 2 \qquad \frac{3}{4} \qquad 0.8$$

The **coefficient** of a term is the numerical part. When there is no number in front of a variable, the coefficient 1 is understood. Coefficients may be fractions or decimals as well as integers.

EXAMPLES OF COEFFICIENTS OF TERMS

Term:	$-7xy$	m	$-x$	$\frac{3}{4}x$ or $\frac{3x}{4}$
Coefficient:	-7	1	-1	$\frac{3}{4}$ or 0.75

A **monomial** is a number, a variable, or a *product* of numbers and variables. So, the terms $\frac{s}{t}$ and $\frac{2}{3b}$ are *not* monomials because division is indicated by the variables in the denominator.

EXAMPLES OF MONOMIALS

$$9xy \qquad 0.5 \qquad -7k \qquad \frac{2}{3}b$$

PRACTICE

Circle the constants.

	a	b	c	d	e	f	g	h
1.	-7	$4m$	9	$\frac{1}{10}$	$-m$	14	$x + y$	$2x$

Circle the monomials.

2.	$5x$	a	$a + b$	$2xy$	$x - 2y$	$\frac{1}{3}a$	$a - 2b$	$12z$

Circle the coefficient of each term.

3.	$5a$	$4s$	$1.5f$	$-42b$	$1250r$	$1.5n$	$-9m$	$\frac{2}{3}x$

Write the coefficient of each term.

4.	$\frac{x}{2}$	$\frac{-3y}{4}$	$\frac{z}{5}$	$\frac{3a}{2}$	$-\frac{2r}{5}$	$\frac{m}{4}$	$-a$	$\frac{3b}{5}$

INTEGERS AND MONOMIALS
Adding Like Terms

Like terms are terms that are the same or which differ only in their coefficients. For example, $4k$ and $3k$ are like terms. However, $2x$ and $6y$ are *not* like terms. To find the sum of $4k$ and $3k$, try writing the multiplication in each term as addition.

$$4k + 3k = (k + k + k + k) + (k + k + k) = 7k$$

This example leads to the following rule for adding like terms.

> **RULE:** The coefficient of the sum of two like terms is the sum of the coefficients.

EXAMPLE 1

> Add: $7x + x$
> $= (7 + 1)x$
> $= 8x$

EXAMPLE 2

> Add: $-8mn + 3mn$
> $= (-8 + 3)mn$
> $= -5mn$

EXAMPLE 3

> Add: $4x + 3y$
> These are not like terms so they cannot be added.

PRACTICE

Add.

	a	b	c	d
1.	$3y + 4y =$	$6n + 5n =$	$3m + 15m =$	$13yz + 12yz =$
2.	$5x + x =$	$2a + a =$	$st + 6st =$	$m + 3m =$
3.	$28y + 52y =$	$12b + 16b =$	$29r + 15s =$	$20mn + 10mn =$
4.	$-3x + (-2x) =$	$-4t + (-6t) =$	$-3cd + (-7cd) =$	$-5v + (-7v) =$
5.	$-2ab + 7ab =$	$-4t + 2t =$	$-8rs + 12rs =$	$-43y + 12y =$
6.	$\frac{1}{2}a + \frac{1}{2}a =$	$\frac{1}{3}n + \frac{1}{3}n =$	$\frac{3}{4}x + \frac{1}{4}x =$	$d + \frac{1}{2}d =$
7.	$0.5b + 1.3b =$	$3.2y + 0.8y =$	$0.8k + 0.2y =$	$0.05t + 0.07t =$
8.	$3a + 2a + 4a =$	$5xy + xy + 8xy =$	$6m + 9m + 3m =$	$7h + h + 2h =$

Subtracting Like Terms

The following rule can be used to subtract like terms, as shown in Example 1. However, sometimes it is easier to subtract by adding the opposite. Write the opposite of a term by changing the sign of the coefficient. Then use the rule for adding like terms.

RULE:	The coefficient of the difference of two like terms is the difference of the coefficients.

EXAMPLE 1

Add: $7x - 5x$

$= (7 - 5)x$
$= 2x$

EXAMPLE 2

Add: $-8ab - 3ab$

$= -8ab + (-3ab)$
$= -(8 + 3)ab$
$= -11ab$

EXAMPLE 3

Add: $\frac{1}{6}n - \left(-\frac{3}{6}n\right)$

$= \frac{1}{6}n + \frac{3}{6}n$
$= \left(\frac{1}{6} + \frac{3}{6}\right)n$
$= \frac{4}{6}n = \frac{2}{3}n$

PRACTICE

Subtract.

	a	*b*	*c*	*d*
1.	$7y - 5y =$	$8a - 7a =$	$14rt - 7rt =$	$26w - 14w =$
2.	$3h - 5h =$	$8yz - 11yz =$	$2f - 9f =$	$8mn - 17mn =$
3.	$-2x - 7x =$	$-4g - 8g =$	$-5z - 9z =$	$-24b - 35b =$
4.	$6n - n =$	$4p - p =$	$-3k - k =$	$-5r - 5r =$
5.	$7t - 5t =$	$m - 7m =$	$a - 12a =$	$xy - 28xy =$
6.	$-5ab - (-9ab) =$	$-4k - (-8k) =$	$-7t - (-6t) =$	$-8x - (-3x) =$
7.	$\frac{3}{4}t - \frac{1}{4}t =$	$\frac{4}{5}x - \frac{3}{5}x =$	$\frac{2}{3}h - \frac{1}{3}h =$	$\frac{3}{2}b - \frac{1}{2}b =$
8.	$0.3n - 0.1n =$	$3.2a - 2.7a =$	$5.4k - 4.7k =$	$6st - 4.2st =$

Simplifying Expressions

The **simplest form** of an expression has no like terms and no parentheses. Also, the terms are usually arranged in alphabetical order, with the constants last.

To **simplify** an expression means to write it in simplest form. Combine the constants and the like terms using the methods shown previously. Study the following examples.

EXAMPLE 1

> **Simplify: $-2 + 8y + y - 3$**
> $= (8y + 1y) + (-2 + (-3))$
> $= 9y + (-5)$
> $= 9y - 5$

EXAMPLE 2

> **Simplify: $6 + 7x - 8$**
> $= 7x + 6 + (-8)$
> $= 7x + (-2)$
> $= 7x - 2$

EXAMPLE 3

> **Simplify: $-4ab + 7a + ab$**
> $= (-4ab + 1ab) + 7a$
> $= -3ab + 7a$

PRACTICE

Simplify.

	a	*b*	*c*
1.	$5a + 4a - 2a =$	$8g + 3g - 7g =$	$4x - 12x + 7x =$
2.	$6y - 4y + y =$	$3m - 5m + 4m =$	$12b - 8b - 4b =$
3.	$9a - 6a + 3b =$	$7t + 4s + 5t =$	$6ab - 3ac - 8ac =$
4.	$5r - 7r + 8m =$	$11 - 4k - 9k =$	$5x - 7 + 9 =$
5.	$16xy - 18 + 7xy =$	$4f - 9f - 3f + 10 =$	$-8rs + 9rs + st =$
6.	$-4g - 5 - 3g + 8 =$	$e + ef + 5f =$	$3x - 7x - 9x =$
7.	$19 + 15bc - 3bd =$	$31p - 54p - 82p =$	$-36 + 74r - 53 + r =$

Multiplying Monomials

Recall that a monomial is a number, a variable, or a product of numbers and variables. To multiply two or more monomials together, rearrange the factors and simplify. Study the following examples.

Remember, $ab = ba$.

EXAMPLE 1

Multiply: (4b)(8a)
$$= (4 \cdot 8)ab$$
$$= 32ab$$

EXAMPLE 2

Multiply: $-7(-4pq)$
$$= -7(-4)pq$$
$$= 28pq$$

EXAMPLE 3

Multiply: $3t(-7m)(-a)$
$$= 3(-7)(-1)amt$$
$$= 21amt$$

PRACTICE

Multiply.

	a	*b*	*c*	*d*
1.	$4(5a) =$	$5(6b) =$	$9m(6) =$	$3(7a) =$
2.	$3(7xy) =$	$(9mn)(4)$	$2(6rs) =$	$(8ab)(8) =$
3.	$(-4)(-5x) =$	$(7a)(-4) =$	$(3b)(-9) =$	$-2(-25c) =$
4.	$(4a)(3b) =$	$5t(10s) =$	$(-4x)(-9z) =$	$2mn(-7p) =$
5.	$\frac{1}{2}y(6) =$	$4\left(\frac{1}{2}x\right) =$	$20t\left(\frac{1}{4}a\right) =$	$25\left(\frac{1}{2}m\right) =$
6.	$3s(0.4r) =$	$5c(0.6b) =$	$5v(0.8t) =$	$6(0.7z) =$
7.	$6(3b)(2c) =$	$7(5t)(3r) =$	$(4x)(3y)(9z) =$	$(-3)(4m)(10n) =$
8.	$(6t)(-5s)(-2) =$	$(-10a)(-4b)(-8c) =$	$(-6m)(-5d)(-5r) =$	$-12(-4t)(8s) =$
9.	$(-19rs)(-5t)(-3) =$	$(-4f)(16e)(12) =$	$-35y(-4x)(5z) =$	$t(32s)(4r) =$

Dividing Monomials by Integers

Monomials with fractional coefficients may be written in two ways. For example, $\frac{2}{3}m$ is equal to $\frac{2m}{3}$. Thus, to divide a monomial by an integer, simply divide the coefficient by the integer and then write the variables. Study the following examples.

EXAMPLE 1

Divide: $\dfrac{-8k}{2}$

$= \dfrac{-8}{2}(k)$

$= -4k$

EXAMPLE 2

Divide: $\dfrac{-100ab}{-20}$

$= \dfrac{-100}{-20}(ab)$

$= 5ab$

EXAMPLE 3

Divide: $\dfrac{7.8w}{3}$

$= \dfrac{7.8}{3}(w)$

$= 2.6w$

PRACTICE

Divide.

	a	b	c	d
1.	$\dfrac{20a}{5} =$	$\dfrac{15a}{3} =$	$\dfrac{12x}{4} =$	$\dfrac{16y}{4} =$
2.	$\dfrac{16ab}{4} =$	$\dfrac{20xy}{5} =$	$\dfrac{12mn}{6} =$	$\dfrac{28rs}{4} =$
3.	$\dfrac{-20a}{-2} =$	$\dfrac{-45b}{5} =$	$\dfrac{-54c}{-9} =$	$\dfrac{-125x}{25} =$
4.	$\dfrac{20a}{-2} =$	$\dfrac{75b}{-15} =$	$\dfrac{-64c}{-4} =$	$\dfrac{180d}{-20} =$
5.	$\dfrac{-15x}{5} =$	$\dfrac{20a}{-4} =$	$\dfrac{-32b}{8} =$	$\dfrac{96c}{-24} =$
6.	$\dfrac{15x}{-5} =$	$\dfrac{-64x}{8} =$	$\dfrac{-72a}{9} =$	$\dfrac{56b}{-14} =$
7.	$\dfrac{2.4z}{4} =$	$\dfrac{2.1x}{3} =$	$\dfrac{1.5a}{5} =$	$\dfrac{2.4n}{8} =$

Simplifying Expressions with Parentheses

Sometimes an expression in parentheses is preceded by an integer or an operation sign. When such expressions are simplified, each term within the parentheses must be multiplied separately by the integer. A negative sign in front of parentheses indicates multiplication by −1. Study the following examples.

Remember, do multiplication before addition.

EXAMPLE 1

Simplify: $-3(8a + 5b)$
$= -3(8a) + (-3)(5b)$
$= -24a + (-15b)$
$= -24a - 15b$

EXAMPLE 2

Simplify: $-(-8x + 2)$
$= -1(-8x + 2)$
$= -1(-8x) + (-1)(2)$
$= 8x - 2$

EXAMPLE 3

Simplify: $4 - (r + 7)$
$= 4 + (-1)(r + 7)$
$= 4 + (-1)(r) + (-1)(7)$
$= 4 - r - 7$
$= -r - 3$

PRACTICE

Simplify.

	a	*b*	*c*
1.	$4(-7x + 3y) =$	$-2(4m + 9n) =$	$8(7 - 5ab) =$
2.	$-(4p + 3q) + 7p =$	$-(6x + y - z) =$	$-(-2r + 7s) + 2(r + s) =$
3.	$8y - (3 - 6y) =$	$-7 + (9x - 8) =$	$2x + 3y - (x + 5y) =$
4.	$2a + 3b + 2(a - 2b) =$	$3x - 5y + 4(x - 3y) =$	$5m + 4n + 3(2m - 5n) =$
5.	$5t - 4s - 3(2t - 3s) =$	$4m + 3n - 2(m + 3n) =$	$7x - 4y - 5(2y - x) =$
6.	$2(3b + 4) - (b - 5) =$	$3(5x - 2y) - (4x + 3y) =$	$3(m + 2n) - 4(2m + n) =$

Simplifying Fractional Expressions

Expressions with negative and positive fractions are simplified using the same rules as for integers. Study the following examples. Notice in Example 3 that dividing by 2 is the same as multiplying by $\frac{1}{2}$.

EXAMPLE 1

Simplify: $-a + \frac{a}{4}$

$$= -1a + \frac{1}{4}a$$

$$= \left(-1 + \frac{1}{4}\right)a$$

$$= \left(-\frac{4}{4} + \frac{1}{4}\right)a = -\frac{3}{4}a$$

EXAMPLE 2

Simplify: $-\frac{y}{4} \cdot \frac{x}{5}$

$$= \left(-\frac{1}{4}\right)y \cdot \left(\frac{1}{5}\right)x$$

$$= \left(-\frac{1}{4} \cdot \frac{1}{5}\right)xy$$

$$= -\frac{1}{20}xy \text{ or } -\frac{xy}{20}$$

EXAMPLE 3

Simplify: $\dfrac{-8m - 6n}{2}$

$$= \frac{1}{2}(-8m + (-6n))$$

$$= \frac{1}{2}(-8m) + \frac{1}{2}(-6n)$$

$$= -4m - 3n$$

PRACTICE

Simplify.

	a	*b*	*c*
1.	$\dfrac{k}{3} - \dfrac{4k}{3} =$	$-\dfrac{r}{4} + s - \dfrac{3r}{4} =$	$\dfrac{-5n}{6} + \dfrac{5n}{6} =$
2.	$-\dfrac{2}{3} \cdot \dfrac{a}{5} =$	$\dfrac{x}{6} \cdot \dfrac{n}{-2} =$	$\dfrac{1}{8}(-16p + 2) =$
3.	$-\dfrac{1}{3}(6y + 1) =$	$\dfrac{2}{5}(10a - 5) =$	$\dfrac{3}{4}(-7x - x) =$
4.	$\dfrac{7x + 21y}{7} =$	$\dfrac{-24a + 2b}{4} =$	$\dfrac{a + 4a}{-5} =$
5.	$\dfrac{x}{2} - 6\left(\dfrac{x}{4} + 1\right) =$	$-8\left(\dfrac{1}{2}y + 4 - y\right) =$	$\dfrac{7(3x + 2) + 1}{-3} =$

PROBLEM-SOLVING STRATEGY

Use Estimation

Many problems do not need an exact answer, so you can estimate instead. An estimate is found by rounding some or all of the numbers and then doing mental math.

Read the problem.

Pamela Yaku owns 62 shares of a certain company's stock. One day the change in value for each share was $+2\frac{1}{8}$. About how much change was there in the total value of Pamela's shares? (Hint: $+1$ means an increase of 1 dollar.)

Identify the important facts.

The value of each share increased $2\frac{1}{8}$ dollars.

She owns 62 shares.

Round.

Round 62 to 60. Round $2\frac{1}{8}$ to 2.

Solve the problem.

$60(2) = 120$
The total value of the shares increased about 120 dollars.

Use estimation to solve each problem.

1. Bobby deposited $890 in a savings account that has an annual interest rate of 5.9%. About how much interest will be earned in one year?	**2.** Teresa borrowed $1950 to buy a used car. The interest rate is 14.8% per year. If she pays back the full amount in one year, about how much interest will she owe?
Answer _____	Answer _____
3. Marcella owns 229 shares of stock. She received dividends of $2.17 per share. About how much money did she receive in all?	**4.** About how many square yards of carpet would be needed for a room that is 22 feet long and 17 feet wide?
Answer _____	Answer _____

Use estimation to solve each problem.

---

5. A box is 41 cm long, 32 cm wide, and 26 cm high. Is the volume closer to 3600 or 36,000 cubic centimeters?

Answer _____

6. The floor of a room has an area of about 196 square feet. The width of the room is $10\frac{1}{4}$ feet. Estimate the length of the room.

Answer _____

---

7. Brad typed a report that was 2876 words long in 48 minutes. About how many words per minute did Brad type?

Answer _____

8. The radius of a circular patio is 3.2 meters. Estimate the diameter of the patio.

Answer _____

---

9. When Lakeesha drives between cities, her average speed is 58 miles per hour. About how many hours will it take for her to drive 367 miles?

Answer _____

10. Estimate the perimeter of a rectangular field that is 734 meters long and 492 meters wide.

Answer _____

---

11. Pat owns 89 shares of stock in a certain company. The value changed $-4\frac{3}{8}$ on Friday. About how much did the total value of Pat's shares change?

Answer _____

12. The total take-home pay for members of the Rose family is $3240 per month. About 18% of this money is spent for food. About how much money does the Rose family spend each month for food?

Answer _____

Unit 2 Review

Write the opposite of each integer.

	a	b	c	d
1.	8	−13	−1	75

Simplify.

	a	b	c	d
2.	$-10 + (-20) =$	$13 + 8 =$	$25 + 42 =$	$-87 + (-4) =$
3.	$-9 + 8 =$	$-4 + 10 =$	$32 + (-7) =$	$18 + (-22) =$
4.	$20 - 17 =$	$11 - 23 =$	$-5 - (-3) =$	$-9 - 2 =$
5.	$8(-6) =$	$(-4)(-22) =$	$(-1)(99) =$	$5(-2)(7) =$
6.	$\dfrac{18}{3} =$	$\dfrac{24}{-2} =$	$\dfrac{-75}{-5} =$	$\dfrac{-63}{9} =$
7.	$8k + k =$	$12m - 3m =$	$7ab - 10ab =$	$10n + (-3n) =$
8.	$5y + 2z - y =$	$-2b + 4c + 3b =$	$-t + 2t - 8t =$	$5jk - (-8jk) + jk =$
9.	$-4(16p) =$	$(-8x)(9y) =$	$5(-32ac) =$	$(-5k)(2.4y) =$
10.	$\dfrac{15x}{5} =$	$\dfrac{-25rs}{-5} =$	$\dfrac{54y}{-6} =$	$\dfrac{10.5mn}{-3} =$

Simplify.

	a	b	c
11.	$k + 7 - (2k + 5) =$	$r + 2 - 3(5 - 2r) =$	$2(3a + 5b) + 3(5a - 3b) =$
12.	$\dfrac{a}{2} + b + \dfrac{a}{2} =$	$\dfrac{3}{4}(-12x + 20) =$	$\dfrac{42b + 70}{7} =$

Cumulative Review

Write an algebraic expression for each verbal expression.

a	b
1. n increased by 10 _____	7 divided by w _____

Evaluate each expression if $x = 9$, $y = 1$, and $z = 5$.

a	b	c	d
2. $xyz =$	$\dfrac{x + y}{z} =$	$3z + xy =$	$9y - x =$

Solve.

a	b	c	d
3. $8 + 5 = r$	$y = \dfrac{38}{2} + 1$	$9x = 90$	$22 + b = 50$

Simplify.

a	b	c	d
4. $-10 + 1 =$	$3 - (-9) =$	$-12 + (-63) =$	$42 - 50 =$
5. $(-2)(-13) =$	$(-7)(11) =$	$\dfrac{54}{-6} =$	$\dfrac{-100}{-5} =$
6. $2a + 7a + 5a =$	$15x - 7x + 4y =$	$4b - (-9b) =$	$-16rs + 12rs + 4rs =$
7. $3(15a) =$	$(-4x)(0.5r) =$	$\dfrac{-32ab}{4} =$	$\dfrac{1.6t}{4} =$
8. $4(7a + 10) =$	$-4(3b - c) =$	$\dfrac{2}{5}(10m - 4n) =$	$\dfrac{-4m + 20}{-4} =$

Solve.

9. In the formula $V = lwh$, find V when l is 10 feet, w is 6 feet, and h is 2 feet.

10. In the formula $D = rt$, find t when D is 240 miles and r is 80 miles per hour.

Answer _____

Answer _____

Solving Addition Equations

To solve the equation $4 + x = 10$, find the value of x that makes the equation true. Since x is a missing addend, the solution is $10 - 4$ or 6. It is important to check the solution by substituting 6 for x in the original equation. Since $4 + 6$ is 10, the solution is correct.

When an addition equation involves integers, a slightly different process is used to find the solution. You can add the same number to both sides of an equation without changing its solution. The goal is to isolate the variable on one side of the equation so the solution will be obvious. In Example 1, the number 4 is added to each side because 4 is the **opposite** of -4. The left side of the equation becomes $x + 0$ or simply x.

EXAMPLE 1

Solve: $x + (-4) = 9$

$x + (-4) + 4 = 9 + 4$

$\qquad x = 13$

The solution is 13.

Check: $13 + (-4) = 9$

EXAMPLE 2

Solve: $5 + n = -2$

$-5 + 5 + n = -5 + (-2)$

$\qquad n = -7$

The solution is -7.

Check: $5 + (-7) = -2$

EXAMPLE 3

Solve: $a + 9 = 7$

$a + 9 + (-9) = 7 + (-9)$

$\qquad a = -2$

The solution is -2.

Check: $-2 + 9 = 7$

PRACTICE

Solve. Check.

	a	b	c	d
1.	$x + 2 = 5$	$x + 15 = 23$	$x + 4 = 8$	$x + 2 = -9$
2.	$x + 23 = 23$	$a + 4 = -1$	$n + 5 = 1$	$t + 33 = 36$
3.	$r + 15 = 2$	$h + 9 = -9$	$y + 12 = 0$	$d + 7 = 9$
4.	$k + 10 = 1$	$c + 17 = 27$	$x + 54 = 36$	$m + 9 = 72$
5.	$f + 19 = 0$	$m + 5 = 19$	$z + 9 = -10$	$x + 3 = 3$

Solving Subtraction Equations

To isolate the variable in a subtraction equation, you can add the same number to both sides. Or, you can rewrite the equation as addition and then solve.

EXAMPLE 1

Solve: $x - 6 = 4$

$x - 6 + 6 = 4 + 6$

$x = 10$

The solution is 10.

Check: $10 - 6 = 4$

EXAMPLE 2

Solve: $n - (-4) = 8$

$n + 4 = 8$

$n + 4 + (-4) = 8 + (-4)$

$n = 4$

The solution is 4.

Check: $4 - (-4) = 8$

EXAMPLE 3

Solve: $z - 9 = 0$

$z - 9 + 9 = 0 + 9$

$z = 9$

The solution is 9.

Check: $9 - 9 = 0$

PRACTICE

Solve. Check.

	a	b	c	d
1.	$x - 13 = 15$	$z - 7 = 4$	$y - 12 = -10$	$r - 6 = 0$
2.	$y - 3 = 3$	$m - 9 = -7$	$z - 4 = 9$	$x - 25 = 10$
3.	$x - 3 = -3$	$p - 6 = -4$	$y - 8 = 19$	$h - 16 = 15$
4.	$r - (-12) = 5$	$t - 11 = -11$	$a - 1 = 0$	$b - (-2) = -1$

SOLVING EQUATIONS
Solving Multiplication Equations

One way to solve a multiplication equation such as $7n = 28$ is to think of the missing factor. The solution to $7n = 28$ is $28 \div 7$ or 4.

Remember that another way to solve an equation is to isolate the variable so the solution is obvious. You can multiply or divide both sides of an equation by any number (except zero) without changing its solution.

In Example 1, both sides are multiplied by $\frac{1}{4}$ because $\frac{1}{4}$ is the **reciprocal** of 4. The equation could also have been solved by dividing both sides by 4. The left side of the equation becomes $1x$ or simply x.

EXAMPLE 1

Solve: 4x = −32
$$\left(\frac{1}{4}\right)4x = \left(\frac{1}{4}\right)(-32)$$
$$x = -8$$
The solution is −8.

Check: $4(-8) = -32$

EXAMPLE 2

Solve: −m = 5
$$(-1)(-m) = (-1)(5)$$
$$m = -5$$
The solution is −5.

Check: $-(-5) = 5$

EXAMPLE 3

Solve: −3y = −3
$$\left(-\frac{1}{3}\right)(-3y) = \left(-\frac{1}{3}\right)(-3)$$
$$y = 1$$
The solution is 1.

Check: $-3(1) = -3$

PRACTICE

Solve. Check.

	a	b	c	d
1.	$6x = 36$	$-8y = 48$	$-n = 9$	$3m = -10$
2.	$-2x = 16$	$23y = 92$	$3x = 18$	$2a = -24$
3.	$25k = 50$	$-3x = -9$	$6r = 24$	$-14y = 56$
4.	$-7x = -14$	$-m = -2$	$3n = -18$	$5x = 25$

58

Solving Division Equations

To solve division equations, use the same methods as for multiplication equations. To isolate the variable in a division equation, you can multiply both sides by the same number.

EXAMPLE 1

Solve: $\dfrac{x}{2} = 6$

$(2)\dfrac{x}{2} = (2)6$

$x = 12$

Check: $\dfrac{12}{2} = 6$

EXAMPLE 2

Solve: $-\dfrac{b}{3} = 9$

$(-3)\left(-\dfrac{b}{3}\right) = (-3)9$

$b = -27$

Check: $-\left(\dfrac{-27}{3}\right) = 9$

EXAMPLE 3

Solve: $\dfrac{y}{5} = 0$

$(5)\dfrac{y}{5} = (5)0$

$y = 0$

Check: $\dfrac{0}{5} = 0$

PRACTICE

Solve. Check.

	a	*b*	*c*	*d*
1.	$\dfrac{x}{4} = 8$	$\dfrac{x}{3} = -2$	$\dfrac{w}{5} = 2$	$\dfrac{z}{9} = 10$
2.	$-\dfrac{f}{8} = -8$	$\dfrac{p}{9} = -9$	$\dfrac{t}{6} = 3$	$\dfrac{h}{7} = 0$
3.	$\dfrac{a}{10} = 7$	$\dfrac{b}{2} = -20$	$-\dfrac{m}{1} = 6$	$\dfrac{z}{1} = 1$
4.	$-\dfrac{y}{15} = 1$	$\dfrac{w}{4} = 25$	$\dfrac{d}{25} = 4$	$-\dfrac{t}{1} = 0$

Practice in Solving Equations

Remember that when isolating the variable in an equation, you can add, subtract, multiply, or divide both sides by the same number. Always check your solution in the original equation.

PRACTICE

Solve. Check.

	a	b	c	d
1.	$a + (-5) = 8$	$r - 9 = 13$	$\dfrac{y}{2} = 5$	$3m = 9$
2.	$t + 2 = 1$	$b - (-4) = 0$	$\dfrac{n}{3} = -2$	$7k = 7$
3.	$s + 6 = 0$	$z - 6 = -3$	$-\dfrac{d}{3} = -9$	$-x = 4$
4.	$\dfrac{k}{3} = 5$	$r + 7 = -1$	$-2c = 4$	$y - 5 = 7$
5.	$w - 18 = 27$	$9m = 12$	$\dfrac{s}{4} = 5$	$b + 12 = 11$
6.	$-\dfrac{h}{3} = 8$	$t - 9 = -4$	$f + 7 = -11$	$7y = -35$
7.	$g + 5 = 4$	$-z = 12$	$\dfrac{a}{3} = 0$	$m - 5 = 7$
8.	$5b = -8$	$l + 24 = -2$	$z - 3 = -15$	$\dfrac{n}{12} = 9$
9.	$x + 73 = 27$	$7r = -49$	$-\dfrac{a}{13} = -1$	$h - 81 = 9$
10.	$c + 15 = -93$	$t - 1 = -60$	$16x = -4$	$-\dfrac{a}{1} = 8$

The Fractional Equation

One method for solving an equation such as $\frac{3x}{4} = 15$ would be to multiply both sides by 4, then divide both sides by 3. This is shown in Example 1.

A simpler method to solve the same equation is to think of $\frac{3x}{4}$ as $\frac{3}{4}x$. This is a multiplication equation with a fractional coefficient. It can be solved by multiplying both sides by the reciprocal of $\frac{3}{4}$, which is $\frac{4}{3}$. This method is shown in Example 2 and Example 3.

EXAMPLE 1

Solve: $\dfrac{3x}{4} = 15$

$(4)\dfrac{3x}{4} = (4)15$

$3x = 60$

$\left(\dfrac{1}{3}\right)3x = \left(\dfrac{1}{3}\right)60$

$x = 20$

EXAMPLE 2

Solve: $\dfrac{3x}{4} = 15$

$\left(\dfrac{4}{3}\right)\dfrac{3x}{4} = \left(\dfrac{4}{3}\right)15$

$x = 20$

Check: $\dfrac{3(20)}{4} = 15$

EXAMPLE 3

Solve: $\dfrac{2n}{3} = -4$

$\left(\dfrac{3}{2}\right)\dfrac{2n}{3} = \left(\dfrac{3}{2}\right)(-4)$

$n = -6$

Check: $\dfrac{2(-6)}{3} = -4$

PRACTICE

Solve. Check.

	a	*b*	*c*	*d*
1.	$\dfrac{2n}{3} = 14$	$\dfrac{7r}{3} = 7$	$\dfrac{2n}{3} = -6$	$\dfrac{2a}{5} = 8$
2.	$\dfrac{3x}{5} = -12$	$\dfrac{2y}{5} = 24$	$\dfrac{3r}{4} = 12$	$\dfrac{3y}{7} = 6$
3.	$\dfrac{3a}{4} = 15$	$\dfrac{3z}{10} = 9$	$\dfrac{5x}{8} = -10$	$\dfrac{4z}{5} = 24$
4.	$\dfrac{5a}{8} = 25$	$-\dfrac{7m}{10} = 21$	$\dfrac{3x}{10} = 3$	$-\dfrac{2r}{3} = 48$

SOLVING EQUATIONS

Combining Like Terms

Some equations contain the same variable in more than one term. Combine the like terms on each side of the equation. Then solve and check.

EXAMPLE 1

> **Solve: $5a + 4a = 45$**
> $$9a = 45$$
> $$\left(\frac{1}{9}\right)9a = \left(\frac{1}{9}\right)45$$
> $$a = 5$$
>
> **Check:** $5(5) + 4(5) = 45$
> $$25 + 20 = 45$$

EXAMPLE 2

> **Solve: $3b - 5b = 4$**
> $$-2b = 4$$
> $$\left(-\frac{1}{2}\right)(-2b) = \left(-\frac{1}{2}\right)4$$
> $$b = -2$$
>
> **Check:** $3(-2) - 5(-2) = 4$
> $$-6 + 10 = 4$$

EXAMPLE 3

> **Solve: $4r + r = -5$**
> $$5r = -5$$
> $$\left(\frac{1}{5}\right)5r = \left(\frac{1}{5}\right)(-5)$$
> $$r = -1$$
>
> **Check:** $4(-1) + (-1) = -5$
> $$-4 + -1 = -5$$

PRACTICE

Solve. Check.

	a	b	c	d
1.	$-15c + 10c = 100$	$4m + 7m = 66$	$-2x + 3x = 24$	$5z + 2z = 41 - 6$
2.	$8a - 5a = 60$	$15a - 3a = 60$	$-8x + 6x = 38$	$-8z - 3z = 24 - 2$
3.	$14b - 6b = 48$	$-6b + 5b = 55$	$3x - x = 46$	$3r + 2r = 31 - 6$
4.	$5x - 2x = 120$	$14b - 9b = 65$	$7x - 3x = 12$	$x - 3x = 18 + 6$

Using Equations to Solve Problems

A problem may include information about the relationship between a number and an unknown quantity. To solve such a problem, first define a variable to represent the unknown quantity. Then write and solve an equation to find the value for the unknown. Study the following example.

EXAMPLE

Three-fifths of a certain number is 18. What is the number?

Define a variable.	Write an equation.	Solve the equation.	State the answer.
Let n = the number.	Three-fifths of n is 18. $$\frac{3}{5}n = 18$$	$$\left(\frac{5}{3}\right)\frac{3}{5}n = \left(\frac{5}{3}\right)18$$ $$n = 30$$	The solution is 30.

Check:
$$\frac{3}{5}(30) = 18$$

Write an equation. Solve. Check.

1. Three-fourths of a number is 36. What is the number?

Answer _____

2. Find the number, one-fifth of which is equal to 14.

Answer _____

3. One-third of a certain number is equal to 15. What is the number?

Answer _____

4. Five times a certain number is equal to 35. What is the number?

Answer _____

5. A certain number, when divided by 3, is equal to 20. What is the number?

Answer _____

6. One and one-half times a certain number is 30. What is the number?

Answer _____

More About Using Equations

A problem may contain more than one unknown quantity. Use the following steps to solve such a problem:

1. Define a variable to represent one unknown quantity. Then use the same variable to write an expression for the other unknown.
2. Write an equation.
3. Solve the equation and check the solution.
4. State the answer to the problem that is asked. Sometimes the answer must include both unknowns.

EXAMPLE

> **Joe's father is three times as old as Joe. The sum of their ages is 60 years. How old is each?**
>
> Define a variable.
>
> Let a = Joe's age.
> $3a$ = his father's age.
>
> Write an equation.
>
> The sum of a and $3a$ is 60.
> $a + 3a = 60$
>
> Solve the equation.
>
> $a + 3a = 60$
> $4a = 60$
> $a = 15$
>
> State the answer.
> Since a = Joe's age, Joe is 15. His father's age is $3a$, which is 3(15) or 45.

Write an equation. Solve. Check.

1. Arlo's father is four times as old as Arlo, and the sum of their ages is 50 years. How old is each?

Answer _____

2. Julia and Ana have $7.20. Ana has five times as much as Julia. How much does each girl have?

Answer _____

3. Together, Tim and Tom have $2.40. Tim has three times as much as Tom. How much does each have?

Answer _____

4. Carla is twice as old as her sister. The sum of their ages is 42 years. How old is each?

Answer _____

5. Bridget and Susan inherited an estate of $2000. Bridget is to receive four times as much as Susan. How much does each receive?

Answer _____

6. From Kansas City to Denver is twice as far as from Kansas City to St. Louis. The two distances together total 900 miles. What is the mileage in each case?

Answer _____

Solving Two-Step Equations

Recall that when you evaluate an expression, you do the multiplication and division before the addition and subtraction. To isolate the variable in an equation, however, first add or subtract. Then multiply or divide. Study the examples.

EXAMPLE 1

Solve: $2x - 5 = 71$

Step 1 $2x = 71 + 5$

          $2x = 76$

Step 2 $x = 76\left(\dfrac{1}{2}\right)$

          $x = 38$

Check: $2(38) - 5 = 71$

            $71 = 71$

EXAMPLE 2

Solve: $4a + 7 = -49$

Step 1 $4a = -49 - 7$

          $4a = -56$

Step 2 $a = -56\left(\dfrac{1}{4}\right)$

          $a = -14$

Check: $4(-14) + 7 = -49$

           $-49 = -49$

EXAMPLE 3

Solve: $-3y - 4 = 11$

Step 1 $-3y = 11 + 4$

         $-3y = 15$

Step 2 $y = 15\left(-\dfrac{1}{3}\right)$

          $y = -5$

Check: $-3(-5) - 4 = 11$

           $11 = 11$

PRACTICE

Solve. Check.

	a	b	c	d
1.	$3x - 5 = 16$	$-14r - 7 = 49$	$25a - 4 = 96$	$60y - 7 = 173$
2.	$7x + 3 = -4$	$23y + 6 = 75$	$17a + 9 = 77$	$-2m + 9 = 7$
3.	$8a - 7 = 65$	$19b - 4 = 72$	$52x + 4 = -100$	$-6z + 15 = 3$
4.	$2r + 45 = 15$	$33b - 3 = 96$	$-75x + 5 = 230$	$35z + 12 = 82$

Work Backwards

Sometimes you are told what happened at the end of a problem and asked to find what happened at the beginning. You can find the solution to a problem like this by working backwards. Another way to find the solution is to write an equation.

Read the problem.

Some people get on an elevator on the ground floor of an office building. On the second floor, 3 people get off the elevator. On the third floor, 4 people get off and 2 get on. On the fifth floor, 5 people get off and 1 gets on. On the top floor, 6 people get off and the elevator is empty. How many people got on the elevator on the ground floor?

Work backwards.

Begin at the end with the empty elevator at the top floor. Work backwards toward the ground floor. If people got off, put them back on by adding. If people got on, take them off by subtracting.

Top floor	Put 6 people on.	$0 + 6 = 6$
Fifth floor	Put 5 people on and take 1 off.	$6 + 5 - 1 = 10$
Third floor	Put 4 people on and take 2 off.	$10 + 4 - 2 = 12$
Second floor	Put 3 people on.	$12 + 3 = 15$

There were 15 people on the elevator when it started.

Write an equation.

Let x = the number of people who got on the elevator on the ground floor. Use positive integers for the people who get on the elevator. Use negative integers for the people who get off.

$$x + (-3) + (-4) + 2 + (-5) + 1 + (-6) = 0$$
$$x + (-18) + 3 = 0$$
$$x + (-15) = 0$$
$$x = 15$$

Solve by working backwards or writing an equation.

1. Miguel went shopping at a factory outlet. He bought a sweater for $35.95, a pair of pants for $19.95, and a shirt for $18.95. After paying for it all, he had $9.15 left. How much did Miguel have before he bought anything.
[Hint: One possible equation would be: $x + (-\$35.95) + (-\$19.95) + (-\$18.95) = \$9.15$]

2. Chim and Hoa bought a new refrigerator that was on sale. They got a discount of $100 off the original price. A sales tax of $33 was added to their cost of the refrigerator. If they paid $583, what was the original price of the refrigerator?

Answer _____

Answer _____

Solve.

3. An elevator starts on the ground floor with some people on it. At the first stop, 6 people get off and 3 get on. At the second stop, 8 get off and 2 get on. At the third stop, 6 get off and 1 gets on. At the last stop, 4 people get off and the elevator is empty. How many people were on the elevator when it started.

Answer _____

4. Sheila was born in New York. She moved to California and lived there twice as long as she lived in New York. Then she moved to Montana, where she has lived for 8 years. She is now 62 years old. How long did she live in New York?

Answer _____

5. Uncle Walter says, ''If you divide my age by 4 and then subtract 11, the answer will be the number of eggs in a dozen.'' How old is Uncle Walter?

Answer _____

6. Marsha bought a new car for $21,152.25. The options she picked cost $2,150. The sales tax was $1,007.25. What was the base price of Marsha's car?

Answer _____

7. Darren wants to save $750.00 for his vacation. When he has saved 3 times as much as he has already saved, he will need only $27 more. How much has he saved so far?

Answer _____

8. Heather buys 2 loaves of bread at $1.45 each, 3 cans of soup at $0.50 each, and a pound of butter for $2.50. She gives the check-out clerk a bill and gets $3.10 in change. What bill did she give the clerk?

Answer _____

SOLVING EQUATIONS

Another Step in Combining Terms

Sometimes you need to rewrite an equation so that the variables are on one side of the equation. To accomplish this, add the opposite of the term to both sides of the equation. Study the example.

EXAMPLE 1

Solve: $4x - 5 = 3x + 1$

$4x - 5 + (-3x) = 3x + 1 + (-3x)$
$x - 5 = 1$
$x - 5 + 5 = 1 + 5$
$x = 6$

Check: $4(6) - 5 = 3(6) + 1$
$19 = 19$

EXAMPLE 2

Solve: $3x + 5 = x + 13$

$3x + 5 - 5 = x + 13 - 5$
$3x = x + 8$
$3x - x = x + 8 - x$
$2x = 8$
$x = 4$

Check: $3(4) + 5 = 4 + 13$
$17 = 17$

EXAMPLE 3

Solve: $7x - 1 = 15 + 3x$

$7x - 1 + 1 = 15 + 3x + 1$
$7x = 16 + 3x$
$7x - 3x = 16 + 3x - 3x$
$4x = 16$
$x = 4$

Check: $7(4) - 1 = 15 + 3(4)$
$27 = 27$

PRACTICE

Solve. Check.

	a	b	c	d
1.	$8x + 5 = 5x - 10$	$5x - 1 = 4x + 3$	$3x - 5 = x - 7$	$5x + 3 = 4x + 8$
2.	$5x - 16 = x + 4$	$6x + 3 = 5x + 3$	$15x + 5 = 10x - 15$	$2x + 3 = x + 10$
3.	$5x - 9 = 5 - 2x$	$5x + 20 = 4x - 24$	$3x + 6 = x + 8$	$5x - 6 = 2x + 12$
4.	$3x - 2 = 2x - 4$	$4x - 12 = 2x + 2$	$3x + 1 = 2x + 5$	$3x - 4 = x + 8$

SOLVING EQUATIONS

Clearing Fractions

When an equation contains fractions on both sides, it is helpful to multiply both sides by the common denominator of the fractions. This process of eliminating fractions is called **clearing fractions.**

EXAMPLE 1

Solve: $\dfrac{x}{2} + 5 = \dfrac{x}{3} + 8$

$(6)\left(\dfrac{x}{2} + 5\right) = (6)\left(\dfrac{x}{3} + 8\right)$

$3x + 30 = 2x + 48$

$3x - 2x = 48 - 30$

$x = 18$

Check: $\dfrac{18}{2} + 5 = \dfrac{18}{3} + 8$

$14 = 14$

EXAMPLE 2

Solve: $\dfrac{3x}{2} + 2 = x + 3$

$(2)\left(\dfrac{3x}{2} + 2\right) = (2)(x + 3)$

$3x + 4 = 2x + 6$

$3x - 2x = 6 - 4$

$x = 2$

Check: $\dfrac{3(2)}{2} + 2 = 2 + 3$

$5 = 5$

EXAMPLE 3

Solve: $\dfrac{2x}{3} - 6 = \dfrac{x}{9} + 4$

$(9)\left(\dfrac{2x}{3} - 6\right) = (9)\left(\dfrac{x}{9} + 4\right)$

$6x - 54 = x + 36$

$6x - x = 36 + 54$

$5x = 90$

$x = 18$

Check: $\dfrac{2(18)}{3} - 6 = \dfrac{(18)}{9} + 4$

$6 = 6$

PRACTICE

Solve. Check.

a

1. $\dfrac{3x}{2} + 2 = \dfrac{x}{4} + 7$

2. $\dfrac{x}{3} + 5 = \dfrac{x}{6} - 6$

3. $\dfrac{x}{3} - 6 = \dfrac{x}{9}$

b

$\dfrac{x}{2} - 3 = \dfrac{x}{7} + 2$

$\dfrac{x}{2} + 4 = \dfrac{x}{4} - 1$

$\dfrac{x}{7} + 8 = x + 2$

c

$\dfrac{x}{5} + 7 = \dfrac{x}{10} + 8$

$\dfrac{x}{4} + 5 = \dfrac{x}{8} + 6$

$x - 5 = \dfrac{2x}{7} - 10$

SOLVING EQUATIONS
Cross Multiplication

If an equation contains only one fraction, the fraction can be cleared by multiplying both sides by the denominator. When there are two fractions, the fractions could be cleared one at a time. For equations that contain only one term on each side, a faster method is to **cross multiply.** With this shortcut, each numerator is multiplied by the opposite denominator. Study the following examples.

EXAMPLE 1

Solve: $\dfrac{2x}{3} = \dfrac{12}{9}$

$9(2x) = 3(12)$
$18x = 36$
$x = 2$

Check: $\dfrac{2(2)}{3} = \dfrac{12}{9}$

$\dfrac{4}{3} = \dfrac{4}{3}$

EXAMPLE 2

Solve: $\dfrac{x}{2} = \dfrac{3}{4}$

$4x = 2(3)$
$4x = 6$

$x = \dfrac{3}{2}$

Check: $\dfrac{3}{2}\left(\dfrac{1}{2}\right) = \dfrac{3}{4}$

EXAMPLE 3

Solve: $\dfrac{3}{x} = \dfrac{6}{4}$

$4(3) = 6x$
$12 = 6x$
$2 = x$

Check: $\dfrac{3}{2} = \dfrac{6}{4}$

$\dfrac{3}{2} = \dfrac{3}{2}$

PRACTICE

Solve. Check.

	a	b	c	d
1.	$\dfrac{x}{3} = \dfrac{2}{5}$	$\dfrac{x}{4} = \dfrac{1}{3}$	$\dfrac{x}{5} = \dfrac{3}{4}$	$\dfrac{2x}{9} = \dfrac{2}{3}$
2.	$\dfrac{3x}{10} = \dfrac{3}{5}$	$\dfrac{5c}{12} = \dfrac{5}{6}$	$\dfrac{4x}{7} = \dfrac{3}{5}$	$\dfrac{2a}{5} = \dfrac{3}{8}$
3.	$\dfrac{x}{6} = \dfrac{7}{12}$	$\dfrac{x}{7} = \dfrac{5}{8}$	$\dfrac{3}{4} = \dfrac{x}{8}$	$\dfrac{4}{5} = \dfrac{m}{5}$
4.	$\dfrac{3x}{7} = \dfrac{4}{9}$	$\dfrac{10}{x} = \dfrac{5}{2}$	$\dfrac{3}{x} = \dfrac{3}{5}$	$\dfrac{5}{x} = \dfrac{2}{8}$

SOLVING EQUATIONS
Equations with Parentheses

When an equation contains parentheses, simplify each side before solving the equation. When you remove parentheses, remember to multiply each term within the parentheses by the coefficient. If the coefficient is negative, the sign of each term within the parentheses must be changed when the parentheses are removed.

EXAMPLE 1

> **Solve:** $5(x + 4) = 4(x + 6)$
>
> $5x + 20 = 4x + 24$
> $5x - 4x = 24 - 20$
> $\qquad x = 4$
>
> **Check:** $5(4 + 4) = 4(4 + 6)$
> $\qquad\qquad 40 = 40$

EXAMPLE 2

> **Solve:** $5b - 3(4 - b) = 2(b + 21)$
>
> $5b - 12 + 3b = 2b + 42$
> $5b + 3b - 2b = 42 + 12$
> $\qquad\quad 6b = 54$
> $\qquad\quad\; b = 9$
>
> **Check:** $5(9) - 3(4 - 9) = 2(9 + 21)$
> $\qquad\qquad\qquad\quad 60 = 60$

PRACTICE

Solve. Check.

	a	b	c
1.	$3(x + 2) = 2(x + 5)$	$3x - (2x - 7) = 15$	$2b - 7(3 + b) = b + 3$
2.	$4(x - 3) = 2(x - 1)$	$7x - (x - 1) = 25$	$9a - 3(2a - 4) = 15$
3.	$4(x - 1) = 2(x + 4)$	$7 - 12(3 + b) = 31$	$5x - 2(4 - x) = 20$
4.	$5x + 3 = 4(x + 2)$	$5x - (x + 6) = 10$	$4(2x - 5) - 3(x + 10) = -15$
5.	$3(x - 1) = 2x + 3$	$3x - (x + 2) = 4$	$2(x + 5) - (x - 3) = 8$

Solving Problems

Solve.

1. Together, Tom and Dick have $3.10. Tom has $0.10 more than 4 times as much as Dick. How much does each have?

$$Let \; x = Dick's \; money$$
$$Then, \; 4x + \$0.10 = Tom's \; money$$
$$And \; x + 4x + \$0.10 = \$3.10$$
$$5x = \$3.10 - \$0.10 = \$3.00$$
$$x = \$0.60$$
$$4x + \$0.10 = \$2.50$$

Answer ____ *Dick has $0.60. Tom has $2.50.* ____

2. If 5 is added to 4 times a certain number, the result is 21. What is the number?

$$Let \; x = the \; number$$
$$Then, \; 4x + 5 = 21$$
$$4x + 5 - 5 = 21 - 5$$
$$4x = 16$$
$$x = 4$$

Answer ____ *The number is 4.* ____

3. If 15 is added to 2 times a certain number, the result is 55. What is the number?

Answer _____

4. If 5 times a number is decreased by 20, the result is equal to the number increased by 12. Find the number.

Answer _____

5. If 8 is added to 5 times a certain number, the result is 43. What is the number?

Answer _____

6. If 3 times a number is decreased by 30, the result is equal to 2 times the number. What is the number?

Answer _____

7. If 15 is added to twice a certain number, the result will be equal to the number increased by 23. Find the number. (If x represents the number, then $x + 23$ represents the number *increased* by 23.)

Answer _____

8. If 6 times a certain number is decreased by 100, the result is equal to the number increased by 150. What is the number?

Answer _____

9. Five times a number added to 3 times the number is equal to the number increased by 56. Find the number.

Answer _____

10. Frank is 4 times as old as his brother. The difference in their ages is 24 years. How old is each?

Answer _____

Solving Problems

Solve.

---

1. The length of a lot is three times the width. The perimeter is 560 feet. Find the length and width.

$$Let\ x = width$$
$$3x = length$$
$$(2l + 2w = P)$$
$$2x + 6x = 560\ feet$$
$$8x = 560\ feet$$
$$x = 70\ feet$$
$$3x = 210\ feet$$

Answer _____ *Length = 210 ft. Width = 70 ft.*_____

2. The sum of two consecutive numbers is 85. Find the numbers.

$$Let\ x = the\ first\ number$$
$$x + 1 = the\ second\ number$$
$$x + x + 1 = 85$$
$$2x + 1 = 85$$
$$2x = 84$$
$$x = 42$$
$$x + 1 = 43$$

Answer _____ *First number = 42. Second number = 43.*_____

---

3. The perimeter of another rectangular-shaped lot is 420 meters. The length is twice the width. Find both dimensions.

Answer _____

4. Three numbers added together total 180. The second number is twice the first, and the third is three times the first. Find each number.

Answer _____

---

5. The length of a rectangular-shaped garden is four times the width. The perimeter is 100 feet. Find both dimensions.

Answer _____

6. Three numbers added together total 300. The second number is four times the first, and the third is five times the first. Find these three numbers. (Let x = first number.)

Answer _____

---

7. The width of a rectangle is one-fifth as much as the length. The perimeter is 120 cm. Find the length and width. (Let x equal the width, thus avoiding fractions.)

Answer _____

8. The sum of three consecutive numbers is 42. What are the numbers? (Remember that the third number is 2 more than the first.)

Answer _____

Identify Substeps

As you already know, solving a problem requires several steps such as reading the problem, deciding what to do, and then finding the answer. Some of these steps may need to be broken down into substeps. Identifying the substeps is an important part of planning how to solve the main problem.

Read the problem.

Kira needs to drive $640\frac{3}{4}$ miles to reach her destination. She has been driving for $4\frac{1}{2}$ hours at a rate of 60 miles per hour. She will drive at an average rate of $63\frac{1}{2}$ miles per hour for the rest of the trip. To the nearest hour, how much longer must she drive?

Identify the substeps.

(1) How far has Kira driven so far?
(2) How much further does she need to drive?
Find the answer for each substep.
(1) $4\frac{1}{2} \times 60 = \frac{9}{2} \times \frac{60}{1} = 270$ miles so far
(2) $640\frac{3}{4} - 270 = 370\frac{3}{4}$ miles to go

Solve the problem.

Solve the problem using the distance formula.
Distance = Rate × Time
$$370\frac{3}{4} = 63\frac{1}{2} \times t$$
$$\frac{1483}{4} = \frac{127}{2}t$$
$$4\left(\frac{1483}{4}\right) = 4\left(\frac{127}{2}\right)t$$
$$1483 = 254t$$
$$5.84 = t$$
To the nearest hour, Kira has to drive 6 hours longer.

Solve.

1. Mrs. Pappos is three times as old as her daughter Nina. Her son Nikos, who is 5 years old, is half as old as Nina. How old is Mrs. Pappos?

   Substep _____

   Answer to Substep _____

   Answer to main problem _____

2. One week Ginny worked 36 hours at $6.00 per hour. The next week she worked 40 hours at $7.00 per hour. How much more did she earn the second week?

   Substep 1 _____

   Answer to Substep 1 _____

   Substep 2 _____

   Answer to Substep 2 _____

   Answer to main problem _____

Solve.

3. Mrs. Kwan painted a wall measuring 20 feet by 9 feet. One gallon of paint covered 120 square feet of wall space. How many gallons of paint did she use?

Answer _____

4. There are 88 keys on a piano. Thirty-six of the keys are black and the rest are white. How many more white keys are there than black keys?

Answer _____

5. A truck driver needs to drive 640 miles to reach his destination. He has been driving for $4\frac{1}{2}$ hours at a rate of 55 miles per hour. How much farther does he have to drive?

Answer _____

6. Pencils sell for $1.68 per dozen. A teacher bought 276 pencils for his math classes. How much did the pencils cost?

Answer _____

7. When Randy started his job, he earned $5.40 per hour. Now he makes $234 for working a 40-hour week. How much more does he earn per hour than he did when he started?

Answer _____

8. A rectangle with a perimeter of 72 inches is $\frac{1}{2}$ as wide as it is long. What is the area of the rectangle?

Answer _____

SOLVING EQUATIONS
Unit 3 Review

Solve. Check.

	a	*b*	*c*
1.	$5x = 45$	$-15y = 105$	$r + 12 = 3$
2.	$a + 5 = 7$	$x - 3 = 4$	$25x = 10$
3.	$\dfrac{2a}{3} = 4$	$\dfrac{x}{2} = 6$	$\dfrac{x}{2} = 6 + \dfrac{x}{5}$
4.	$5x + 6 = 1$	$4r + 3 = 3$	$2x - 5 = 7$
5.	$5x + 7 = 2x + 8$	$3m + 1 = 6m - 5$	$x + (x + 5) = x + 2$
6.	$a + 2(a - 2) = 2a + 3$	$5y - 2(y + 2) = 5$	$6y - 4 = 2(2y + 1)$

Solve.

7. Henry is 7 years older than his brother, Ted. The sum of their ages is 23 years. How old is each?

8. Together, Leslie and Elena have $5.25. Elena has $0.25 more than Leslie. How much does each have?

Answer _____

Answer _____

Cumulative Review

Simplify.

	a	*b*	*c*
1.	$(-2)(-7) =$	$5(-8 + 9) =$	$4 + 6(2) =$
2.	$-3a + 4(a + 2) =$	$7(-3a) + 6(-a) =$	$3(a + 3b) - (a + 2b) =$

Solve. Check.

	a	*b*	*c*
3.	$5x = 90$	$\dfrac{2a}{5} = 4$	$x - 10 = 35$
4.	$r + 17 = 20$	$\dfrac{y}{9} = -8$	$3x - 10 = 2$
5.	$8x + 5 = 5x - 10$	$\dfrac{y}{3} = \dfrac{2}{5}$	$3(x + 2) = 2(x + 5)$
6.	$\dfrac{3x}{2} + 2 = \dfrac{x}{4} + 7$	$8a + 3 = 6a - 7$	$\dfrac{2a}{7} = \dfrac{2}{3}$

Solve.

7. In the formula $V = lwh$ find l when $h = 4$ in., $w = 7$ in., and $V = 252$ cu in.

Answer _____

8. In the formula $I = prt$ find p when $I = \$20$, $r = 5\%$, and $t = 1$ year.

Answer _____

9. Twice a number decreased by 8 is equal to the number increased by 10. Find the number.

Answer _____

10. The sum of two consecutive numbers is 41. What are the numbers? (Hint: Let x be the first number.)

Answer _____

4

Exponents

Recall that the formula for finding the volume of a prism is $V = lwh$. A cube is a prism that has equal dimensions. Let s represent the length of each edge. So, the formula for volume of a cube is $V = s \times s \times s$ or $V = s^3$ (pronounced s *cubed*). The 3 in the expression s^3 is called the **exponent.** The s is called the **base.** The exponent indicates the number of times the base is listed as a factor.

When no exponent is used, as in $A = lw$, the exponent of each variable is understood to be 1. If an expression contains factors that are repeated, you can rewrite the expression using exponents.

Remember, $y \times y$, $y \cdot y$, and $(y)(y)$ all mean multiply.

EXAMPLE 1

A cube has edges 5 inches long. What is its volume?
$5^3 = 5 \times 5 \times 5 = 125$
The volume is 125 cubic inches.

EXAMPLE 2

Write r · r · r · r using an exponent.
$r \cdot r \cdot r \cdot r = r^4$

EXAMPLE 3

Write y using an exponent.
$y = y^1$

PRACTICE

Write using exponents.

	a	*b*	*c*
1.	$5 \times 5 =$	$4 \times 4 \times 4 =$	$(y)(y) =$
2.	$2 \times 2 \times 2 \times 2 =$	$a \cdot a \cdot a =$	$8 \cdot 8 \cdot 8 \cdot 8 =$
3.	$9 \times 9 \times 9 =$	$(r)(r)(r) =$	$p =$
4.	$s \cdot s \cdot s \cdot s \cdot s =$	$1 \times 1 \times 1 \times 1 \times 1 =$	$15 \times 15 =$
5.	$(3)(3)(3) =$	$w \cdot w =$	$(5)(5)(5) =$

Find the volume of each cube.

6. A cube has edges 3 inches long.

7. A cube has edges 2 inches long.

8. A cube has edges 6 inches long.

9. A cube has edges 5 inches long.

EXPONENTS AND POLYNOMIALS

Powers of Integers

The exponent in an expression indicates the number of times the base is used as a factor.

Remember,
  · zero with any exponent is zero. $0^2 = 0 \cdot 0 = 0$
  · one with any exponent is one. $1^2 = 1 \cdot 1 = 1$

EXAMPLE 1

Simplify: 4^3

$4^3 = 4 \cdot 4 \cdot 4$
$\quad = 64$

EXAMPLE 2

Simplify: $(-2)^4$

$(-2)^4 = (-2)(-2)(-2)(-2)$
$\quad\quad = 4 \cdot 4$
$\quad\quad = 16$

EXAMPLE 3

Simplify: $-2^4 \cdot 3^2$

$-2^4 \cdot 3^2 = -(2 \cdot 2 \cdot 2 \cdot 2)(3 \cdot 3)$
$\quad\quad\quad = -16 \cdot 9$
$\quad\quad\quad = -144$

PRACTICE

Simplify.

	a	*b*	*c*	*d*
1.	$4^2 =$	$3^2 =$	$-2^2 =$	$5^2 =$
2.	$3^3 =$	$-6^3 =$	$(-5)^3 =$	$2^3 =$
3.	$-8^2 =$	$0^3 =$	$(-10)^2 =$	$9^2 =$
4.	$2^5 =$	$(-3)^4 =$	$4^4 =$	$-3^5 =$
5.	$(-1)^3 =$	$-10^3 =$	$-2^5 =$	$(-4)^4 =$
6.	$(-11)^3 =$	$10^1 =$	$21^2 =$	$-3^6 =$
7.	$14^2 =$	$-20^3 =$	$17^2 =$	$0^{50} =$
8.	$2^3 \cdot 3^2 =$	$4^2 \cdot 5^2 =$	$(-3)^3 \cdot 4^2 =$	$8^2 \cdot 2^3 =$
9.	$10^2 \cdot 5^3 =$	$(-9)^2 \cdot 3^3 =$	$-6^2 \cdot 7^3 =$	$(-1)^2 \cdot 5 =$
10.	$(-3^4)(2^2) =$	$(4^3)(7^2) =$	$(6^2)(4^2) =$	$(8^2)(-8^3) =$

Find a Pattern

Sometimes the numbers in a problem follow a definite pattern. In order to solve the problem, you must first discover the pattern. Then you can use the pattern to find the answer.

Read the problem.

Anna drew a diagram of her family tree. She wrote her own name in the bottom row and her parents' names in the row above. Then she wrote her grandparents' and great-grandparents' names in the rows above her parents'. Suppose she continued until there were 7 rows in all. How many names would be in the seventh row from the bottom?

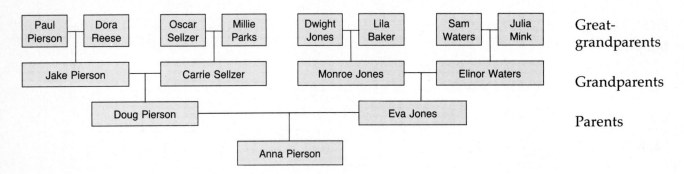

Use the strategy.

Count the number of names in each row, starting at the bottom. Anna has 2 parents, 4 grandparents, and 8 great-grandparents. The pattern is doubling the number of names.

Solve the problem.

The fifth row from the bottom would have 2 × 8 or 16 names. The sixth row from the bottom would have 2 × 16 or 32 names. The seventh row from the bottom would have 2 × 32 or 64 names.

The pattern 1, 2, 4, 8, 16, 32, 64 can be expressed using exponents.

Rows	1	2	3	4	5	6	7
Names	1 2^0	2 2^1	4 2^2	8 2^3	16 2^4	32 2^5	64 2^6

Write the next three numbers in each pattern.

1. 3, 9, 27, 81, _____, _____, _____

2. 6, 12, 24, 48, _____, _____, _____

3. 7, 13, 19, 25, _____, _____, _____

4. 75, 64, 53, 42, _____, _____, _____

5. 448, 224, 112, _____, _____, _____

6. −5, 10, −20, 40, _____, _____, _____

Find a pattern. Solve.

7. The number of students at Jefferson High School has been decreasing steadily from 911 two years ago to 862 last year to 813 today. If the trend continues, how many students will be at Jefferson High School next year?

Answer _____

8. Jake's hourly wage has increased steadily every 6 months. It has gone from $4.85 per hour to $5.60 per hour to $6.35 per hour. If the pattern continues, how much will he be making in 6 months?

Answer _____

9. A person mails a recipe to six friends. Each of the six friends mails the recipe to six of their friends and so on. How many people receive a recipe in the fourth mailing?

Answer _____

10. Suppose that ten 9s were multiplied together.

$9 \times 9 \times 9 \times 9 \times 9 \times 9 \times 9 \times 9 \times 9 \times 9$

What is the ones digit of the answer? (Hint: Multiply two nines together; three nines; four nines. Look for a pattern in the ones digit.)

Answer _____

11. Seven people were at a meeting. Each person shook hands with each other person exactly once. How many handshakes took place? (Hint: Decide how many handshakes would take place if there were 2 people, 3 people, 4 people, and so on.)

Answer _____

12. Maria had 3 employees in 1990. Her business grew to 9 employees in 1991. Then there were 27 employees in 1992. At that growth rate, how many employees were there in 1994?

Answer _____

Multiplying Monomials

When like bases are multiplied, the exponents are added. When monomials have coefficients other than 1, remember to multiply the coefficients.

EXAMPLE 1

Multiply: $s \cdot s$

$s^1 \cdot s^1 = s^{1+1}$
$ = s^2$

EXAMPLE 2

Multiply: $(3m^2)(3m^3)$

$(3m^2)(3m^3) = (3 \cdot 3)m^{2+3}$
$ = 9m^5$

EXAMPLE 3

Multiply: $(d^3ef)(de^4)$

$(d^3ef)(de^4) = d^{3+1}e^{1+4}f^1$
$ = d^4e^5f$

PRACTICE

Multiply.

	a	b	c	d
1.	$(a^3)(a^5) =$	$(b^3)(b^4) =$	$(c^5)(c^3) =$	$(d^3)(d^7) =$
2.	$(a^3x)(ax) =$	$(a^3b)(ab^2) =$	$(m^5n)(m^2n) =$	$(x^6y)(xy^3) =$
3.	$(abc)(a) =$	$(xyz)(x^2) =$	$(rst)(s^2) =$	$(def)(e^5) =$
4.	$(a^3xy)(ax^2) =$	$(a^4bc)(ab^2) =$	$(c^5de^2)(c^2d) =$	$(b^3df^3)(b^5d) =$
5.	$(7m^2n^2)(m^3n^2) =$	$(6a^5b^6)(3ab) =$	$(8b^3cd)(2b) =$	$(5x^2y^3)(5x^2y^3) =$
6.	$(9ax)(-8y) =$	$(-6ab^2)(-9bc) =$	$(2xy^3)(6z^4) =$	$(2rs^5)(-6mr^6) =$
7.	$(4x^5)(12yz) =$	$(5a^6)(10xy) =$	$(-16z^3)(9yz) =$	$(-15c^6)(-5rs) =$
8.	$(15x^3y^2)(2axy) =$	$(-10bc^3d)(-5acd) =$	$(6x^3y)(-6axy) =$	$(8c^2d)(6abd^2) =$

EXPONENTS AND POLYNOMIALS
Powers of Powers

When a base with an exponent also has an exponent, such as $(2^2)^3$, simplify by multiplying the two exponents. You can check multiplication by showing the factors and adding the exponents.

Remember to multiply the exponents of *all* the factors in each expression.

EXAMPLE 1

Simplify: $(2^2)^3$

$(2^2)^3 = 2^{2\cdot3} = 2^6 = 64$

Check:

$(2^2)^3 = (2^2 \cdot 2^2 \cdot 2^2)$
$= 2^{2+2+2} = 2^6 = 64$

EXAMPLE 2

Simplify: $(2x^3)^3$

$(2x^3)^3 = (2^{1\cdot3})(x^{3\cdot3})$
$= 2^3x^9 = 8x^9$

Check:

$(2x^3)^3 = (2\cdot2\cdot2)(x^3 \cdot x^3 \cdot x^3)$
$= 8x^{3+3+3} = 8x^9$

EXAMPLE 3

Simplify: $(2ab^2)^2 (a^2)^3$

$(2ab^2)^2 (a^2)^3 = (2^2a^2b^4)(a^6)$
$= 2^2a^{2+6}b^4$
$= 4a^8b^4$

PRACTICE

Simplify.

	a	b	c	d
1.	$(3^2)^3 =$	$(4^2)^2 =$	$(5^2)^3 =$	$(6^3)^2 =$
2.	$(2a^4)^2 =$	$(3h^3)^4 =$	$(2n^5)^4 =$	$(5k^7)^3 =$
3.	$(ab)^4 =$	$(st)^6 =$	$(xyz)^5 =$	$(mnp)^8 =$
4.	$(a^4b)^2 =$	$(y^2z)^2 =$	$(mn^4)^3 =$	$(p^6q)^3 =$
5.	$(m^2n^4)^2 =$	$(p^5q^2)^2 =$	$(r^2s^4)^3 =$	$(x^4y^2)^4 =$
6.	$(2c^2de^3)^2 =$	$(4x^3y^2z)^2 =$	$(2mn^5p^3)^4 =$	$(5r^4s^2t^3)^3 =$

Simplify.

	a	b	c
7.	$(ab^2)(a^2b)^2 =$	$(m^2n)(m^3n)^2 =$	$(j^2k^3)(j^2k^2)^3 =$
8.	$(xy)^2(x^3y^2)^3 =$	$(mn^2)^3(m^2n^3)^4 =$	$(g^4h)^3(g^4h^2)^3 =$
9.	$(-3y^2)^2(x^2y^2)^3 =$	$(7pq^3)^2(p^4q^6)^3 =$	$(3x)^3(xy^4)^2 =$

83

Dividing Monomials

In algebra, as in arithmetic, division is the reverse of multiplication. When monomials are multiplied, exponents of like bases are added. When monomials are divided, exponents of like bases are subtracted. Study the examples. When monomials have coefficients other than 1, remember to divide the coefficients.

Recall that expressions such as $\frac{5}{5}$ and $\frac{a}{a}$ equal 1. If you use the rule for dividing monomials, you see that $\frac{a}{a} = a^{1-1} = a^0$. Since $\frac{a}{a} = 1$, it follows that $a^0 = 1$. Therefore, *Any base raised to the zero power equals one.* See Example 3.

EXAMPLE 1

Divide: $\dfrac{a^7}{a^4}$

$\dfrac{a^7}{a^4} = a^{7-4} = a^3$

Check:

$\dfrac{a^7}{a^4} = \dfrac{\overset{1}{\cancel{a}} \cdot \overset{1}{\cancel{a}} \cdot \overset{1}{\cancel{a}} \cdot \overset{1}{\cancel{a}} \cdot a \cdot a \cdot a}{\underset{1}{\cancel{a}} \cdot \underset{1}{\cancel{a}} \cdot \underset{1}{\cancel{a}} \cdot \underset{1}{\cancel{a}}} = a^3$

EXAMPLE 2

Divide: $\dfrac{b^3}{b}$

Recall that $b = b^1$.

$\dfrac{b^3}{b} = b^{3-1} = b^2$

Check: $\dfrac{\overset{1}{\cancel{b}} \cdot b \cdot b}{\underset{1}{\cancel{b}}} = b^2$

EXAMPLE 3

Divide: $\dfrac{3c^2}{c^2}$

$\dfrac{3c^2}{c^2} = 3c^{2-2} = 3c^0 = 3$

Check:

$\dfrac{3c^2}{c^2} = \dfrac{3}{1} \cdot \dfrac{\overset{1}{\cancel{c}} \cdot \overset{1}{\cancel{c}}}{\underset{1}{\cancel{c}} \cdot \underset{1}{\cancel{c}}} = 3$

PRACTICE

Divide.

	a	b	c	d	e
1.	$\dfrac{a^4}{a^4} =$	$\dfrac{d^6}{d^3} =$	$\dfrac{b^5}{b} =$	$\dfrac{m^8}{m^3} =$	$\dfrac{c^9}{c^5} =$
2.	$\dfrac{x^5}{x^3} =$	$\dfrac{y^5}{y^3} =$	$\dfrac{a^6}{a^4} =$	$\dfrac{m^5}{m^2} =$	$\dfrac{s^5}{s^2} =$
3.	$\dfrac{x^2}{x} =$	$\dfrac{a^5}{a^4} =$	$\dfrac{c^2}{c} =$	$\dfrac{c^9}{c^3} =$	$\dfrac{m^2}{m^2} =$
4.	$\dfrac{4z}{2z} =$	$\dfrac{3a^5}{a^3} =$	$\dfrac{5e^6}{e} =$	$\dfrac{9t}{t} =$	$\dfrac{6d^4}{3d} =$
5.	$\dfrac{2x^3}{x^3} =$	$\dfrac{10a^2}{a^2} =$	$\dfrac{20b^5}{4b^2} =$	$\dfrac{2d^6}{d^4} =$	$\dfrac{3b^5}{b^4} =$
6.	$\dfrac{4a}{2} =$	$\dfrac{2y^3}{y} =$	$\dfrac{5e^6}{5e} =$	$\dfrac{6d^6}{6} =$	$\dfrac{8f^8}{2f^2} =$

More About Dividing Monomials

When subtracting exponents, you may get a negative exponent. A negative exponent means that the variable will remain in the denominator.

EXAMPLE 1

Divide: $\dfrac{x^2}{x^3}$

$\dfrac{x^2}{x^3} = x^{2-3} = x^{-1} = \dfrac{1}{x}$

Check:

$\dfrac{x^2}{x^3} = \dfrac{\overset{1}{\cancel{x}} \cdot \overset{1}{\cancel{x}}}{x \cdot \cancel{x} \cdot \cancel{x}} = \dfrac{1}{x}$

EXAMPLE 2

Divide: $\dfrac{18y^2}{9y^4}$

$\dfrac{18y^2}{9y^4} = \dfrac{18}{9}(y^{2-4})$

$= 2 \cdot y^{-2} = 2 \cdot \dfrac{1}{y^2} = \dfrac{2}{y^2}$

EXAMPLE 3

Divide: $\dfrac{-30}{15x^3}$

$\dfrac{-30}{15x^3} = \dfrac{-30}{15} \cdot \dfrac{1}{x^3}$

$= -2 \cdot \dfrac{1}{x^3} = \dfrac{-2}{x^3}$

PRACTICE

Divide.

	a	b	c	d	e
1.	$\dfrac{x^2}{x^3} =$	$\dfrac{y^2}{y^4} =$	$\dfrac{a^2}{a^5} =$	$\dfrac{b}{b^2} =$	$\dfrac{s^2}{s^3} =$
2.	$\dfrac{x^4}{x^6} =$	$\dfrac{a^3}{a^4} =$	$\dfrac{y^2}{y^5} =$	$\dfrac{b^9}{b^{10}} =$	$\dfrac{d^{12}}{d^{14}} =$
3.	$\dfrac{-y}{y^2} =$	$\dfrac{-x^2}{x^3} =$	$\dfrac{-z}{z^3} =$	$-\dfrac{r^3}{r^5} =$	$-\dfrac{d}{d^4} =$
4.	$\dfrac{15}{5c^2} =$	$\dfrac{21x}{7x^3} =$	$\dfrac{27}{3b} =$	$-\dfrac{18r^2}{6r^3} =$	$\dfrac{12}{2e^4} =$
5.	$\dfrac{12x^4}{6x^5} =$	$\dfrac{15y}{5y^2} =$	$\dfrac{6a^4}{a^8} =$	$\dfrac{10b^2}{2b^6} =$	$\dfrac{27z^2}{9z^3} =$
6.	$\dfrac{-12a^2}{4a^3} =$	$\dfrac{16b^2}{-4b^3} =$	$\dfrac{-18x^2}{2x^3} =$	$\dfrac{-90r^2}{10r^4} =$	$\dfrac{-14z^3}{-7z^4} =$

Reducing Algebraic Fractions to Lowest Terms

Algebraic fractions are reduced to lowest terms just as fractions in arithmetic are reduced. First, reduce the fraction formed by the coefficients to lowest terms and then divide the like bases.

Remember, when dividing, subtract the exponents.

EXAMPLE 1

Reduce: $\dfrac{x^3y}{x^2y^2}$

$\dfrac{x^3y}{x^2y^2} = x^{3-2} \cdot y^{1-2}$

$= x^1 \cdot y^{-1} = x \cdot \dfrac{1}{y} = \dfrac{x}{y}$

EXAMPLE 2

Reduce: $\dfrac{a^2b^3c}{a^3b^5}$

$\dfrac{a^2b^3c}{a^3b^5} = a^{2-3} \cdot b^{3-5} \cdot c^1$

$= a^{-1} \cdot b^{-2} \cdot c^1 = \dfrac{1}{a} \cdot \dfrac{1}{b^2} \cdot c$

$= \dfrac{c}{ab^2}$

EXAMPLE 3

Reduce: $\dfrac{8rst}{16st^2}$

$\dfrac{8rst}{16st^2} = \dfrac{8}{16} \cdot r^1 \cdot s^{1-1} \cdot t^{1-2}$

$= \dfrac{1}{2} \cdot r^1 \cdot s^0 \cdot t^{-1} = \dfrac{r}{2t}$

Remember, $s^0 = 1$.

PRACTICE

Reduce to lowest terms.

	a	b	c	d	e
1.	$\dfrac{x^3y^2}{x^2y^2} =$	$\dfrac{a^2b^2}{a^3b} =$	$\dfrac{a^4b^2}{a^2b^4} =$	$\dfrac{x^6y^3z}{x^4yz^2} =$	$\dfrac{xy^3z^6}{x^2y^2z^4} =$
2.	$\dfrac{6x^2y^4}{2x^3y^2} =$	$\dfrac{12x^3y^5}{3x^4y^2} =$	$\dfrac{8ab^2c^3}{16a^2b^2c^3} =$	$\dfrac{25a^3b^2c}{5ab^2c^3} =$	$\dfrac{6a^4b^2c}{24a^2b^3c^4} =$
3.	$\dfrac{15x^3y}{-5x^2y^2} =$	$\dfrac{-5x^2y}{10xy^2} =$	$\dfrac{16x^4y}{-4x^3y^2} =$	$\dfrac{10x^3y^2}{-5x^4y} =$	$\dfrac{-8xy^5}{24x^2y^3} =$
4.	$\dfrac{4ab^2}{-20a^3b} =$	$\dfrac{-15x^2y^3}{5x^3y^2} =$	$\dfrac{-24x^2y^4}{6x^4y^2} =$	$\dfrac{7a^3b^2}{-35a^2b^3} =$	$\dfrac{-48xy^2z^3}{8x^3y^2z} =$
5.	$\dfrac{-15xy}{-5x^2y^2} =$	$\dfrac{-6xy^3z^5}{-36x^2y^3z^4} =$	$\dfrac{-7x^4y^3}{-14x^2y^4} =$	$\dfrac{-16a^3b^4}{-8a^4b^3} =$	$\dfrac{-35ab^3}{-7a^2b} =$
6.	$\dfrac{8a^2y}{12ay^2} =$	$\dfrac{16xy^2}{10x^3y} =$	$\dfrac{12ab^2c}{18a^2bc} =$	$\dfrac{10ab^2c^3}{15a^3b^2c} =$	$\dfrac{14a^4b^2c}{12a^3b^3c^3} =$

Adding Binomials

You have already learned to add monomials. You can now use these skills
to add binomials. A **binomial** is the sum or difference of two monomials.
To add binomials, group the like terms and add the coefficients.

EXAMPLE 1

Add: $(a + b) + (a − b)$

$= (a + a) + (b − b)$
$= 2a + 0 = 2a$

EXAMPLE 2

Add: $(5a + 3b) + (3a − b)$

$= (5a + 3a) + (3b − b)$
$= 8a + 2b$

EXAMPLE 3

Add: $(8xy − 2y) + (−5y)$
$= 8xy + (−2y − 5y)$
$= 8xy + (−7y)$
$= 8xy − 7y$

PRACTICE

Add.

a	b	c
1. $(4a − 2b) + (4a + 2b) =$	$(3x − y) + (3x + y) =$	$(6m − 7n) + (4m − 7n) =$
2. $(4a + 2b) + (4a + 2b) =$	$(6x − 3y) + (x + 4y) =$	$(5m − 6n) + (−2m − n) =$
3. $(−7a + b) + (−3a − b) =$	$(9r − s) + (4r − s) =$	$(6m − n) + (−3m + 3n) =$
4. $(r + 5st) + (r + st) =$	$(4b − 3cd) + (−b − cd) =$	$(−6xy − 8z) + (−8z − 6xy) =$
5. $(7x + 2y) + (−3y + x) =$	$(18p − 19q) + (10p − 14q) =$	$(7ab − 6yz) + (−9yz + 3ab) =$
6. $(xy − x) + (x − xy) =$	$(2ab − a) + (−2ab + a) =$	$(cd + d) + (cd + d) =$
7. $(xyz + z) + (xyz − z) =$	$(6ab − abc) + (ab + 6abc) =$	$(−rst + t) + (6rst + 6t) =$
8. $(5ab − abc) + (5ab − abc) =$	$(10xy − z) + (xy − 10z) =$	$(7y − yz) + (7y − yz) =$

EXPONENTS AND POLYNOMIALS

Subtracting Binomials

Recall that subtracting is the same as adding the opposite. So, to subtract binomials, first change the sign of each term of the subtrahend. Then add.

EXAMPLE 1

Subtract:
$(x + y) - (2x + y)$
$= (x + y) + (-2x - y)$
$= (x - 2x) + (y - y)$
$= -x + 0 = -x$

EXAMPLE 2

Subtract:
$(x + y) - (-3x + y)$
$= (x + y) + (3x - y)$
$= (x + 3x) + (y - y)$
$= 4x + 0 = 4x$

EXAMPLE 3

Subtract:
$(-7rs - 5t) - (5rs + t)$
$= (-7rs - 5t) + (-5rs - t)$
$= (-7rs - 5rs) + (-5t - t)$
$= -12rs + (-6t)$
$= -12rs - 6t$

PRACTICE

Subtract.

	a	*b*	*c*
1.	$(x + y) - (x - y) =$	$(2a + 4b) - (3a - b) =$	$(8m + 6n) - (7m - 5n) =$
2.	$(x - y) - (x + y) =$	$(3a - b) - (6a + 2b) =$	$(10m - n) - (6m + 2n) =$
3.	$(x - y) - (-x + y) =$	$(b - 4c) - (-3b - c) =$	$(-6r - 2s) - (-r - 3s) =$
4.	$(3b - 2cd) - (2b + 3cd) =$	$(6m + 2np) - (3m - 5np) =$	$(8rs - t) - (6t + 5rs) =$
5.	$(-2x + yz) - (x - 5yz) =$	$(6pq - 4rs) - (6pq - 4rs) =$	$(-7rs - 5t) - (5t + rs) =$
6.	$(8x - 5yz) - (-x - 4yz) =$	$(7x + 5wy) - (-2x + 3wy) =$	$(-8mn + 6p) - (-5mn + 6p) =$
7.	$(-4 + xyz) - (5 + xyz) =$	$(4p - 5qt) - (-5qt + 4p) =$	$(-t + rs) - (t - rs) =$
8.	$(10z + xyz) - (10xyz + z) =$	$(3abc - c) - (2abc + c) =$	$(rst - 2rs) - (3rst - 4rs) =$

Simplifying Polynomials with Exponents

A **polynomial** is an expression that can be written as a sum of monomials. Simplifying polynomials with exponents is done by adding and subtracting like terms. Group the like terms. Like terms must have the same exponents.

Remember, when subtracting terms in parentheses, change the sign of *each* term. Then add.

EXAMPLE 1	EXAMPLE 2	EXAMPLE 3
Simplify: $3x^2 + 5y + 2x^2 + y$ $= (3x^2 + 2x^2) + (5y + y)$ $= 5x^2 + 6y$	**Simplify:** $8x^3 - 5y^2 - (3x^3 + 2y^2 + y)$ $= (8x^3 - 3x^3) + (-5y^2 - 2y^2) - y$ $= 5x^3 - 7y^2 - y$	**Simplify:** $2x^4 + 3x^3 - (-6x^4) + 2$ $= (2x^4 + 6x^4) + 3x^3 + 2$ $= 8x^4 + 3x^3 + 2$

PRACTICE

Simplify.

	a	b	c
1.	$4x^3 + 3y^2 + 3x^3 + 4y^2 =$	$5a^2 + 4b^2 + 3a^2 + 5b^2 =$	$b^2 + 9c^2 + 4b^2 + 3c^2 =$
2.	$9m^2 + n - (m^2 + 6n^2) =$	$5x^2 + 3y - (3x^2 + 5y) =$	$9a^2 + 4b - (6a^2 + 7b) =$
3.	$5b^2 - 7b - (3b^2 - 9b) =$	$7m^2 - 3n^4 - (4m^2 - 7n^4) =$	$4x^2 - 5y - (3x^2 - 2y) =$
4.	$9x^3 - 4y^2 - (-x^3 - 3y^2) =$	$5a^3 - 4b^2 - (-3a^3 - 5b^2) =$	$8b^3 - 7b^2 - (-b^3 - b^2) =$
5.	$-4m^2 - 3m - (-4m^2 - 2m) =$	$-5x^2 + 4y^3 - (3x^2 + 2y^3) =$	$-6x + 9y^2 - (-6x - 2y^2) =$
6.	$-(8a^3 + 7a^2 + a) + 3a^2 + 5a =$	$-(4b^3 - 5b^2) + b^3 - b^2 + b =$	$-(9m + 9m^2) + 3m^2 + 3m =$
7.	$-(3 + 2x^2 + 4x^4) - (4x^4) =$	$-(c^2 - b^2) + c^2 + b^2 + 1 =$	$-(-4 - x^2) - (-2 + 4x^2 + x) =$
8.	$-3x^4 - x^3 + 3x^2 - (3x^4 + x^3) =$	$-(15m - 6m^2) + (-5m + 4m) =$	$-(7a^4 - 7a^4) + (3a^4 + 9a^4) =$

Multiplying Fractions

Algebraic fractions are multiplied in exactly the same way as fractions in arithmetic are multiplied. Cancel whenever possible. Then multiply the numerators and multiply the denominators. When negative numbers are multiplied, remember the following rule.

> **RULE:** The product of an even number of negative factors is positive.
> The product of an odd number of negative factors is negative.

EXAMPLE 1

Multiply: $\dfrac{x}{a} \cdot \dfrac{a}{b}$

$$\dfrac{x}{\overset{1}{\cancel{a}}} \cdot \dfrac{\overset{1}{\cancel{a}}}{b} = \dfrac{x}{b}$$

EXAMPLE 2

Multiply: $\dfrac{-x^2}{a^2} \cdot \dfrac{a}{b}$

$$\dfrac{-x^2}{a^2} \cdot \dfrac{a}{b} = \dfrac{-x^2}{a \cdot \overset{1}{\cancel{a}}} \cdot \dfrac{\overset{1}{\cancel{a}}}{b}$$

$$= \dfrac{-x^2}{ab}$$

EXAMPLE 3

Multiply: $\dfrac{-2xy}{a^2} \cdot \dfrac{-a^4}{x^2}$

$$= \dfrac{-2xy}{\underset{1\ 1}{\cancel{a}\cdot\cancel{a}}} \cdot \dfrac{-(\overset{1}{\cancel{a}}\cdot\overset{1}{\cancel{a}}\cdot a \cdot a)}{\underset{1}{\cancel{x}\cdot x}}$$

$$= \dfrac{(-2y)}{1} \cdot \dfrac{(-a^2)}{x} = \dfrac{2a^2y}{x}$$

PRACTICE

Multiply.

	a	*b*	*c*
1.	$\dfrac{p}{q} \cdot \dfrac{q}{p} =$	$\dfrac{x}{2a} \cdot \dfrac{2a}{9y} =$	$\dfrac{3x^2}{4b} \cdot \dfrac{40y}{x^2} =$
2.	$\dfrac{x^2}{4} \cdot \dfrac{4a}{2x} =$	$\dfrac{a^2}{x^3} \cdot \dfrac{1}{a} =$	$\dfrac{6a^2}{x^3} \cdot \dfrac{12x^3}{b} =$
3.	$\dfrac{-4b^2}{x} \cdot \dfrac{2x^5}{b} =$	$\dfrac{-9a^2}{y} \cdot \dfrac{6y}{15a} =$	$\dfrac{-15c}{6b^2} \cdot \dfrac{12b^3}{5c} =$
4.	$\dfrac{-5x^2}{12a} \cdot \dfrac{-6x}{10a} =$	$\dfrac{-9a^3}{4x^2} \cdot \dfrac{-8x^4}{3a} =$	$\dfrac{5a}{-6x^2} \cdot \dfrac{3x^3}{-10a^2} =$
5.	$\dfrac{4ab}{c} \cdot \dfrac{c}{2a} =$	$\dfrac{3y^2z}{4x} \cdot \dfrac{2xz}{9y^2} =$	$\dfrac{p}{pq^2} \cdot \dfrac{-pq^2}{p^2} =$
6.	$\dfrac{a+b}{c} \cdot \dfrac{c}{a+b} =$	$\dfrac{3(x+y)}{x-y^2} \cdot \dfrac{2(x-y^2)}{3} =$	$\dfrac{5}{a^2+b^2} \cdot \dfrac{-(a^2+b^2)}{10x} =$

Dividing Fractions

In arithmetic, you learned to divide fractions by writing the reciprocal of the second fraction, then multiplying. The same rule holds true in algebra. Study the following examples.

Remember to cancel when possible.

EXAMPLE 1

Divide: $\dfrac{3a^2}{x} \div \dfrac{3a}{x^2}$

$= \dfrac{\cancel{3a^2}^{\,a}}{\cancel{x}_{\,1}} \cdot \dfrac{\cancel{x^2}^{\,x}}{\cancel{3a}_{\,1}} = ax$

EXAMPLE 2

Divide: $\dfrac{2x^2y}{3} \div 4a$

$= \dfrac{\cancel{2}^{\,1}x^2y}{3} \cdot \dfrac{1}{\cancel{4}_{\,2}a} = \dfrac{x^2y}{6a}$

EXAMPLE 3

Divide: $\dfrac{a+b}{2} \div \dfrac{a+b}{4}$

$= \dfrac{\cancel{a+b}^{\,1}}{\cancel{2}_{\,1}} \cdot \dfrac{\cancel{4}^{\,2}}{\cancel{a+b}_{\,1}} = 2$

PRACTICE

Divide.

	a	*b*	*c*
1.	$\dfrac{x^2}{a} \div \dfrac{x^4}{a^2} =$	$\dfrac{x}{a^3} \div \dfrac{x^3}{a} =$	$\dfrac{x^4}{a^2} \div \dfrac{x}{a^3} =$
2.	$\dfrac{2x^2y}{3} \div \dfrac{4xy^2}{15} =$	$\dfrac{6ab}{7xy} \div \dfrac{18a^2b^2}{28x^2y^2} =$	$\dfrac{15x^2y}{9ab} \div \dfrac{5xy^2}{3ab} =$
3.	$\dfrac{2xy}{9} \div 4 =$	$\dfrac{5ab}{6x} \div 10 =$	$\dfrac{9x^2y^2}{ab} \div 3 =$
4.	$\dfrac{10x^2y}{3} \div 5xy =$	$\dfrac{9a^2b^2}{4} \div 3ab =$	$\dfrac{3ab^3}{2} \div 6b^2 =$
5.	$\dfrac{-12a^3}{5} \div 4 =$	$\dfrac{-15x^2y}{2} \div 5xy =$	$\dfrac{-16xy^2}{3} \div 4xy =$
6.	$\dfrac{18a^2}{5} \div \dfrac{1}{10} =$	$\dfrac{15x^2y}{4} \div \dfrac{1}{2} =$	$\dfrac{21a^3b^2}{5} \div \dfrac{3}{20} =$
7.	$\dfrac{a+b}{2} \div \dfrac{2(a+b)}{4a} =$	$\dfrac{a-b}{4a} \div \dfrac{a-b}{8} =$	$\dfrac{a^2+b^2}{6} \div \dfrac{a^2+b^2}{12x} =$

Multiplying Polynomials by Monomials

You have learned how to multiply and divide with monomials. Now you will study these operations on polynomials. To multiply a polynomial by a monomial, multiply each term of the polynomial by the monomial. Multiply each term separately.

Remember,
- when like bases are multiplied, add the exponents.
- use the rules for products of negative and positive numbers.

EXAMPLE 1

Multiply: $a(a + b)$

$a(a + b) = (a \cdot a) + (a \cdot b)$
$\quad = a^2 + ab$

EXAMPLE 2

Multiply: $2a^2(a + b + 2c)$

$= (2a^2 \cdot a) + (2a^2 \cdot b) + (2a^2 \cdot 2c)$
$= 2a^3 \cdot 2a^2b + 4a^2c$

EXAMPLE 3

Multiply: $-2xy(5x^2 + 2y)$

$= (-2xy \cdot 5x^2) + (-2xy \cdot 2y)$
$= -10x^3y - 4xy^2$

PRACTICE

Multiply.

	a	b	c
1.	$x(x + y) =$	$y(2x + y) =$	$x^3(x + 2y) =$
2.	$2x(x + y) =$	$3x(2x + 3y) =$	$6a^3(2a - b) =$
3.	$-2b(2a + b) =$	$-2b(3a + b) =$	$-3b^3(-4a + 3b) =$
4.	$4x(x^2 + y) =$	$2b(2b^2 - a^2) =$	$-5c^2(-3c^3 - 4) =$
5.	$2x(3x - 5y - 2z) =$	$-2y(-2x + 3y - 4z) =$	$3b^2(5a + 4b + 2c) =$
6.	$4b(4a^2 - 5b^2 - 3c^2) =$	$-2b(7a - 3b^4 - 1) =$	$-3c^2(-4c^2 - 3c + 2) =$
7.	$2xy(5x - 2y + 3z) =$	$xz(x + y - z) =$	$-2ab^2(-4a - 4b - 4) =$
8.	$-xyz(5x - 3y + 4z) =$	$2abc(a^2 + b^2 + c^2) =$	$-4xy^2z(xy + yz) =$

Dividing Polynomials by Monomials

When dividing a polynomial by a monomial, divide each term of the polynomial by the monomial. Divide each term separately.

Remember, when dividing, subtract exponents of like bases.

EXAMPLE 1

Divide: $\dfrac{x^2 + xy}{x}$

$= \dfrac{x^2}{x} + \dfrac{xy}{x} = x^{2-1} + (x^{1-1}y)$

$\qquad = x + y$

EXAMPLE 2

Divide: $\dfrac{-6a^3 + 12a^2 - 9a}{3a}$

$= \dfrac{-6a^3}{3a} + \dfrac{12a^2}{3a} - \dfrac{9a}{3a}$

$= -2a^2 + 4a - 3$

EXAMPLE 3

Divide:

$\dfrac{-9a^3y + 12a^2y^2 - 6ay^3}{-3ay}$

$= \dfrac{-9a^3y}{-3ay} + \dfrac{12a^2y^2}{-3ay} + \dfrac{-6ay^3}{-3ay}$

$= 3a^2 - 4ay + 2y^2$

PRACTICE

Divide.

	a	*b*	*c*
1.	$\dfrac{a^2 + a}{a} =$	$\dfrac{6xy + 4z}{2} =$	$\dfrac{8xy + 6xz}{2x} =$
2.	$\dfrac{10ab + 15ac + 20ad}{5a} =$	$\dfrac{18x^2 + 24xy + 16xz}{2x} =$	$\dfrac{6a^2y + 12ay^2 + 18ay^3}{6a} =$
3.	$\dfrac{-4a^2 + 10a + 2}{2} =$	$\dfrac{12x^4 - 16x^3 - 24x^2}{4x^2} =$	$\dfrac{-25x^3 - 20x^2 + 15x}{5x} =$
4.	$\dfrac{9x^4 + 15x^3 + 21x^2}{-3x^2} =$	$\dfrac{18a^3y + 24a^2y^2 + 30ay^3}{-6ay} =$	$\dfrac{10x^2y + 15xy^2 + 20y^2}{-5y} =$
5.	$\dfrac{-12x^3 - 9x^2 - 15x}{-3x} =$	$\dfrac{-16a^4 - 24a^3 - 16a^2}{-8a} =$	$\dfrac{-24x^3y - 12x^2y^2 - 18xy^3}{-6xy} =$
6.	$\dfrac{4x^2y + 12xy - 8xy^2}{2xy} =$	$\dfrac{-15x^3y + 12x^2y^2 - 18xy^3}{-3xy} =$	$\dfrac{-18c^2d - 24c^2d^2 + 12cd^3}{-6cd} =$

PROBLEM-SOLVING STRATEGY

Use Logic

Some problems can be solved using logic. Using logic is like looking for clues to solve a mystery. First, read the problem and look for clues. Then, make a chart or draw pictures to keep track of the clues. Next, solve the problem.

Read the problem.

Adam, Bernardo, and Charles live in New York, Chicago, and Los Angeles, although not necessarily in that order. Adam is the uncle of the man who lives in Los Angeles. Either Bernardo or Charles lives in New York. Charles has no uncles.

Look for clues.

Clue 1: Adam is the uncle of the man from Los Angeles.
Logical conclusion: Adam is not from Los Angeles.

Clue 2: Either Bernardo or Charles lives in New York.
Logical conclusion: Adam is not from New York.

Clue 3: Charles has no uncles.
Logical conclusion: Charles does not live in Los Angeles.

Make a chart.

Use what you learned from the clues to fill in parts of the chart.

	New York	Chicago	Los Angeles
Adam	no	YES	no
Bernardo	no	no	YES
Charles	YES	no	no

Solve the problem.

Adam lives in Chicago, Bernardo lives in Los Angeles, and Charles lives in New York.

Solve. Use logic.

1. Diane, Ella, and Felicia are a farmer, lawyer, and teacher, although not necessarily in that order. Ella has never been to a farm. Neither Ella nor Diane is a lawyer. Which person is in which profession?

	Farmer	Lawyer	Teacher
Diane			
Ella			
Felicia			

Farmer _____   Lawyer _____   Teacher _____

Solve. Use logic.

2. The hobbies of Jan, Kelly, and Laura are bowling, swimming, and basketball, although not necessarily in that order. Jan often has lunch with the bowler. Laura is either the basketball player or the swimmer. Jan is either the swimmer or the bowler. Which person has which hobby?

	Bowling	Swimming	Basketball
Jan			
Kelly			
Laura			

Bowling _____

Swimming _____

Basketball _____

3. Manuel, Norman, Oliver, and Penny live in houses of four different colors. The colors are white, yellow, green, and blue. Penny lives in the green or blue house. Norman's friend lives in the yellow house. The blue house is not Manuel's, Norman's, or Penny's. Use the clues to figure out which person lives in which house.

	White	Yellow	Green	Blue
Manuel				
Norman				
Oliver				
Penny				

White _____   Yellow _____

Green _____   Blue _____

4. Four cars are parked along a street. The colors of the cars are silver, black, tan, and red. Here are the license numbers: AB 764, MDY 340, GX 2378, and 816 ZPN. The red car's license number has a 6 in it. The silver car's license number has the letters after the numbers. The tan car's license number does not have four digits. What is the license number for each car?

Silver _____

Black _____

Tan _____

Red _____

5. Allan, Bill, Carl, and Dean are the names of Wesley's son, father, brother, and grandfather, but not necessarily in that order. Carl is younger than Allan. Dean is older than Bill. Dean's grandfather is Allan. Write the name for each of Wesley's relatives.

Son _____

Father _____

Brother _____

Grandfather _____

Removing Common Monomial Factors

If you know one factor of a number, division can be used to find another factor. For example, since 3 is a factor of 24, you can divide 24 by 3 to find another factor, 8. Similarly, if you know one factor of a polynomial, you can divide to find another factor.

The **common monomial factor** of a polynomial is a monomial that is a factor of all the terms. In the example below, the common factors are 3 and a, since 3 and a are factors of each term. So, the common monomial factor of the entire polynomial is $3a$. To find the other factor, divide the polynomial by $3a$.

EXAMPLE

Find the common monomial factor of $12ab - 6ac + 3ad$. Divide to find another factor. Write the polynomial as the product of the monomial and a polynomial.

Since 3 and a are factors of each term, the common monomial factor is $3a$. Divide by $3a$.

$$\frac{12ab - 6ac + 3ad}{3a} = 4b - 2c + d$$

The two factors are $3a$ and $4b - 2c + d$.

So, $12ab - 6ac + 3ad = 3a(4b - 2c + d)$

PRACTICE

Find the common monomial factor. Divide to find another factor. Then write the polynomial as the product of the monomial and a polynomial.

a	b
1. $7mn - 14mp - 21mq =$	$5x^3 - 10x^2 + 15x =$
2. $4ax + 8ay - 12az =$	$6a^3b - 12a^2b^2 + 18ab^3 =$
3. $10x^3 + 8x^2 - 2x =$	$9a^2b^2 + 6ab + 15 =$
4. $8x^2y + 4xy - 12xy^2 =$	$10x^3 - 12x^2 - 6x =$
5. $20a^3b - 15a^2b^2 + 10ab^3 =$	$16xy^3 - 12x^2y^2 + 20x^2y^3 =$
6. $3a^2 - 15a^3y + 18a^4y^2 =$	$20ab^3 - 15a^2b^2 - 25a^3b =$
7. $-12a^3 + 8a^2b - 16ab^3 =$	$-9x^2 + 6xy - 18y^2 =$

Multiplying Polynomials by Binomials

Multiplying binomials by binomials may be thought of as multiplying a binomial by two monomials. Parentheses are often used to show multiplication of binomials. Multiply each term of the first binomial by each term of the second binomial. Combine like terms. Polynomials are multiplied in the same way.

Remember, ab^2 is the same as b^2a and thus can be added or subtracted as in Example 2.

EXAMPLE 1

Multiply: $(x - y^2)(x - y^2)$
$= x(x - y^2) - y^2(x - y^2)$
$= x^2 - xy^2 - y^2x + y^4$
$= x^2 - 2xy^2 + y^4$

EXAMPLE 2

Multiply: $(4a + 3b)(2a + b)$
$= 4a(2a + b) + 3b(2a + b)$
$= 8a^2 + 4ab + 6ab + 3b^2$
$= 8a^2 + 10ab + 3b^2$

EXAMPLE 3

Multiply: $(ab + c)(ab + c)$
$= ab(ab + c) + c(ab + c)$
$= a^2b^2 + abc + abc + c^2$
$= a^2b^2 + 2abc + c^2$

PRACTICE

Multiply.

	a	*b*	*c*
1.	$(a + b)(a + b) =$	$(a + 2b)(a + 2b) =$	$(2x + y)(2x + y) =$
2.	$(3a - 2b)(3a - 2b) =$	$(2x + 3y)(-3x + 2y) =$	$(-2c + d)(c + 2d) =$
3.	$(x - 4y)(-3x - 2y) =$	$(-a + 2b)(a - 2b) =$	$(x + 2y)(x - 2y) =$
4.	$(-y - 2z)(y - 2z) =$	$(3a - 4b)(a + 3b) =$	$(-6x + 2y)(6x - y) =$
5.	$(xy + z)(xy + z) =$	$(2ab - c)(4ab - 3c) =$	$(-ab + c)(-ab - c) =$
6.	$(x^2y - z)(xy + z) =$	$(3xy^4 + y^3)(4x^3y - x) =$	$(-2abc + d)(3a - 4) =$
7.	$(a + b + c)(a + b) =$	$(2x^2 - x + 1)(x + y) =$	$(4x^2 - 2xy - y^2)(x - y) =$

Dividing Polynomials by Binomials

Polynomials are divided by binomials in much the same way that numbers are divided in arithmetic. Look at Example 1. Divide the first term of the dividend (a^2) by the first term of the divisor (a). The result is a. Place the a in the quotient, multiply *both* terms of the divisor by a, and subtract. Continue in this manner until you cannot divide again.

EXAMPLE 1

Divide:

$$
\begin{array}{r}
a + b \\
a + b \overline{\smash{\big)}\, a^2 + 2ab + b^2} \\
\underline{a^2 + ab} \downarrow \\
ab + b^2 \\
\underline{ab + b^2} \\
0
\end{array}
$$

EXAMPLE 2

Divide:

$$
\begin{array}{r}
a - b \\
a - b \overline{\smash{\big)}\, a^2 - 2ab + b^2} \\
\underline{a^2 - ab} \downarrow \\
-ab + b^2 \\
\underline{-ab + b^2} \\
0
\end{array}
$$

EXAMPLE 3

Divide:

$$
\begin{array}{r}
x + 3 \\
2x + 7 \overline{\smash{\big)}\, 2x^2 + 13x + 21} \\
\underline{2x^2 + 7x} \downarrow \\
6x + 21 \\
\underline{6x + 21} \\
0
\end{array}
$$

PRACTICE

Divide.

	a	*b*	*c*
1.	$a + 2b \overline{\smash{\big)}\, a^2 + 4ab + 4b^2}$	$x - y \overline{\smash{\big)}\, x^2 - 2xy + y^2}$	$a - 2b \overline{\smash{\big)}\, a^2 - 4ab + 4b^2}$
2.	$2x + 3y \overline{\smash{\big)}\, 4x^2 + 12xy + 9y^2}$	$3x - 2y \overline{\smash{\big)}\, 9x^2 - 12xy + 4y^2}$	$5a + 2b \overline{\smash{\big)}\, 25a^2 + 20ab + 4b^2}$
3.	$x + 1 \overline{\smash{\big)}\, x^2 + 3x + 2}$	$x - 6 \overline{\smash{\big)}\, x^2 - 9x + 18}$	$x - 5 \overline{\smash{\big)}\, x^2 - 4x - 5}$

More Practice Multiplying and Dividing Polynomials

Multiply.

	a	*b*	*c*
1.	$2b(3b^2 - 4b + 6) =$	$3xy(4x^2 - 2xy - 3y^2) =$	$4x^2(10 + 3y^2) =$
2.	$(x + 2)(x^2 - 3x + 5) =$	$(2a + 3b)(2a^2 - 3ab + b^2) =$	$(2x - 1)(3x^3 - 2x^2 - x) =$
3.	$3x - 2(2x^2 - 5x) =$ $= 3x - 4x^2 + 10x$ $= -4x^2 + 13x$	$3x(2x^2 - 5x + 4) - 2 =$	$2(6 + 2a - 3a^2) - 12 =$
4.	$3(x - y + z)(x + y - z) =$	$(6x^2 - x)(2y + 3)3y =$	$7b(-4b^2) + 3b(-b) =$

Divide.

	a	*b*	*c*
5.	$\dfrac{x^2 + 4x}{x} =$	$\dfrac{6x^2 + 3x}{3x} =$	$\dfrac{2y^2 - 4y}{2y} =$
6.	$\dfrac{2x(x + 2x)}{2x^2} =$ $= \dfrac{2x(3x)}{2x^2} = \dfrac{6x^2}{2x^2} = 3$	$\dfrac{6y(3y^2 - xy + x^2y)}{y^2} =$	$\dfrac{xy(6 + 6x - 6x^2)}{6x} =$
7.	$5 + x \overline{)\, 25 + 10x + x^2}$	$4 + 2x \overline{)\, 16 + 16x + 4x^2}$	$3 - 2x \overline{)\, 6 + 5x - 6x^2}$

EXPONENTS AND POLYNOMIALS

Unit 4 Review

Simplify.

	a	*b*	*c*
1.	$5^2 =$	$(-9)^3 =$	$(-10)^2 \cdot 3^2 =$
2.	$(cd^3)(c^2) =$	$(5xy^5)(5x^5y) =$	$(xy^3z^4)^3 =$
3.	$\dfrac{m^9}{m^3} =$	$\dfrac{3xy}{x^2y^2} =$	$-\dfrac{8a^3b^2c}{12ab^2c^3} =$
4.	$(xy - x) + (5xy + 3x) =$	$(-b - 4) - (b + 2) =$	$-(15m^2 + 6m^3) - (-5m) =$
5.	$\dfrac{4ab}{6a} \cdot \dfrac{3b}{2ab} =$	$\dfrac{3x^2y}{z} \cdot \dfrac{z^2}{3} =$	$\dfrac{-12x^3}{5} \div 4 =$
6.	$\dfrac{x^2 - x}{x} =$	$\dfrac{6xy - 4z}{2} =$	$\dfrac{16a^4 - 12a^2 - 4a}{4a} =$
7.	$x(x - y) =$	$-2y(-2x^2y + 3) =$	$6ab(a^2 + b^2) =$
8.	$(a + b)(a - b) =$	$(2ab + c)(2ab - c) =$	$(a^2 + b^2 + 3)(ab - b) =$

Divide.

	a	*b*	*c*
9.	$x + 1 \,\overline{)\, x^2 - x - 2}$	$x + 2y \,\overline{)\, x^2 + 4xy + 4y^2}$	$2x - 3y \,\overline{)\, 4x^2 - 12xy + 9y^2}$

Cumulative Review

Solve.

	a	b	c
1.	$5x = 135$	$y - 5 = -10$	$5(a + 3) = 25$
2.	$7 + 37 = k$	$-6 + r = -2$	$3(n - 2) = -n - 10$
3.	$\dfrac{2s}{3} = 16$	$\dfrac{x}{4} = \dfrac{3}{8}$	$7b - 10b = -18$

Simplify.

	a	b	c
4.	$-6 - (-11) =$	$-2(-1)(-8) =$	$\dfrac{-48}{2} =$
5.	$2(4 + 3) - 6(0) =$	$\dfrac{-125rs^5}{-25s^3} =$	$\dfrac{a}{4} + \dfrac{3a}{4} - \dfrac{1}{2} =$
6.	$\dfrac{-15a^4b^{10}c^6}{-3ab^2c^3} =$	$\dfrac{10x^3}{(a + b)} \cdot \dfrac{6(a + b)}{20x^2} =$	$\dfrac{4ab^2}{3} \div \dfrac{12a^2b^2}{a} =$
7.	$(-1)^{99}(-2)^4 =$	$(4a^2x)^2 =$	$(4a + 2b)(3a - b) =$
8.	$\dfrac{-9a^3}{x^4} \cdot \dfrac{3x^4}{a} =$	$\dfrac{-24x^2y - 20y^4z^6 + 10y}{-2y} =$	$5x - 6 \overline{\smash{)}5x^2 + 9x - 18}$

Solve.

9. The sum of three consecutive numbers is 279. Find the numbers.

Answer _____

10. Find the circumference of a circle if the diameter is 24 feet. $(C = \pi d)$

Answer _____

Equations with Two Variables

The equation $x + 2y = 15$ is a special type of equation. It has two variables and no single solution. If a value for x is selected, the equation can be solved to find a corresponding value for y. Study the following examples.

EXAMPLE 1

Solve: $x + 2y = 15$ when $x = 7$

$$7 + 2y = 15$$
$$2y = 8$$
$$y = 4$$

So, the equation $x + 2y = 15$ is true when x is 7 and y is 4.

EXAMPLE 2

Solve: $x + 2y = 15$ when $x = -3$

$$-3 + 2y = 15$$
$$2y = 18$$
$$y = 9$$

So, the equation $x + 2y = 15$ is true when x is -3 and y is 9.

Solutions to an equation in two variables are pairs of numbers that make the equation true. Each solution may be written as an ordered pair in the form (x, y). The value for x is always written first in the ordered pair. So, two solutions to $x + 2y = 15$ are $(7, 4)$ and $(-3, 9)$. The ordered pair $(4, 7)$ is not a solution because $4 + 2(7)$ does not equal 15.

PRACTICE

Solve each equation for the given value of x or y. Write the ordered pair which makes the equation true.

a	b	c
1. $x + 2y = 10$ when $x = 0$	$x + 2y = 15$ when $x = 1$	$x + 2y = 15$ when $x = 2$
$0 + 2y = 10$		
$y = 5$		
Ordered pair ____(0,5)____	Ordered pair _____	Ordered pair _____
2. $2x + 2y = 4$ when $y = 0$	$2x + 2y = 4$ when $y = 2$	$2x + 2y = 4$ when $y = 4$
Ordered pair _____	Ordered pair _____	Ordered pair _____
3. $x + y = -1$ when $x = 0$	$x + y = -1$ when $x = -1$	$x + y = -1$ when $x = 1$
Ordered pair _____	Ordered pair _____	Ordered pair _____

GRAPHS AND SYSTEMS OF EQUATIONS

Graphing Ordered Pairs

In the graph at the right, the line labeled x is called the **horizontal axis** or **x-axis**. The line labeled y is called the **vertical axis** or **y-axis**. The point where the axes cross is called the **origin**. The position of a point on the graph is determined by its coordinates. The x-coordinate tells the distance right or left of the origin. The y-coordinate tells the distance up or down.

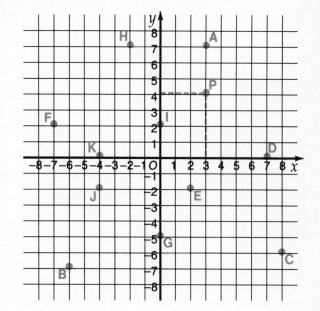

The scale on the x-axis shows that the x-coordinates to the right of the origin are positive and to the left are negative. Similarly, the y-coordinates above the origin are positive and below the origin are negative. The coordinates of point P are the ordered pair (3, 4). Find point P on the graph.

To graph an ordered pair, such as (−7, 2), draw a dot above −7 on the x-axis, across from 2 on the y-axis. This point is plotted on the graph and labeled F.

PRACTICE

Give the coordinates of each point. Refer to the graph above.

	a	b	c	d	e

1. E (__,__) B (__,__) H (__,__) K (__,__) C (__,__)

2. D (__,__) G (__,__) J (__,__) A (__,__) I (__,__)

Plot each point on the graph provided.

3. A (2, 6)
   B (3, −5)
   C (−5, 3)
   D (−4, −6)
   E (0, 1)

4. F (−5, −8)
   G (0, 8)
   H (−8, 0)
   I (0, −7)
   J (0, 0)

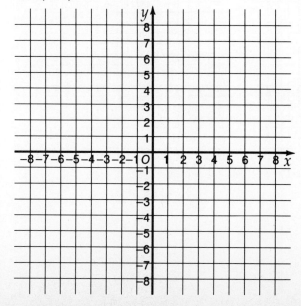

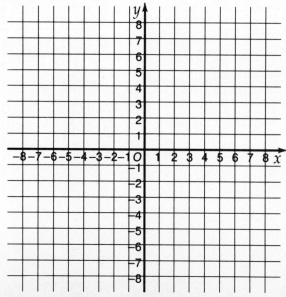

103

Graphing Solutions

You can graph solutions to equations in two variables.

EXAMPLE

Graph the solutions to $2x - y = 6$, when $x = 0, 1, 3,$ and 4.

Substitute each value for x into the equation and find the corresponding value for y. Write each solution in a table. Plot each solution on the coordinate graph.

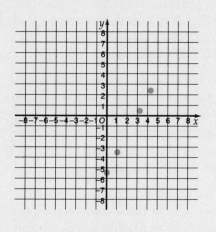

Find y when $x = 0$.
$$2(0) - y = 6$$
$$0 - y = 6$$
$$y = -6$$

Find y when $x = 1$.
$$2(1) - y = 6$$
$$2 - y = 6$$
$$y = -4$$

Find y when $x = 3$.
$$2(3) - y = 6$$
$$6 - y = 6$$
$$y = 0$$

Find y when $x = 4$.
$$2(4) - y = 6$$
$$8 - y = 6$$
$$y = 2$$

x	y
0	−6
1	−4
3	0
4	2

PRACTICE

Complete each table of solutions to the given equation. Graph each solution.

1. $3x + 4y = 12$

x	y
−4	___
0	___
4	___
8	___

2. $3x - 5y = 15$

x	y
−5	___
0	___
5	___

3. $y = 6 - 3x$

x	y
0	___
___	0
1	___
3	___

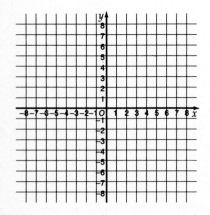

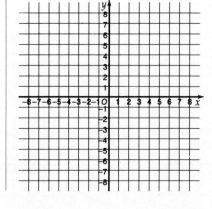

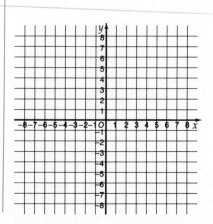

Graphing Linear Equations

When you graphed solutions to equations in two variables, you may have noticed that the points were in a line. If more solutions to an equation were graphed, each solution would be on the same line. For this reason, equations with two variables are called **linear equations.** Although it is impossible to list all the ordered pairs that are solutions, you can show a graph of the solutions by connecting the points with a straight line.

EXAMPLE

Draw a graph of the solutions to the equation $x - 2y = 6$.

Select values of x and find the corresponding values of y. Try starting with $x = 0$. Make a table like the one at the right. Notice that when $x = 2$, $y = -2$. When $y = 0$, $x = 6$.

x	y
0	-3
2	-2
6	0

Plot the points and draw a straight line to show the graph of the solutions.

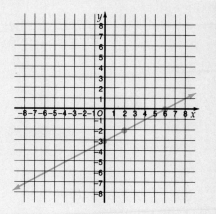

PRACTICE

Make a table of 3 solutions. Graph each solution. Draw a straight line.

1. $4x - y = 4$

x	y

2. $2x + 3y = 6$

x	y

3. $x + y = -8$

x	y

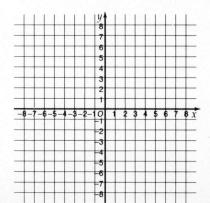

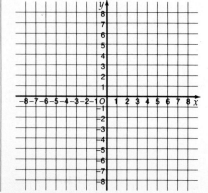

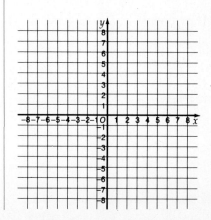

Make a List

Problems sometimes ask you to find the number of ways that something can be done. To solve such problems, it helps to make an organized list. Then count the number of items on your list. This number will be the number of ways that something can be done.

Read the problem.

Two six-sided number cubes are tossed. How many different ways can a sum of 7 turn up?

Make a list.

Label the number cubes A and B. Then make a list of the possibilities. Be sure the list is organized carefully.

A	B	
1	6	$1 + 6 = 7$
6	1	$6 + 1 = 7$
2	5	$2 + 5 = 7$
5	2	$5 + 2 = 7$
3	4	$3 + 4 = 7$
4	3	$4 + 3 = 7$

or

A	B
1	6
2	5
3	4
4	3
5	2
6	1

Solve the problem.

Count the number of combinations listed. There are 6 different ways a sum of 7 can turn up.

Make a list. Use your list to solve the problem.

1. Two number cubes are tossed. How many different ways can a sum of 10 turn up?	**2.** A 2-digit number is a perfect square. (A perfect square is the product of a whole number times itself, such as 9, 16, 25, and so on.) The difference between the digits is 5. How many such numbers are there?

Answer _____

Answer _____

Make a list. Use your list to solve the problem.

3. A baseball team has 4 catchers and 5 pitchers. How many different combinations of a catcher and a pitcher are possible?

Answer _____

4. A soft drink from a vending machine costs $0.50. The machine accepts nickels, dimes, and quarters. How many different coin combinations can it accept?

Answer _____

5. A penny is tossed three times. In how many different orders can heads and tails turn up?

Answer _____

6. At a picnic, 3 different main courses were offered, along with 2 different salads and 2 different desserts. How many different main course-salad-dessert combinations were possible?

Answer _____

7. An easy chair is offered in 4 different colors, 2 different sizes, and 2 different styles. How many different color-size-style combinations are possible?

Answer _____

8. Al, Bob, Carla, and Ana are to sit in 4 seats side-by-side. Al and Bob may not sit next to each other. How many different ways can the four be seated?

Answer _____

Systems of Equations

Systems of equations are two equations that are solved together to find the solution that satisfies both equations. Since both sides of an equation have the same value, you can create a new equation by adding the two equations together, or subtracting one equation from the other. The goal of combining equations in this way is to eliminate one of the variables in order to solve for the other variable.

EXAMPLE

Solve: $x + y = 13$
$\qquad x - y = 1$

Add.
$\begin{array}{r} x + y = 13 \\ x - y = 1 \\ \hline 2x = 14 \\ x = 7 \end{array}$

Subtract.
$\begin{array}{r} x + y = 13 \\ x - y = 1 \\ \hline 2y = 12 \\ y = 6 \end{array}$

Check: Substitute into the original equations.

$x + y = 13 \qquad x - y = 1$
$7 + 6 = 13 \qquad 7 - 6 = 1$

The solution to the system of equations is (7, 6).

PRACTICE

Solve each system of equations. Check by substitution.

	a	*b*	*c*
1.	$a + b = 15$ $a - b = 5$	$a + b = 13$ $a - b = 5$	$a + b = 14$ $a - b = 6$
2.	$x + y = 6$ $x - y = 4$	$x + y = 7$ $x - y = 3$	$a + b = 25$ $a - b = 5$

GRAPHS AND SYSTEMS OF EQUATIONS

Practice with Systems of Equations

Solve these systems of equations as shown in the example on the previous page.

PRACTICE

Solve each system of equations. Check by substitution.

	a	b	c

1.
$$x + y = 17$$
$$x - y = 7$$

$$m + n = 27$$
$$m - n = 17$$

$$d + e = 51$$
$$d - e = 9$$

2.
$$x + y = 37$$
$$x - y = 7$$

$$b + c = 55$$
$$b - c = 17$$

$$a + b = 23$$
$$a - b = 9$$

3.
$$m + n = 35$$
$$m - n = 5$$

$$a + b = 45$$
$$a - b = 15$$

$$x + y = 25$$
$$x - y = 15$$

4.
$$c + d = 33$$
$$c - d = 9$$

$$s + t = 43$$
$$s - t = 7$$

$$r + s = 18$$
$$r - s = 2$$

Larger Coefficients

Systems of equations with coefficients greater than 1 are solved in exactly the same way as before.

EXAMPLE

Solve: $3x + 2y = 26$
$3x - 2y = 10$

Check: Substitute the values of x and y into the original equations.

Add.

$$3x + 2y = 26$$
$$\underline{3x - 2y = 10}$$
$$6x \quad\;\; = 36$$
$$x = \;\; 6$$

The solution is (6, 4).

Subtract.

$$3x + 2y = 26$$
$$\underline{3x - 2y = 10}$$
$$4y = 16$$
$$y = \;\; 4$$

$$3x + 2y = 26 \qquad 3x - 2y = 10$$
$$3(6) + 2(4) = 26 \qquad 3(6) - 2(4) = 10$$
$$18 + 8 = 26 \qquad 18 - 8 = 10$$

PRACTICE

Solve each system of equations.

	a	b	c
1.	$2a + 3b = 28$ $2a - 3b = \;\; 4$	$3x + 2y = 14$ $3x - 2y = 10$	$5a + 4b = 23$ $5a - 4b = \;\; 7$
2.	$8y + 6z = 40$ $8y - 6z = -8$	$3r + 7s = \;\; 57$ $3r - 7s = -27$	$9x + 5y = \;\; 67$ $9x - 5y = -13$
3.	$4b + 5c = \;\; 61$ $4b - 5c = -29$	$4r + 6s = 58$ $4r - 6s = -2$	$3m + 8n = \;\; 58$ $3m - 8n = -22$

Changing the Coefficients

Recall that multiplying both sides of an equation by the same number does not change its solution. When you are solving a system of equations, you may need to change the form of one or both equations. By multiplying, you can change the coefficients so that the system can be solved. The following example shows this method. Step 1 shows multiplying the second equation by 2. In Step 2, the new equation is subtracted from the first equation. This eliminates the terms with x so the equation can be solved for y. Then, in Step 3, the value of y is substituted into one of the original equations. When you use this method, remember to check the solution in both original equations.

EXAMPLE

Solve: $2x + 3y = 9$
$\quad\quad x - 2y = 1$

Check: Substitute the values of x and y into the original equations.

Step 1.
Multiply by 2.

Step 2.
Subtract.

Step 3.
Substitute.

$2(x - 2y) = 2(1)$
$2x - 4y = 2$

$\begin{aligned} 2x + 3y &= 9 \\ 2x - 4y &= 2 \\ \hline 7y &= 7 \\ y &= 1 \end{aligned}$

$x - 2y = 1$
$x - 2(1) = 1$
$x = 3$

$2x + 3y = 9$
$2(3) + 3(1) = 9$
$9 = 9$

$x - 2y = 1$
$3 - 2(1) = 1$
$1 = 1$

The solution is (3, 1).

PRACTICE

Solve each system of equations.

a	*b*	*c*

1. $5a + 2b = 23$
$\quad a + 3b = 15$

$5d - 3e = 5$
$\quad d - e = -1$

$x + 4y = 9$
$2x - 4y = 6$

Practice in Changing Coefficients

This page will give you more practice in changing coefficients and solving systems of equations. Remember, an equation can be changed provided the same change is made to both sides.

PRACTICE

Solve each system of equations. Check.

	a	*b*	*c*
1.	$x + y = 4$ $2x + 3y = 10$	$x - y = -4$ $2x - 3y = -14$	$x + y = 4$ $3x - 2y = 7$
2.	$2x - y = 0$ $4x + 2y = 16$	$5x + y = 8$ $2x - 3y = -7$	$3x - y = 1$ $4x - 2y = -2$
3.	$5x - 2y = 11$ $2x - y = 4$	$2x + 4y = 22$ $4x + 2y = 14$	$2x + 4y = 22$ $4x + 2y = 32$

GRAPHS AND SYSTEMS OF EQUATIONS

Changing Coefficients in Both Equations

In the systems of equations you have solved so far, it was necessary to change coefficients in only one equation. In many systems of equations, however, it is necessary to change coefficients in both equations in order to solve. Remember, multiplying both sides of an equation by the same number will not change the solution.

EXAMPLE

Solve: $2x + 3y = 9$
$3x + 2y = 11$

Step 1.
Multiply the first equation by 3.

$3(2x + 3y) = 3(9)$
$6x + 9y = 27$

Step 2.
Multiply the second equation by 2.

$2(3x + 2y) = 2(11)$
$6x + 4y = 22$

Step 3.
Subtract the new equations.

$6x + 9y = 27$
$6x + 4y = 22$
$\overline{5y = 5}$
$y = 1$

Step 4.
Substitute $y = 1$ in any equation.

$6x + 9(1) = 27$
$6x = 18$
$x = 3$

The solution is (3, 1).

PRACTICE

Solve each system of equations. Check.

a	b	c
1. $5a - 2b = 3$ $2a + 5b = 7$	$2a + 3b = 14$ $3a - 2b = 8$	$3x - 2y = 11$ $4x - 3y = 14$
2. $2x + 3y = 12$ $3x + 2y = 13$	$3x - 2y = 0$ $2x - 3y = -5$	$2x - 3y = 1$ $3x - 2y = 9$

Solving in Terms of One Variable

Sometimes it is helpful to isolate one of the variables in an equation that has two variables. To isolate a variable, change the form of the equation by adding, subtracting, multiplying, or dividing both sides by the same number or expression. Study the examples. Remember, multiply both sides of an equation by −1 to change the signs, as shown in Example 2.

EXAMPLE 1

Solve: $2x + 3y = 6$ for y in terms of x

$$2x + 3y = 6$$
$$2x - 2x + 3y = 6 - 2x$$
$$3y = 6 - 2x$$
$$\frac{1}{3}(3y) = \frac{1}{3}(6 - 2x)$$
$$y = 2 - \frac{2}{3}x$$

EXAMPLE 2

Solve: $y - x = 2$ for x in terms of y

$$y - x = 2$$
$$y - y - x = 2 - y$$
$$-x = 2 - y$$
$$-1(-x) = -1(2 - y)$$
$$x = -2 + y$$
$$x = y - 2$$

PRACTICE

Solve each equation for y in terms of x.

	a	*b*	*c*
1.	$12x - 4y = 48$	$6x + 2y = 10$	$3x + 4y = 60$
2.	$-x + 2y = 8$	$x + 3y = 6$	$4x + 2y = -1$

Solve each equation for x in terms of y.

	a	*b*	*c*
3.	$x - 3y = -1$	$-2x + 4y = 8$	$3x + y = 9$
4.	$3x - 2y = 3$	$2x - 2y = 20$	$7x + 4y = 28$

The Substitution Method

In working with equations, you have substituted a value for a variable. To solve a system of equations, you can use a slightly different type of substitution. The following example shows you how to substitute for one variable in terms of the other variable. This method is called the **substitution method** for solving a system of equations.

EXAMPLE

Solve: $x + 2y = 7$
$\quad\quad 3x + y = 11$

Check: $\quad x + 2y = 7$
$\quad\quad\quad 3 + 2(2) = 7$

$\quad\quad\quad 3x + y = 11$
$\quad\quad\quad 3(3) + 2 = 11$

Step 1.
Solve for x in terms of y.
$$x + 2y = 7$$
$$x + 2y - 2y = 7 - 2y$$
$$x = 7 - 2y$$

Step 2.
Substitute $7 - 2y$ for x in the second equation.
$$3x + y = 11$$
$$3(7 - 2y) + y = 11$$
$$21 - 6y + y = 11$$
$$-5y = -10$$
$$y = 2$$

Step 3.
Substitute 2 for y in either equation.
$$x + 2(2) = 7$$
$$x = 3$$

The solution is (3, 2).

PRACTICE

Use the substitution method to solve each system of equations.

	a	*b*	*c*
1.	$x + 4y = 12$ $2x - y = 6$	$x - y = 1$ $5x + 3y = 45$	$3x + 2y = 13$ $x + y = 5$
2.	$x + y = 5$ $x + 3y = 9$	$x - y = 2$ $4x + y = 18$	$2x + 3y = 9$ $x - 2y = 1$

Practice with the Substitution Method

Remember, to use the substitution method, solve for one variable in terms of the other. Then substitute and solve.

PRACTICE

Use the substitution method to solve each system of equations. Check.

a	b	c
1. $x + 2y = 9$ $x - y = 3$	$x + 3y = 10$ $x + y = 6$	$x + 3y = 11$ $x + y = 7$
2. $x + 5y = 10$ $x - 2y = 3$	$2x + y = 8$ $x + 2y = 7$	$3x - y = 9$ $2x + y = 11$
3. $3x + 2y = 22$ $x + y = 9$	$2x + 3y = 29$ $x - y = -3$	$5x + y = 23$ $5x - y = 17$

Choose a Method

You have used several methods to solve systems of equations. Study each system of equations and decide which method is best to use. Then solve.

PRACTICE

Choose a method and solve.

	a	*b*	*c*
1.	$2x + 3y = 16$ $3x - y = 2$	$5x - 2y = 6$ $2x + 5y = 14$	$6x + 5y = 6$ $3x + 5y = -12$
2.	$x + y = 5$ $x - 3y = 1$	$4x + 3y = 14$ $2x + 3y = 10$	$3x - y = 3$ $2x - 3y = -19$
3.	$10x + 7y = 45$ $3x + 7y = 38$	$2a - b = 5$ $7a + b = 49$	$a + b = 8$ $a - 2b = -1$

Solving Problems with Systems of Equations

Some word problems can be solved by using systems of equations.

EXAMPLE

The sum of two numbers is 13. Their difference is 1. What are the numbers?	Add. $\begin{array}{r} x + y = 13 \\ x - y = 1 \\ \hline 2x = 14 \\ x = 7 \end{array}$	**Check:** $\begin{array}{r} x + y = 13 \\ 7 + 6 = 13 \end{array}$

Let x = one number.
Let y = the other number.

Then, $x + y = 13$ (the sum)
$\quad\quad x - y = 1$ (the difference)

Add. $x + y = 13$
$\quad\quad \underline{x - y = 1}$
$\quad\quad\quad 2x = 14$
$\quad\quad\quad\; x = 7$

Substitute. $x + y = 13$
$\quad\quad\quad\quad 7 + y = 13$
$\quad\quad\quad\quad\quad\; y = 6$

Check: $x + y = 13$
$\quad\quad 7 + 6 = 13$

$x - y = 1$
$7 - 6 = 1$

The two numbers are 7 and 6.

PRACTICE

Use a system of equations to solve each problem.

1. Find the numbers whose sum is 15, if twice the first number minus the second number equals 6.

Answer _____

2. The sum of two numbers is 18. Twice the first number plus three times the second number equals 40. Find the numbers.

Answer _____

3. Four times a certain number increased by three times a second number is 25. Four times the first number decreased by three times the second number is 7. Find the two numbers.

Answer _____

4. The difference of two numbers is −1. If twice the first number is added to three times the second number, the result is 13. What are the numbers?

Answer _____

Solving Problems

Use a system of equations to solve each problem.

1. Three times the first of two numbers decreased by the second number equals 9. Twice the first number increased by the second number equals 11. Find the two numbers.

Answer _____

2. The first of two numbers decreased by five times the second number equals −10. The first number decreased by two times the second number equals −1. Find the numbers.

Answer _____

3. The first of two numbers added to two times the second number equals 9. The first number decreased by the second number is 3. Find the numbers.

Answer _____

4. Find the numbers whose sum is 9, if three times the first number increased by two times the second number equals 22.

Answer _____

5. The difference of two numbers is −3. Twice the first number increased by three times the second number is 29. Find the numbers.

Answer _____

6. There are two numbers. Three times the first number increased by two times the second number equals 28. Two times the first number increased by three times the second number equals 27. Find the two numbers.

Answer _____

7. Twice a number decreased by a second number equals 6. Three times the first number increased by twice the second number equals 23. Find the two numbers.

Answer _____

8. Three times the length of a field increased by four times the width equals 24. Two times the length decreased by three times the width is −1. Find the two dimensions.

Answer _____

Systems of Equations with Fractional Coefficients

The methods for solving systems of equations with fractional coefficients are the same as for solving systems of equations with integer coefficients.

EXAMPLE

Solve: $\frac{1}{2}a + b = 5$

$\frac{1}{2}a - b = 1$

Check: Substitute the values of a and b into the original equations.

Step 1.
Add.

Step 2.
Subtract.

$\frac{1}{2}a + b = 5$

$\frac{1}{2}a - b = 1$

$\overline{\quad 1a \quad = 6}$

$\quad a \quad = 6$

$\frac{1}{2}a + b = 5$

$\frac{1}{2}a - b = 1$

$\overline{\quad 2b = 4}$

$\quad b = 2$

$\frac{1}{2}a + b = 5$

$\frac{1}{2}(6) + 2 = 5$

$3 + 2 = 5$

$\frac{1}{2}a - b = 1$

$\frac{1}{2}(6) - 2 = 1$

$3 - 2 = 1$

The solution is (6, 2).

PRACTICE

Solve each system of equations. Check.

a	*b*	*c*
1. $\frac{1}{2}m + n = 3$ $\frac{1}{2}m - n = 1$	$\frac{1}{2}x + y = 6$ $\frac{1}{2}x - y = 2$	$\frac{3}{4}x + y = 6$ $\frac{1}{4}x - y = -2$
2. $\frac{3}{5}x + y = 11$ $\frac{2}{5}x - y = -1$	$\frac{2}{3}x + y = 0$ $\frac{2}{3}x - y = 8$	$\frac{3}{4}x + y = 11$ $\frac{1}{4}x - y = 1$

GRAPHS AND SYSTEMS OF EQUATIONS

Solving Problems

Use a system of equations with fractional coefficients to solve each problem.

---

1. One-half of a number added to a second number equals 4. One-half of the same number decreased by the second number equals zero. Find the two numbers.

Answer _____

2. One-half of a certain number increased by a second number equals 8. One-half of the same number decreased by the second number equals −2. Find the two numbers.

Answer _____

---

3. Seven-tenths of a number increased by a second number equals 19. Three-tenths of the first number decreased by the second number is equal to 1. What are the two numbers?

Answer _____

4. One-third of a number increased by a second number equals 7. One-third of the number decreased by the second number is equal to −3. What are the numbers?

Answer _____

---

5. Two-thirds of the first of two numbers added to the second number equals 6. One-third of the first number decreased by the second number is equal to zero. Find the numbers.

Answer _____

6. Three-fourths of a certain number increased by a second number equals 6. One-fourth of the same number decreased by the second number equals −2. What are the two numbers?

Answer _____

PROBLEM-SOLVING STRATEGY

Use a Graph

A graph can be used to find the solution to a system of equations. Graph each equation. The point of intersection (where the lines cross) is the solution to the system of equations.

Read the problem.

> Mr. Isler mixes peanuts that sell for $3.00 a pound with pecans that sell for $4.50 a pound. He wants to make 12 pounds of the mixture to sell for $4.00 a pound. How many pounds of each should Mr. Isler use?

Write the equations.

Let x = the number of pounds of peanuts.
Let y = the number of pounds of pecans.

Amount of peanuts	+	Amount of pecans	=	Amount of mixture
x	+	y	=	12

The price of x pounds of peanuts, plus y pounds of pecans, must equal the price of 12 pounds of the mixture. Write the equation as follows.

Price of peanuts	+	Price of pecans	=	Price of mixture
$3.00(x)$	+	$4.50(y)$	=	$4.00(12)$

Graph the equations.

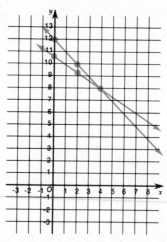

$x + y = 12$ $3x + 4.5y = 48$

x	y
0	12
2	10
4	8

x	y
0	$10\frac{2}{3}$
2	$9\frac{1}{3}$
4	8

The point of intersection has coordinates (4, 8). So $x = 4$ and $y = 8$. Mr. Isler should use 4 pounds of peanuts and 8 pounds of pecans.

Solve by graphing. Write the answer.

---

1. The difference between twice a number and another number is 2. Their sum is 7. Find the numbers. (Hint: Graph $2x - y = 2$ and $x + y = 7$.)

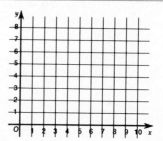

Answer _____

Solve by graphing. Write the answer.

2. Twice one number is equal to 1 more than a second number. The sum of the numbers is 5. Find the numbers.

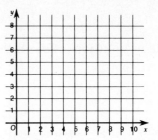

Answer _____

3. The difference between the length and width of a rectangle is 7 cm. The perimeter of the rectangle is 22 cm. Find the length and the width.

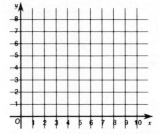

Answer _____

4. The perimeter of a rectangle is 18 inches. The length is twice the width. Find the length and the width.

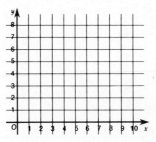

Answer _____

5. Mindy mixes walnuts that sell for $5.00 a pound with peanuts that sell for $3.00 a pound. She wants to make a 10-pound mixture to sell for $3.60 a pound. How many pounds of each should she use?

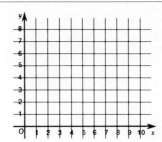

Answer _____

6. Matthew mixes pretzels that sell for $1.50 a pound with cereal that sells for $3.00 a pound. He wants to make 12 pounds of a mixture to sell for $2.00 a pound. How many pounds of each should he use?

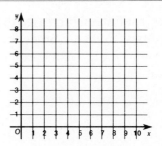

Answer _____

Unit 5 Review

Make a table of solutions. Graph the equation.

a   *b*

1. $2x + 2y = 4$

x	y
-2	
-1	
0	
1	
2	

$x - y = 3$

x	y

Solve each system of equations.

a   *b*   *c*

2. $x + y = 12$
$x - y = 2$

$a + 5b = 14$
$a - 5b = 4$

$x + 5y = 13$
$2x - 3y = 0$

Ordered pair _____

Ordered pair _____

Ordered pair _____

3. $5x + 3y = 45$
$x - y = 1$

$\dfrac{3a}{8} - b = 2$

$\dfrac{7a}{8} + b = 18$

$2x + 3y = 7$
$3x + 2y = 3$

Ordered pair _____

Ordered pair _____

Ordered pair _____

4. Four times a number increased by a second number equals 29. Three times the first number decreased by the second equals 13. What are the numbers?

5. One-half a certain number increased by a second number equals 5. One-half the same number decreased by the second number equals 1. Find the two numbers.

Answer _____

Answer _____

Cumulative Review

Simplify.

	a	*b*	*c*
1.	$4 - 9 + 1 =$	$-3(12 + 5) =$	If $x = 4$, then $-12x =$
2.	$4(a - 3b) + 9(2a + 4b) =$	$\left(\dfrac{r}{5} - y\right) + \left(\dfrac{4r}{5} + y\right) =$	$4a^2b - 2a^2b + 10 =$
3.	$\dfrac{-8x^6}{a^2} \cdot \dfrac{4a^2}{2x^2} =$	$\dfrac{-100r^2st^4 + 10rst}{-10rst} =$	$(6x + 3)(3x - 4) =$

Solve.

	a	*b*	*c*
4.	$x = 10(3^2)$	$17 - y = 24$	$3x + 2y = 6$ for y in terms of x
5.	$3a + 2b = 12$ $3a - 4b = -6$	$\dfrac{3}{5}x + 2y = 22$ $\dfrac{3}{5}x - 2y = 2$	$x - y = 6$ $2x + y = 3$

6. In the formula $I = prt$, find t when p is \$300, r is 6%, and I is \$9.

7. Find the volume of a cylinder if the radius is 12 cm and the height is 15 cm. Use 3.14 for π and round the volume to the nearest whole number.

Answer _____

Answer _____

INEQUALITIES, ROOTS, AND PROPORTIONS

Inequalities

Sometimes the answer to a practical problem is not an exact number, but lies within a certain range. Thus, it is important to study less-than and greater-than relationships. Such relationships are called **inequalities.**

Recall that these symbols are used with inequalities.

> $>$ is greater than $\qquad$ $<$ is less than
> $\geq$ is greater than or equal to $\qquad$ $\leq$ is less than or equal to

On a number line, greater numbers are to the right. If x is greater than y, then $x - y$ is positive. If x is less than y, then $x - y$ is negative.

EXAMPLE 1

Write $>$, $<$, or $=$.

$-4 \underline{\quad < \quad} -1$

$1.001 \underline{\quad > \quad} 0.01$

$16 - 7 \underline{\quad = \quad} 19 - 10$

EXAMPLE 2

Write $>$, $<$, or $=$.

$\left(\frac{1}{2} - \frac{3}{4}\right) \underline{\qquad} \left(\frac{3}{4} - \frac{1}{2}\right)$

$\frac{2}{4} - \frac{3}{4} \underline{\qquad} \frac{3}{4} - \frac{2}{4}$

$-\frac{1}{4} \underline{\quad < \quad} \frac{1}{4}$

EXAMPLE 3

True or False?
$-0.14 \leq -0.12$
$-0.14 - (-0.12) = -0.02$
Since the result is negative, -0.14 is less than -0.12. True

PRACTICE

Use $>$, $<$, or $=$ to complete each statement.

	a	b	c
1.	$-10 \underline{\qquad} -2$	$-3 \underline{\qquad} 4$	$7 \underline{\qquad} -4$
2.	$0.56 \underline{\qquad} 0.43$	$0.004 \underline{\qquad} 0.078$	$1.34 \underline{\qquad} 0.56$
3.	$\frac{15}{18} \underline{\qquad} \frac{61}{72}$	$\frac{17}{72} \underline{\qquad} \frac{5}{24}$	$\frac{13}{18} \underline{\qquad} \frac{15}{24}$
4.	$\left(\frac{5}{8} - \frac{1}{6}\right) \underline{\qquad} \left(\frac{3}{4} - \frac{1}{8}\right)$	$\left(\frac{3}{4} - \frac{5}{8}\right) \underline{\qquad} \left(\frac{3}{8} - \frac{1}{4}\right)$	$\left(\frac{3}{10} - \frac{1}{5}\right) \underline{\qquad} \left(\frac{4}{10} - \frac{1}{2}\right)$

Tell whether each statement is *true* or *false*.

	a	b	c
5.	$-14 > -10$	$0.08 < -0.19$	$-0.20 < -0.16$
6.	$-11 \geq -11$	$15 \geq -13$	$2.63 \leq -2.63$
7.	$\frac{3}{4} > \frac{2}{3}$	$\frac{5}{6} \leq \frac{15}{18}$	$\frac{2}{9} < -\frac{1}{8}$

Solving Inequalities with Addition and Subtraction

Inequalities are solved in much the same way as are equations. You can add or subtract the same amount from both sides of an inequality without changing its solution. If you exchange the left and right sides of an equality, you must reverse the direction. For example, if $7 < x$ then $x > 7$. Study the following examples.

EXAMPLE 1

Solve: $x - 2 > 12$

$$x - 2 > 12$$
$$x - 2 + 2 > 12 + 2$$
$$x > 14$$

EXAMPLE 2

Solve: $2 \leq x + 12$

$$2 \leq x + 12$$
$$2 - 12 \leq x + 12 - 12$$
$$-10 \leq x$$
$$\text{or}$$
$$x \geq -10$$

EXAMPLE 3

Solve: $-x + 16 \leq -2x - 8$

$$-x + 16 - 16 \leq -2x - 8 - 16$$
$$-x \leq -2x - 24$$
$$-x + 2x \leq -2x + 2x - 24$$
$$x \leq -24$$

PRACTICE

Solve.

	a	b	c
1.	$x - 7 > 15$	$x - 4 \leq 11$	$14 > x - 6$
2.	$x + 9 \leq 10$	$20 < x + 5$	$8 \leq x + 12$
3.	$x - 10 \geq -4$	$-17 < x + 7$	$x - 3 > -11$
4.	$11 + x < 7$	$-15 + x < 16$	$-12 \geq 4 + x$
5.	$2x + 3 < x - 1$	$4x + 2 > 4 + 3x$	$6x - 1 \leq 5x - 5$
6.	$7 + 2x \leq x + 8$	$15 - 4x > 9 - 5x$	$22 + 9x \leq -12 + 8x$

Solving Inequalities with Multiplication and Division

As with equations, you can multiply or divide both sides of an inequality by the same number. However, if you multiply or divide by a negative number, you must change the direction of the inequality sign. This is shown in Example 2.

EXAMPLE 1

Solve: $\dfrac{x}{2} \geq 3$

Multiply both sides by 2.

$2\left(\dfrac{x}{2}\right) \geq 2(3)$

$x \geq 6$

EXAMPLE 2

Solve: $-2x < 6$

Divide both sides by -2 and reverse the sign.

$\dfrac{-2x}{-2} > \dfrac{6}{-2}$

$x > -3$

EXAMPLE 3

Solve: $-2x + 3 \leq 5x + 17$

$-2x + 3 - 3 \leq 5x + 17 - 3$

$-2x \leq 5x + 14$

$-2x - 5x \leq 5x - 5x + 14$

$\dfrac{-7x}{-7} \geq \dfrac{14}{-7}$

$x \geq -2$

PRACTICE

Solve.

	a	*b*	*c*
1.	$\dfrac{x}{5} > 2$	$\dfrac{x}{2} \leq -6$	$3 \leq \dfrac{x}{-4}$
2.	$4x < 8$	$-10 \geq 2x$	$-6x \leq -18$
3.	$3x + 2 \geq 8$	$8x - 13 > 19$	$-2 - 3x > 7$
4.	$8x - 10 > 7x - 4$	$2 - 5x < 11 + 4x$	$3x - 2 \geq 2x + 18$
5.	$-7x + 13 > -2x + 9$	$3x - \dfrac{2}{5} \leq 5x + \dfrac{3}{5}$	$4 + 2x < 6 + 3x$

Solving Problems with Inequalities

Certain problems can be solved using inequalities.

EXAMPLE

Margaret is 2 years older than Sam, and their combined age is, at most, 20. What is the oldest Sam could be? What is the oldest Margaret could be?

Let x = Sam's age.
$x + 2$ = Margaret's age.

Their combined age is, at most, 20.

$$x + (x + 2) \qquad \leq \qquad 20$$
$$2x + 2 \leq 20$$
$$2x \leq 18$$
$$x \leq 9$$

The oldest Sam could be is 9 years old.
The oldest Margaret could be is $x + 2$ or $9 + 2 = 11$ years old.

PRACTICE

Solve using inequalities.

1. In order to race, jockeys must weigh-in at less than 130 pounds. This includes the jockey's weight plus the weight of the blanket, saddle, and bridle. If the combined weight of the equipment is $\frac{1}{8}$ of the jockey's weight, what is the maximum the jockey can weigh in order to race?

Answer _____

2. The Rodriguez family has a fixed income of $2000 a month. Their fixed expenditures are $1200 a month. They save at least one-half of the remaining income each month. What is the minimum amount saved by the Rodriguez family in a year?

Answer _____

3. The sum of three consecutive integers is less than 186. What is the maximum value for the first integer?

Answer _____

4. The sum of four consecutive odd integers is greater than 48. What is the minimum value for the first integer?

Answer _____

PROBLEM-SOLVING STRATEGY

Make a Table

For some problems, it is necessary to make many calculations before finding the final answer. It is easier to solve this type of problem if the information is organized in a table.

Read the problem.

The sum of the first three consecutive odd integers is 9. What is the sum of the first five consecutive odd integers? the first 50 consecutive odd integers? the first 100?

Make a table.

Number of consecutive odd integers	3	5	50	100
Sum	9			

Solve the problem.

Find the sum of the first five consecutive odd integers.

$$1 + 3 + 5 + 7 + 9 = 25$$

Record the answer in the table. Notice that $3^2 = 9$ and $5^2 = 25$. Use this observation to complete the table.

Number of consecutive odd integers	3	5	50	100
Sum	9	25	2500	10,000

Solve.

1. A number can be divided evenly by its *factors*. For example, the factors of 12 are 1, 2, 3, 4, 6, and 12 since each of these numbers divides into 12 evenly. Complete the tables at the right to show the factors of numbers up to 20.

Number	Factors
1	1
2	1, 2
3	
4	1, 2, 4
5	1, 5
6	
7	
8	
9	
10	1, 2, 5, 10

Number	Factors
11	1, 11
12	
13	
14	
15	
16	
17	
18	
19	
20	1, 2, 4, 5, 10, 20

2. Which integers less than 20 have an odd number of factors?

3. Which integers less than 20 have four factors?

Answer _____

Answer _____

Make a table. Solve.

4. In January, canned apricots cost 68¢. Canned peaches cost 78¢. The price of apricots increased 4¢ per month. The price of peaches increased 2¢ per month. Find the month when both items sold for the same price.

Answer _____

5. Jeff had 250 baseball cards and Jason had 82 baseball cards. At the first meeting of the Card Club and at every meeting thereafter, Jeff sold 12 cards to Jason. After which meeting did the two have the same number of cards?

Answer _____

6. Domingo took a job at $18,000 the first year with $450 a year raises thereafter. Brenda took a job at $19,020 a year with $590 a year increases. During which year will Brenda be earning $2000 a year more than Domingo?

Answer _____

7. In November, the Sport Shop sold 74 pairs of snow skis and 3 pairs of water skis. Each month the shop sold 11 more pairs of water skis and 6 fewer pairs of snow skis than the previous month. When was the first month the shop sold more water skis than snow skis?

Answer _____

8. Betty tore a sheet of paper in half. Then she tore each of the remaining pieces in half. She continued this process 6 more times. How many pieces of paper did she have at the end?

Answer _____

9. Mr. Hassan's house number is composed of 3 consecutive digits. It is a multiple of his age, which is 63. What is Mr. Hassan's house number?

Answer _____

Square Roots

The sign $\sqrt{}$ tells you to find the positive square root of the number under the sign. The expression $\sqrt{9}$ is called a **radical.** The 9 is called a **radicand** and the $\sqrt{}$ is called a **radical sign.**

You may remember from arithmetic that the square root of a number is that factor which when multiplied by itself gives the number. Here are three examples:

Number	Square
1	1
2	4
3	9
4	16
5	25
6	36
7	49
8	64
9	81
10	100
11	121
12	144
13	169
14	196
15	225
16	256
17	289
18	324
19	361
20	400

$$\sqrt{4} = 2 \qquad\qquad \sqrt{9} = 3 \qquad\qquad \sqrt{81} = 9$$

You may also take the square root of a monomial. To do this, first take the square root of the coefficient. Next, take the square root of each variable expression.

$$\sqrt{4x^2} = 2x \qquad \sqrt{9x^4} = 3x^2 \qquad \sqrt{x^4y^2} = x^2y$$
$$\text{Check: } 2x \cdot 2x = 4x^2 \quad \text{Check: } 3x^2 \cdot 3x^2 = 9x^4 \quad \text{Check: } x^2y \cdot x^2y = x^4y^2$$

Use the chart to help you find larger square roots. To find $\sqrt{400}$, find 400 in the *square* column. The square root of 400 is in the first column. So, $\sqrt{400}$ is 20 since $20 \times 20 = 400$.

Remember, the square root of 1 is always 1.

PRACTICE ─────────────────────────────

Find each square root.

	a	b	c	d	e
1.	$\sqrt{121} =$	$\sqrt{49} =$	$\sqrt{144} =$	$\sqrt{25} =$	$\sqrt{169} =$
2.	$\sqrt{225} =$	$\sqrt{81} =$	$\sqrt{16} =$	$\sqrt{324} =$	$\sqrt{196} =$
3.	$\sqrt{a^2} =$	$\sqrt{a^4} =$	$\sqrt{x^6} =$	$\sqrt{y^8} =$	$\sqrt{b^4} =$
4.	$\sqrt{a^2b^2} =$	$\sqrt{x^4y^4} =$	$\sqrt{x^2y^4} =$	$\sqrt{a^2b^2c^2} =$	$\sqrt{x^4b^2c^4} =$
5.	$\sqrt{9a^2} =$	$\sqrt{16b^4} =$	$\sqrt{36a^2b^2} =$	$\sqrt{64x^2y^4} =$	$\sqrt{81a^2b^4c^8} =$
6.	$\sqrt{169x^{10}y^4} =$	$\sqrt{289x^{12}} =$	$\sqrt{324b^4c^6} =$	$\sqrt{400a^2b^6} =$	$\sqrt{100x^4y^2z^6} =$

Cube Roots

The sign $\sqrt[3]{}$ tells you to find the cube root of the number under the sign. The cube root of a number is used as a factor three times to give the number. Study the following examples.

Number	Cube
1	1
2	8
3	27
4	64
5	125
6	216
7	343
8	512
9	729
10	1000
11	1331
12	1728
13	2197
14	2744
15	3375
16	4096
17	4913
18	5832
19	6859
20	8000

$\sqrt[3]{8} = 2$
Since $2 \cdot 2 \cdot 2 = 8$

$\sqrt[3]{125} = 5$
Since $5 \cdot 5 \cdot 5 = 125$

$\sqrt[3]{1000} = 10$
Since $10 \cdot 10 \cdot 10 = 1000$

You may also take the cube root of a monomial. Take the cube root of any coefficient. Then take the cube root of each variable expression. Use the chart if needed.

Remember, the cube root of 1 is 1.

EXAMPLE 1

$\sqrt[3]{8y^3} = 2y$
Check: $2y \cdot 2y \cdot 2y = 8y^3$

EXAMPLE 2

$\sqrt[3]{1000x^6y^3} = 10x^2y$
Check: $10x^2y \cdot 10x^2y \cdot 10x^2y$
$= 1000x^6y^3$

PRACTICE

Find each cube root.

        a   *b*   *c*   *d*   *e*

1. $\sqrt[3]{27} =$ $\qquad$ $\sqrt[3]{64} =$ $\qquad$ $\sqrt[3]{512} =$ $\qquad$ $\sqrt[3]{1} =$ $\qquad$ $\sqrt[3]{4096} =$

2. $\sqrt[3]{y^3} =$ $\qquad$ $\sqrt[3]{y^6} =$ $\qquad$ $\sqrt[3]{b^9} =$ $\qquad$ $\sqrt[3]{c^{12}} =$ $\qquad$ $\sqrt[3]{z^{15}} =$

3. $\sqrt[3]{8y^3} =$ $\qquad$ $\sqrt[3]{216x^6} =$ $\qquad$ $\sqrt[3]{1331z^9} =$ $\qquad$ $\sqrt[3]{8000a^3} =$ $\qquad$ $\sqrt[3]{4096b^{12}} =$

4. $\sqrt[3]{343a^3b^3} =$ $\qquad$ $\sqrt[3]{729x^6y^{15}} =$ $\qquad$ $\sqrt[3]{8c^{12}d^9} =$ $\qquad$ $\sqrt[3]{216x^3y^6} =$ $\qquad$ $\sqrt[3]{3375z^{27}} =$

5. $\sqrt[3]{512a^3b^3c^6} =$ $\qquad$ $\sqrt[3]{1000x^3y^6z^9} =$ $\qquad$ $\sqrt[3]{2197r^9s^9} =$ $\qquad$ $\sqrt[3]{5832t^{30}} =$ $\qquad$ $\sqrt[3]{125x^{15}y^{15}} =$

Equations with Squares

Solving some equations involves finding the square root of a number. A number equation such as $x^2 = 9$ has two solutions. The solutions to $x^2 = 9$ are 3 and −3 because $(-3)(-3) = 9$ *and* $(3)(3) = 9$. These solutions can be written as ± 3. The symbol $\pm$ means positive or negative. Study the following example.

EXAMPLE

Solve: $2a^2 - 7 = 43$	**Check:** $2(5)^2 - 7 = 43$
$2a^2 - 7 + 7 = 43 + 7$	$2(5)(5) - 7 = 43$
$2a^2 = 50$	$50 - 7 = 43$
$\dfrac{2a^2}{2} = \dfrac{50}{2}$	$2(-5)^2 - 7 = 43$
	$2(-5)(-5) - 7 = 43$
$a^2 = 25$	$50 - 7 = 43$
Find the square root of both sides.	
$a = \pm 5$	

PRACTICE

Solve.

	a	*b*	*c*	*d*
1.	$2x^2 = 200$	$7x^2 = 175$	$3x^2 = 147$	$2x^2 = 32$
2.	$x^2 + 15 = 40$	$x^2 - 12 = 24$	$x^2 + 17 = 81$	$x^2 - 15 = 85$
3.	$3a^2 + 7 = 34$	$5a^2 - 9 = 116$	$2a^2 - 6 = 44$	$4a^2 + 3 = 19$

Combine like terms and solve.

	a	*b*	*c*
4.	$3x^2 - 7 = x^2 + 1$	$5x^2 + 3 = 2x^2 + 30$	$7x^2 - 15 = 5x^2 + 17$

Equations with Cubes

Solving equations with cubes involves finding the cube root of a number. An equation such as $x^3 = 27$ has only one solution. The solution is 3 because $(3)(3)(3) = 27$. Notice that -3 is not a solution because the product $(-3)(-3)(-3) = -27$.

EXAMPLE

Solve: $3x^3 + 7 = 88$

$$3x^3 + 7 = 88$$
$$3x^3 + 7 - 7 = 88 - 7$$
$$3x^3 = 81$$
$$\frac{3x^3}{3} = \frac{81}{3}$$
$$x^3 = 27$$
$$x = 3$$

Check: $3(3)^3 + 7 = 88$

$$3(3)(3)(3) + 7 = 88$$
$$3(27) + 7 = 88$$
$$81 + 7 = 88$$

PRACTICE

Solve.

	a	b	c	d
1.	$3x^3 = 24$	$2x^3 = 250$	$4x^3 = 864$	$2x^3 = 1458$
2.	$x^3 + 7 = 34$	$x^3 + 9 = 17$	$x^3 - 15 = 49$	$x^3 - 81 = 919$
3.	$5x^3 - 15 = 610$	$2x^3 + 25 = 711$	$4x^3 - 8 = 248$	$3x^3 - 100 = 548$

Combine like terms and solve.

	a	b	c
4.	$3x^3 - 5 = x^3 + 11$	$5x^3 - 17 = 3x^3 + 111$	$2x^3 + 5 = x^3 + 221$

Using Equations with Squares

Equations containing terms with exponents of 2 can be used to solve problems concerning the area of a rectangle ($A = lw$). Drawing a picture may help solve the problem.

EXAMPLE

The area of a rectangle is 200 square feet. The length is twice the width. Find the dimensions.

Let x = width.   Since $A = 200$ square ft,   **Check:** $(2x)x = 200$
    $2x$ = length. $2x^2 = 200$ $(20)10 = 200$
Then $A = (2x)x$ $x^2 = 100$
    $A = 2x^2$ $x = \pm 10$

The width (x) is 10 ft and the length ($2x$) is 20 ft. The negative value of $x = -10$ is not a solution since dimensions cannot be negative.

Solve.

1. Find the dimensions of a rectangle with an area of 288 square cm and a length twice the width.

    Answer _____

2. Find the dimensions of a rectangle with an area of 128 square in. and the length 8 times the width.

    Answer _____

3. The area of a rectangle is 100 square m. The length is 4 times the width. What are the dimensions of the rectangle?

    Answer _____

4. The length of a rectangle is six times the width, and the area is 2166 square in. Find the dimensions of the rectangle.

    Answer _____

5. Find the dimensions of a rectangle with an area of 125 square cm if the width is one-fifth of the length. (Hint: Fractions can be eliminated by letting $5x$ represent the length.)

    Answer _____

6. If the width of a rectangle is one-third the length and the area is 4332 square ft, find the dimensions of the rectangle. (Hint: Eliminate the fraction by letting x = width.)

    Answer _____

Using Equations with Cubes

Equations containing terms with exponents of 3 can be used to solve problems concerning the volume of a rectangular prism ($V = lwh$). Drawing a picture may help solve the problem.

EXAMPLE

Find the dimensions of a rectangular prism with a volume of 256 cubic meters. The height and the length are each twice the width.

Let x = width.　　　Since $V = 256$ cubic m,　　**Check:**　$(2x)(x)(2x) = 256$
　　$2x$ = height.　　　　$4x^3 = 256$　　　　　　　　　　$(8)(4)(8) = 256$
　　$2x$ = length.　　　　　$x^3 = 64$
Then $V = x(2x)(2x)$　　　　$x = 4$
　　　　$= 4x^3$

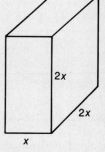

The width (x) is 4 meters, the height ($2x$) is 8 meters, and the length ($2x$) is also 8 meters.

PRACTICE

Solve.

1. Find the dimensions of a rectangular prism with a volume of 512 cubic cm if the width is one-half the length and the height is four times the width. (Hint: Eliminate the fraction by letting x = the base width.)

Answer _____

2. Find the dimensions of a rectangular prism with a volume of 162 cubic m if the width is one-half the length and the height is three times the width.

Answer _____

3. Find the dimensions of a rectangular prism with a volume of 384 cubic m if the length is twice the width and the height is three times the width.

Answer _____

4. Find the dimensions of a cube with a volume of 125 cubic cm. (Hint: Remember that the cube has equal dimensions.)

Answer _____

5. Find the dimensions of a rectangular prism with a volume of 135 cubic ft if the base is a square and the height is five times the base edge. (Hint: In this problem, length = width.)

Answer _____

6. What are the dimensions of a rectangular prism with a volume of 576 cubic m if the width is three-fourths the length and the height is twice the width? (Hint: Fractions can be eliminated by letting $4x$ = the length.)

Answer _____

137

The Meaning of Ratio

Ratio is defined as the comparison of quantities of the same kind. For instance, to compare a quart to a gallon, the gallon must be changed to quarts. The ratio of one quart to a gallon is written $1:4$ or $\frac{1}{4}$ since there are four quarts in a gallon. The ratio is read *one to four*. A ratio in fractional form can be reduced just as any fraction can be reduced to lowest terms. Ratios can be used to solve problems.

EXAMPLE 1

> **Jack is 15 years old. His father is 40 years old. What is the ratio of Jack's age to his father's age?**
>
> Stated in fractional form, the ratio is $\frac{15}{40}$. Reduced to lowest terms, the ratio is $\frac{3}{8}$. Thus, the ratio of Jack's age to the age of his father is $\frac{15}{40}$ or $\frac{3}{8}$.

EXAMPLE 2

> **The perimeter of a rectangle is 60 ft. The length and width are in the ratio of 2 to 1. Find the two dimensions.**
>
> Let $\quad x = $ width
> $\qquad 2x = $ length
> Then $P = 2(x) + 2(2x) = 6x$
> Since $P = 60$ ft.
> $\qquad 6x = 60$
> $\qquad x = 10$
> The width is 10 ft, the length is 20 ft.

PRACTICE

Find each ratio.

$\qquad\qquad\qquad\qquad\qquad a \qquad\qquad\qquad\qquad\qquad\qquad\qquad\qquad\qquad\qquad\qquad\qquad\qquad b$

1. an ounce to a pound $\qquad 1:16$ or $\dfrac{1}{16}$ $\qquad\qquad$ an inch to a foot

2. a gram to a kilogram $\qquad\qquad\qquad\qquad\qquad$ a foot to a mile

3. a millimeter to a centimeter $\qquad\qquad\qquad$ a meter to a centimeter

Solve.

4. Carol is 5 feet 4 inches tall and Adam is 5 feet tall. What is the ratio of Carol's height to that of Adam? (Hint: Remember to change both measurements to inches.)

Answer _____

5. One car has an engine of 90 horsepower. A second has an engine of 75 horsepower. What is the ratio of the horsepower of the first to the horsepower of the second?

Answer _____

6. The perimeter of a rectangle is 70 ft. The length and width are in the ratio of 3 to 2. Find the length and width.

Answer _____

7. The length and width of a rectangle are in the ratio of 10 to 7. The perimeter is 340 meters. Find the length and width.

Answer _____

INEQUALITIES, ROOTS, AND PROPORTIONS

The Meaning of Proportion

Consider this situation. On Monday, Stan earned $20 for working 4 hours. On Tuesday, he earned $35 for working 7 hours.

The ratio of Monday's hours to Tuesday's hours is $\frac{4}{7}$. The ratio of Monday's earnings to Tuesday's earnings is $\frac{20}{35}$. Since these ratios are equal, you can write an equation.

$$\text{Monday's hours} \rightarrow \frac{4}{7} = \frac{20}{35} \leftarrow \text{Monday's dollars} \atop \leftarrow \text{Tuesday's dollars}$$

An equation formed by two fractions is called a **proportion.** The fractions can be ratios *or* rates. Ratios (above) have the same units while rates (below) have different units.

$$\frac{\text{dollars} \rightarrow 20}{\text{hours} \rightarrow 4} = \frac{35 \leftarrow \text{dollars}}{7 \leftarrow \text{hours}}$$

Problems with one part of the proportion missing can be easily solved by cross multiplication.

EXAMPLE

Kathryn earns $9 for working 2 hours. How much would she earn for working 6 hours?

Let x = the amount earned in 6 hours.

Use ratios: $\frac{9}{x} = \frac{2}{6}$ or rates: $\frac{9}{2} = \frac{x}{6}$.

Solve by cross multiplication.
$$9(6) = x(2)$$
$$54 = 2x$$
$$27 = x$$

Check:
$$\frac{9}{27} = \frac{2}{6} = \frac{1}{3}$$

Kathryn would earn $27 for working 6 hours.

PRACTICE

Solve each proportion. Use cross multiplication.

	a	*b*	*c*	*d*
1.	$\frac{x}{4} = \frac{5}{10}$	$\frac{x}{6} = \frac{2}{3}$	$\frac{2}{x} = \frac{6}{9}$	$\frac{8}{x} = \frac{4}{8}$
2.	$\frac{3}{25} = \frac{x}{100}$	$\frac{4}{5} = \frac{x}{20}$	$\frac{3}{7} = \frac{6}{x}$	$\frac{7}{5} = \frac{21}{x}$

Solve.

3. If Roland earned $8.40 in 2 hours, how much would he earn in 3 hours?

4. If it takes 3 hours for a horse to walk 10 miles, how far will he walk in 8 hours?

Answer _____

Answer _____

Problems with Ratio and Proportion

Solve.

1. Find the dimensions of a rectangle, if the area equals 525 square cm and the length and the width are in the ratio of 7 to 3.

   $$\text{Since } l:w = 7:3, \qquad A = lw$$
   $$\text{let } 7x = length \qquad 525 = (7x)(3x)$$
   $$\quad 3x = width \qquad 525 = 21x^2$$
   $$25 = x^2$$
   $$\pm 5 = x$$

   Answer _Length = 35 cm. Width = 15 cm._

2. Find the dimensions of a rectangle, if the area equals 144 square in. and the length and the width are in the ratio of 2 to $\frac{1}{2}$. (Hint: In order to eliminate the fraction, the ratio may be changed to 4 to 1.)

   Answer _____

3. The area of a rectangle is 96 square ft. The two dimensions are in the ratio of two-thirds to one. Find the dimensions. (Hint: Would two-thirds to one be the same as two to three?)

   Answer _____

4. The length and the width of a rectangle are in the ratio of 2 to 1. The area is 200 square feet. Find the two dimensions.

   Answer _____

5. The taxes on a piece of property valued at $4000 were $86. At the same rate, what would be the taxes on property which was valued at $5500?

   Answer _____

6. Another piece of property valued at $4500 was assessed taxes of $91. At this rate, what would be the taxes on property valued at $7200?

   Answer _____

7. Mr. Sanchez paid $300 taxes on his lot, which was valued at $16,000. At the same rate, what is the value of Mr. Muñoz's lot, if he paid $468.75 in taxes?

   Answer _____

8. Trey paid $46.45 fare for a bus trip of 370 miles. At the same rate, how much would he have to pay for a trip of 540 miles?

   Answer _____

Proportion in Measurements

Triangles whose corresponding angles are equal are called **similar triangles.** Similar triangles have the same shape, but not necessarily the same size. If two triangles are similar, the measures of the corresponding sides are proportional. For the triangles at the right you can write these proportions.

$$\frac{AB}{DE} = \frac{BC}{EF} \qquad \frac{AB}{DE} = \frac{AC}{DF} \qquad \frac{AC}{DF} = \frac{BC}{EF}$$

The lengths of some sides of the triangles are indicated in the drawing. Proportions can be used to find the lengths of the other sides.

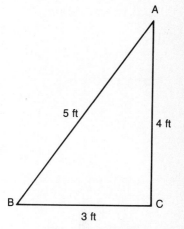

EXAMPLE 1

EXAMPLE 2

Find the length of EF.	Find the length of DE.
$\dfrac{AC}{DF} = \dfrac{BC}{EF}$	$\dfrac{AC}{DF} = \dfrac{AB}{DE}$
$\dfrac{4}{2} = \dfrac{3}{EF}$	$\dfrac{4}{2} = \dfrac{5}{DE}$
$4EF = 6$	$4DE = 10$
$EF = 1.5$ ft	$DE = 2.5$ ft

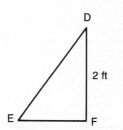

PRACTICE

Solve.

---

1. Triangles ABC and DEF are similar. AB is 10 feet, BC is 15 feet, AC is 20 feet, and DE is 6 feet. Find EF.

Answer _____

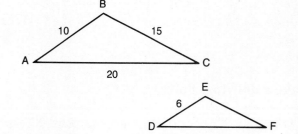

2. Using the same triangles, find DF.

Answer _____

---

3. The drawing at the right shows a person 5 feet tall, casting a shadow 3 feet long. The tree is casting a shadow 15 feet long. How tall is the tree? (Hint: The shadows form the bases of the triangles.)

Answer _____

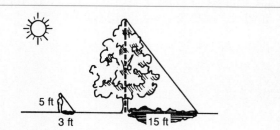

---

4. When a pole 20 feet tall casts a shadow 15 feet long, how tall is a tree which casts a shadow of 24 feet?

Answer _____

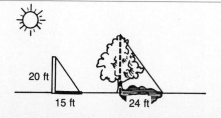

Make a Drawing

It is often easier to solve a problem by making a drawing. Even a rough sketch may give you the clue you need to solve the problem.

Read the problem.

Triangles ABC and DEF are similar. AB is 12 feet, BC is 8 feet, AC is 8 feet, and DE is 9 feet. Find EF.

Make a drawing.

Draw triangle ABC. Then draw a smaller triangle that has the same shape. Write labels D, E, and F to correspond to A, B, and C, respectively. Be sure to label corresponding angles with the corresponding letters.

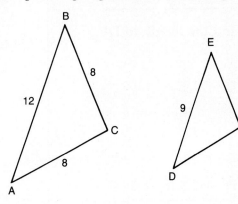

Solve the problem.

Write a proportion. Substitute.

$$\frac{AB}{DE} = \frac{BC}{EF} \qquad\qquad \frac{12}{9} = \frac{8}{EF}$$
$$12EF = 72$$
$$EF = 6 \text{ feet}$$

Make a drawing. Solve.

1. Triangles XYZ and RST are similar. XY is 24 inches, YZ is 16 inches, XZ is 12 inches, and RS is 18 inches. Find ST.

2. Triangles HIJ and MNP are similar. HI is 12 meters, IJ is 16 meters, HJ is 20 meters, and MN is 15 meters. Find NP. Find MP.

Answer _____

Answer _____

Make a drawing. Solve.

3. When a fence post 1 meter tall casts a shadow 1.7 meters long, how tall is a flagpole which casts a shadow of 80 meters? Round to the nearest meter.

Answer _____

4. When a person 6 feet tall casts a shadow 10 feet long, how tall is the tree which casts a shadow of 45 feet?

Answer _____

5. A church steeple casts a shadow 100 feet long when a 15-foot tree casts a shadow 20 feet long. How high is the church steeple?

Answer _____

6. Two rectangles are similar. Each of the sides of the larger rectangle is 3 times the length of the corresponding side of the smaller rectangle. How does the area of the larger rectangle compare with the area of the smaller?

Answer _____

INEQUALITIES, ROOTS, AND PROPORTIONS
Unit 6 Review

Use >, <, or = to complete each statement.

a	b	c
1. 19 _____ −12	0.003 _____ 0.030	$\dfrac{14}{28}$ _____ $\dfrac{1}{2}$

Solve.

a	b	c
2. $x - 10 < 16$	$3y - 7 \geq 8$	$-9m + 10 \leq -7m - 2$
3. $3x^2 = 75$	$4a^2 - 20 = 16$	$y^3 - 2 = 6$
4. $\dfrac{2}{5} = \dfrac{x}{15}$	$\dfrac{18}{4} = \dfrac{r}{6}$	$\dfrac{c}{4} = \dfrac{5}{10}$

Find each square or cube root.

a	b	c	d
5. $\sqrt{49} =$	$\sqrt[3]{27} =$	$\sqrt{25x^2y^4} =$	$\sqrt[3]{216} =$

Solve.

6. The length of a rectangle is twice the width. The area is 450 square cm. Find the two dimensions.

Answer _____

7. The volume of a rectangular prism is 576 cubic cm and the height and length are each three times the width. Find the three dimensions.

Answer _____

8. The length and the width of a rectangle are in the ratio of 4 to 3. The area is 1200 square in. Find the two dimensions.

Answer _____

9. The taxes on a piece of property valued at $16,000 were $300. At this same rate, what would the taxes be on property valued at $25,000?

Answer _____

10. Triangles EFG and XYZ are similar. EF is 4 meters, FG is 10 meters, EG is 12 meters, and XY is 6 meters. Find YZ.

Answer _____

11. When a 40-foot pole casts a shadow of 30 feet, how tall is a tree that casts a shadow of 15 feet?

Answer _____

Cumulative Review

Simplify.

	a	b	c
1.	$-(-38) =$	$46xy + 52xy + 17xy =$	$(4c^2)(2d^3)^2 =$
2.	$\dfrac{-36m^2n^2}{18n^3} =$	$\left(\dfrac{a}{2} + 3y\right) - \left(\dfrac{a}{2} - 6y\right) =$	$\dfrac{4r^2s^4}{5r} \div \dfrac{16rs}{10r^2} =$
3.	$\dfrac{x}{x} + 0(y) =$	$\sqrt{a^2b^6} =$	$a + b \,\overline{)\,a^2 + 2ab + b^2}$

Solve.

	a	b	c
4.	$3(2a - 6) = 0 + 6$	$3k - 3 \geq 15$	$4 - 2x \leq 10$

Solve each system of equations.

	a	b	c
5.	$x + 2y = 7$ $x - 2y = 3$	$\dfrac{1}{2}x + y = 4$ $\dfrac{1}{2}x - 2y = 7$	$3x + 2y = 25$ $x - 3y = -21$

Give the coordinates of each point. **Solve.**

6. A (＿＿ , ＿＿)

   B (＿＿ , ＿＿)

   C (＿＿ , ＿＿)

   D (＿＿ , ＿＿)

   E (＿＿ , ＿＿)

   F (＿＿ , ＿＿)

   G (＿＿ , ＿＿)

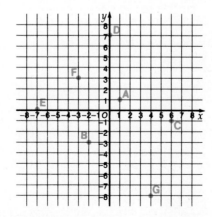

7. The length and width of a rectangle are in the ratio of 5 to 3 and the area is 240 square centimeters. Find the dimensions.

Answer ＿＿＿＿＿＿＿＿

The Square of the Sum of Two Terms

Squaring a binomial is the same as multiplying a binomial by itself. Study Example 1. Notice that the first term of the answer, x^2, is the square of the first term of the binomial. The middle term of the answer, $2xy$, is twice the product of the two terms of the binomial. The last term of the answer, y^2, is the square of the second term of the binomial. This leads to the following shortcut for finding the square of the sum of two terms.

> **RULE:** The square of the sum of two terms is equal to the square of the first term, plus twice the product of the first and the second terms, plus the square of the second term.

EXAMPLE 1

Find: $(x + y)^2$
$$(x + y)^2 = (x + y)(x + y)$$
$$= x(x) + x(y) + x(y) + y(y)$$
$$= x^2 + 2xy + y^2 \text{ Remember, } x(y) = y(x).$$

EXAMPLE 2

Find: $(a + 2b)^2$
$$(a + 2b)^2 = (a + 2b)(a + 2b)$$
$$= a(a) + 2(a)(b) + 2(a)(b) + 2b(2b)$$
$$= a^2 + 4ab + 4b^2$$

PRACTICE

Find the square of each binomial.

	a	b
1.	$(a + b)^2 =$	$(b + a)^2 =$
2.	$(m + n)^2 =$	$(r + s)^2 =$
3.	$(b + c)^2 =$	$(c + d)^2 =$
4.	$(2a + b)^2 =$	$(x + 2y)^2 =$
5.	$(2a + 2b)^2 =$	$(2y + z)^2 =$
6.	$(x + 3y)^2 =$	$(3x + y)^2 =$
7.	$(2x + 3y)^2 =$	$(3x + 2y)^2 =$
8.	$(3x + 5)^2 =$	$(5x + 3)^2 =$
9.	$(m + 4)^2 =$	$(4 + m)^2 =$
10.	$(2x + 3)^2 =$	$(4a + 3)^2 =$

The Square of the Difference of Two Terms

The only difference between squaring the sum of two terms and squaring the difference of two terms is the operation on the middle term of the product. With the sum of two terms, the terms are all added. With the difference of two terms, the middle term is subtracted. Here is a shortcut for squaring the difference of two terms.

> **RULE:** The square of the difference of two terms is equal to the square of the first term, minus twice the product of the first and the second terms, plus the square of the second term.

EXAMPLE 1

Find: $(x - 2)^2$

$$(x - 2)^2 = (x - 2)(x - 2)$$
$$= x(x) - 2(x) - 2(x) + 4$$
$$= x^2 - 4x + 4$$

EXAMPLE 2

Find: $(2x - 5y)^2$

$$(2x - 5y)^2 = (2x - 5y)(2x - 5y)$$
$$= 2x(2x) - 2x(5y) - 2x(5y) + 5y(5y)$$
$$= 4x^2 - 20xy + 25y^2$$

PRACTICE

Find the square of each binomial.

	a	b
1.	$(x - 4)^2 =$	$(x - 3)^2 =$
2.	$(x - 5)^2 =$	$(x - 8)^2 =$
3.	$(5 - x)^2 =$	$(7 - x)^2 =$
4.	$(a - 12)^2 =$	$(a - 10)^2 =$
5.	$(c - 2d)^2 =$	$(x - 3y)^2 =$
6.	$(x - 6y)^2 =$	$(x - 10y)^2 =$
7.	$(x - 5y)^2 =$	$(x - 9y)^2 =$
8.	$(3 - 2x)^2 =$	$(5 - 4x)^2 =$
9.	$(7 - 2x)^2 =$	$(10 - 3x)^2 =$
10.	$(3x - 2y)^2 =$	$(5x - 4y)^2 =$

FACTORING AND QUADRATIC EQUATIONS

Factoring: The Square of the Sum of Two Terms

The result of squaring a binomial is a perfect square **trinomial,** or polynomial with three terms. For example, $(a + b)^2 = a^2 + 2ab + b^2$. To factor a perfect square trinomial such as $a^2 + 2ab + b^2$, think of the reverse of multiplication. Thus, the factors of $a^2 + 2ab + b^2$ are $(a + b)(a + b)$ or $(a + b)^2$.

EXAMPLE 1

Factor: $x^2 + 2xy + y^2$
$= (x + y)(x + y)$
$= (x + y)^2$

EXAMPLE 2

Factor: $25 + 10x + x^2$
$= (5 + x)(5 + x)$
$= (5 + x)^2$

EXAMPLE 3

Factor: $4y^2 + 48y + 144$
$= (2y + 12)(2y + 12)$
$= (2y + 12)^2$

PRACTICE

Factor each trinomial.

a	*b*
1. $a^2 + 2ay + y^2 =$	$m^2 + 2mn + n^2 =$
2. $c^2 + 2cd + d^2 =$	$r^2 + 2rs + s^2 =$
3. $x^2 + 4xy + 4y^2 =$	$4x^2 + 4xy + y^2 =$
4. $m^2 + 6mn + 9n^2 =$	$r^2 + 14rt + 49t^2 =$
5. $x^2 + 8xy + 16y^2 =$	$x^2 + 8x + 16 =$
6. $49y^2 + 56y + 16 =$	$x^2 + 10xy + 25y^2 =$
7. $9 + 6y + y^2 =$	$z^2 + 6z + 9 =$
8. $4 + 4x + x^2 =$	$x^2 + 6xy + 9y^2 =$
9. $64 + 16x + x^2 =$	$49 + 14x + x^2 =$
10. $9x^2 + 12xy + 4y^2 =$	$4x^2 + 16xy + 16y^2 =$
11. $81 + 36x + 4x^2 =$	$64x^2 + 16x + 1 =$
12. $100 + 20x + x^2 =$	$36x^2 + 24x + 4 =$

FACTORING AND QUADRATIC EQUATIONS

Factoring: The Square of the Difference of Two Terms

You already know that $a^2 + 2ab + b^2$ is a perfect square trinomial and factors into $(a + b)^2$. You can see that $a^2 - 2ab + b^2$ is also a perfect square trinomial. Since the only difference between $a^2 + 2ab + b^2$ and $a^2 - 2ab + b^2$ is the operation on the middle term, it follows that the only difference between their factors should be the operation. Thus, $a^2 - 2ab + b^2 = (a - b)(a - b)$ or $(a - b)^2$.

EXAMPLE 1

Factor: $r^2 - 2rs + s^2$
$= (r - s)(r - s)$
$= (r - s)^2$

EXAMPLE 2

Factor: $4p^2 - 12pq + 9q^2$
$= (2p - 3q)(2p - 3q)$
$= (2p - 3q)^2$

PRACTICE

Factor.

a	b
1. $x^2 - 2xy + y^2 =$	$c^2 - 2cd + d^2 =$
2. $b^2 - 2bd + d^2 =$	$m^2 - 2mn + n^2 =$
3. $r^2 - 2rs + s^2 =$	$y^2 - 2yz + z^2 =$
4. $x^2 - 4x + 4 =$	$a^2 - 6a + 9 =$
5. $a^2 - 8a + 16 =$	$x^2 - 12x + 36 =$
6. $x^2 - 16x + 64 =$	$x^2 - 14x + 49 =$
7. $x^2 - 6xy + 9y^2 =$	$x^2 - 8xy + 16y^2 =$
8. $x^2 - 12xy + 36y^2 =$	$x^2 - 16xy + 64y^2 =$
9. $x^2 - 10xy + 25y^2 =$	$x^2 - 14xy + 49y^2 =$
10. $x^2 - 18xy + 81y^2 =$	$x^2 - 22xy + 121y^2 =$
11. $9x^2 - 12x + 4 =$	$16x^2 - 16x + 4 =$
12. $36x^2 - 36x + 9 =$	$49x^2 - 42x + 9 =$

FACTORING AND QUADRATIC EQUATIONS

Solving Quadratic Equations: Type 1

A **quadratic equation** is an equation in which the greatest exponent of any term is 2. An example is $x^2 + 10x + 25 = 0$. This type of quadratic equation has a perfect square trinomial on one side of the equal sign and a zero on the other. To solve, first factor the left side. Then use the **zero-product property**. This property states that if $ab = 0$, then $a = 0$, or $b = 0$. To use this property, write each factor equal to zero, and solve. Check each solution back in the original equation.

EXAMPLE 1

Solve: $x^2 + 10x + 25 = 0$

$\qquad (x + 5)(x + 5) = 0$ Factor.

$x + 5 = 0 \qquad x + 5 = 0$ Use zero-product

$\qquad x = -5 \qquad\quad x = -5$ property.

Check: $(-5)^2 + 10(-5) + 25 = 0$

$\qquad\qquad\quad 25 - 50 + 25 = 0$

$\qquad\qquad\qquad\qquad\quad 0 = 0$

EXAMPLE 2

Solve: $8x + 16x^2 = -1$

$\qquad 16x^2 + 8x + 1 = 0$ Rearrange terms.

$\qquad (4x + 1)(4x + 1) = 0$

$4x + 1 = 0 \qquad 4x + 1 = 0$

$\qquad 4x = -1 \qquad\quad 4x = -1$

$\qquad\quad x = -\dfrac{1}{4} \qquad\quad x = -\dfrac{1}{4}$

Check: $8\left(-\dfrac{1}{4}\right) + 16\left(-\dfrac{1}{4}\right)^2 = -1$

$\qquad\qquad -\dfrac{8}{4} + \dfrac{16}{16} = -1$

$\qquad\qquad\qquad -2 + 1 = -1$

PRACTICE

Solve each quadratic equation.

a	*b*	*c*
1. $x^2 + 4x + 4 = 0$	$x^2 + 6x + 9 = 0$	$x^2 + 8x + 16 = 0$
2. $x^2 + 14x + 49 = 0$	$9x^2 + 12x = -4$	$16x^2 + 24x = -9$
3. $4x^2 + 12x = -9$	$4 + 4x + x^2 = 0$	$9 + 6x + x^2 = 0$

Solving Quadratic Equations: Type 2

A second type of quadratic equation involves factoring a perfect square trinomial where the middle term is subtracted. An example is $x^2 - 10x + 25 = 0$.

To solve, factor the left side and use the zero-product property as before. Check your solutions.

EXAMPLE 1

Solve: $x^2 - 2x + 1 = 0$
$$(x - 1)(x - 1) = 0$$
$$x - 1 = 0 \qquad x - 1 = 0$$
$$x = 1 \qquad x = 1$$

Check: $(1)^2 - 2(1) + 1 = 0$
$$1 - 2 + 1 = 0$$
$$0 = 0$$

EXAMPLE 2

Solve: $4x^2 - 12x = -9$
$$4x^2 - 12x + 9 = 0$$
$$(2x - 3)(2x - 3) = 0$$
$$2x - 3 = 0 \qquad 2x - 3 = 0$$
$$2x = 3 \qquad 2x = 3$$
$$x = \frac{3}{2} \qquad x = \frac{3}{2}$$

Check: $4\left(\frac{3}{2}\right)^2 - 12\left(\frac{3}{2}\right) = -9$

$$4\left(\frac{9}{4}\right) - \frac{36}{2} = -9$$
$$9 - 18 = -9$$

PRACTICE

Solve each quadratic equation.

	a	*b*	*c*
1.	$x^2 - 4x + 4 = 0$	$x^2 - 6x + 9 = 0$	$x^2 - 8x + 16 = 0$
2.	$25 - 10x + x^2 = 0$	$16 - 8x + x^2 = 0$	$36 - 12x - x^2 = 0$
3.	$4x^2 - 16x = -16$	$-8x + 16x^2 = -1$	$-12x + 4 = -9x^2$

The Product of the Sum and the Difference of Two Terms

Example 1 shows the results of multiplying the sum of two terms by the difference of the same two terms. Notice that the first term of the product, x^2, is the square of the first term of each binomial. The second term, y^2, is the square of the second term of each binomial. The two middle terms are added, and will always add to zero. This leads to the following shortcut for finding the product of the sum and the difference of two terms.

> **RULE:** The product of the sum and the difference of two terms is equal to the square of the first term of each binomial minus the square of the second term of each binomial.

EXAMPLE 1

Find: $(x + y)(x - y)$
$$= x(x) + x(-y) + x(y) + y(-y)$$
$$= x^2 - xy + xy - y^2$$
$$= x^2 - y^2$$

EXAMPLE 2

Find: $(2x + 1)(2x - 1)$
$$= 2x(2x) + 2x(-1) + 2x(1) + 1(-1)$$
$$= 4x^2 - 2x + 2x - 1$$
$$= 4x^2 - 1$$

PRACTICE

Find each product.

a	b
1. $(x - 3)(x + 3) =$	$(x + 8)(x - 8) =$
2. $(x + 6)(x - 6) =$	$(x - 7)(x + 7) =$
3. $(a + b)(a - b) =$	$(y + z)(y - z) =$
4. $(5 + x)(5 - x) =$	$(6 - b)(6 + b) =$
5. $(2x + 3)(2x - 3) =$	$(3m + 5)(3m - 5) =$
6. $(8x - 2)(8x + 2) =$	$(6x - 5)(6x + 5) =$
7. $(5 - 3x)(5 + 3x) =$	$(7 + 6x)(7 - 6x) =$
8. $(3 + 7y)(3 - 7y) =$	$(9 - 5a)(9 + 5a) =$
9. $(3x - 4y)(3x + 4y) =$	$(4m + 6n)(4m - 6n) =$

The Product of Two Binomials with a Common Term

You have been studying products, factoring, and equations where both factors have two common terms. For example, $(x - y)(x + y)$. To multiply two binomials with one common term, such as $(x - 2)(x + 3)$, you can use the long method by multiplying each term separately; or follow these steps as a shorter method.

Step 1. Square the common term.

Step 2. Add the unlike terms and multiply by the common term.

Step 3. Multiply the unlike terms.

Step 4. Combine the results from steps 1–3.

EXAMPLE 1: Long method

Find: $(x + 5)(x - 3)$

$$= x(x) + 5(x) + (-3)(x) + (5)(-3)$$
$$= x^2 + 5x - 3x - 15$$
$$= x^2 + 2x - 15$$

EXAMPLE 2: Short method

Find: $(x + 5)(x - 3)$

(1) $(x)(x) = x^2$
(2) $(5) + (-3) = 2, \quad 2 \cdot x = 2x$
(3) $(5)(-3) = -15$
(4) $x^2 + 2x - 15$

PRACTICE ——————————————————————————————————

Find each product. Use the short method.

	a	*b*
1.	$(x + 5)(x + 4) =$	$(x + 2)(x + 6) =$
2.	$(x + 1)(x + 3) =$	$(x + 3)(x + 4) =$
3.	$(x + 7)(x + 2) =$	$(x + 4)(x + 6) =$
4.	$(x + 10)(x + 1) =$	$(x + 6)(x + 7) =$
5.	$(x + 4)(x - 1) =$	$(x + 2)(x - 3) =$
6.	$(x + 8)(x - 2) =$	$(x + 7)(x - 2) =$
7.	$(x - 7)(x + 2) =$	$(x - 10)(x + 1) =$
8.	$(x - 5)(x - 1) =$	$(x - 7)(x - 3) =$
9.	$(x - 4)(x - 5) =$	$(x - 3)(x - 5) =$

Factoring: The Difference of Two Squares

It is easy to recognize the difference of two squares. There are only two terms and both are perfect squares that are subtracted. For example, $y^2 - 9$ is a perfect square.

To factor the difference of two squares, use these steps.

Step 1. Find the square root of each term.

Step 2. Use the sum of these two square roots as the first factor.

Step 3. Use the difference of these two square roots as the second factor.

EXAMPLE

Factor: $4x^2 - 25$ **Check:** $(2x + 5)(2x - 5)$

(1) $2x$ = the square root of $4x^2$ $= 4x^2 + 5x - 5x - 25$
      5 = the square root of 25 $= 4x^2 - 25$

(2) $2x + 5$ = sum of the two square roots

(3) $2x - 5$ = difference

So, $(2x + 5)(2x - 5)$ are the factors

PRACTICE ───────────────────────────────

Factor.

	a	b
1.	$x^2 - y^2 =$	$x^2 - 36 =$
2.	$a^2 - b^2 =$	$a^2 - 81 =$
3.	$m^2 - n^2 =$	$m^2 - 9 =$
4.	$x^2 - 100 =$	$x^2 - 121 =$
5.	$25 - a^2 =$	$64 - a^2 =$
6.	$225 - x^2 =$	$900 - z^2 =$
7.	$4x^2 - 49 =$	$36x^2 - 64 =$
8.	$25a^2 - 16 =$	$49a^2 - 4 =$
9.	$100x^2 - 9 =$	$144x^2 - 100 =$
10.	$25x^2 - 25y^2 =$	$16x^2 - 81y^2 =$

FACTORING AND QUADRATIC EQUATIONS

Factoring for Two Binomials with a Common Term

On page 153, you learned a shortcut for multiplying two binomials with a common term. The product, of course, is a trinomial. For example, $x^2 + 8x - 20$ is a trinomial that can be factored into two binomials with a common term. Now you are going to learn about factoring that trinomial. Use these steps.

Step 1. Find the square root of the first term.

Step 2. Find all factors of the third term.

Step 3. Decide which of these factors can be added to find the coefficient of the middle term.

EXAMPLE

Factor: $x^2 + 2x - 15$

(1) x = square root of first term.

(2) $(-3)(5)$
$(3)(-5)$
$(-1)(15)$
$(1)(-15)$

These are factors of the third term. Note that one factor must be negative in this example because the third term (-15) is negative.

(3) $5 + (-3) = 2$ Two factors are added to find the coefficient of the middle term.

So, $(x + 5)(x - 3)$ are the two binomial factors.

Check: $(x + 5)(x - 3)$
$= x(x) + 5x - 3x - 15$
$= x^2 + 2x - 15$

PRACTICE

Factor.

	a	*b*
1.	$x^2 + 8x + 15 =$	$x^2 + 5x + 6 =$
2.	$x^2 + 3x + 2 =$	$x^2 + 8x + 12 =$
3.	$x^2 + 7x + 10 =$	$x^2 + 9x + 8 =$
4.	$x^2 + 4x - 12 =$	$x^2 + 8x - 20 =$
5.	$x^2 + 2x - 8 =$	$x^2 + 5x - 24 =$
6.	$x^2 - 4x - 12 =$	$x^2 - 8x - 20 =$
7.	$x^2 - 9x - 10 =$	$x^2 - 10x - 24 =$
8.	$x^2 - 7x + 12 =$	$x^2 - 9x + 20 =$

Solving Quadratic Equations: Type 3

A third type of quadratic equation involves factoring the difference of two squares. An example is $4x^2 - 9 = 0$. To solve, factor the left side and use the zero-product property.

EXAMPLE 1

Solve: $y^2 - 100 = 0$

$$(y - 10)(y + 10) = 0$$

$$y - 10 = 0 \qquad y + 10 = 0$$

$$y = 10 \qquad y = -10$$

Check: $(10)^2 - 100 = 0 \qquad (-10)^2 - 100 = 0$

$$100 - 100 = 0 \qquad 100 - 100 = 0$$

EXAMPLE 2

Solve: $4x^2 - 9 = 0$

$$(2x - 3)(2x + 3) = 0$$

$$2x - 3 = 0 \qquad 2x + 3 = 0$$

$$2x = 3 \qquad 2x = -3$$

$$x = \frac{3}{2} \qquad x = -\frac{3}{2}$$

Check: $4\left(\frac{3}{2}\right)^2 - 9 = 0 \qquad 4\left(-\frac{3}{2}\right)^2 - 9 = 0$

$$\cancel{4}\left(\frac{9}{\cancel{4}}\right) - 9 = 0 \qquad \cancel{4}\left(\frac{9}{\cancel{4}}\right) - 9 = 0$$

$$9 - 9 = 0 \qquad 9 - 9 = 0$$

PRACTICE

Solve each quadratic equation.

	a	*b*	*c*
1.	$a^2 - 49 = 0$	$a^2 - 64 = 0$	$a^2 - 81 = 0$
2.	$x^2 - 144 = 0$	$x^2 - 400 = 0$	$x^2 - 16 = 0$
3.	$16x^2 - 100 = 0$	$4x^2 - 25 = 0$	$81x^2 - 36 = 0$
4.	$4x^2 - 36 = 0$	$25x^2 - 100 = 0$	$9x^2 - 36 = 0$

Solving Quadratic Equations: Type 4

A fourth type of quadratic equation involves factoring a trinomial that is the product of two binomials with a common term. To solve, factor the left side of the equation and use the zero-product property.

EXAMPLE 1

Solve: $x^2 - 5x - 14 = 0$

$$(x - 7)(x + 2) = 0$$
$$x - 7 = 0 \qquad x + 2 = 0$$
$$x = 7 \qquad x = -2$$

Check: $(7)^2 - 5(7) - 14 = 0$
$$49 - 35 - 14 = 0$$
$$49 - 49 = 0$$

$$(-2)^2 - 5(-2) - 14 = 0$$
$$4 + 10 - 14 = 0$$
$$14 - 14 = 0$$

EXAMPLE 2

Solve: $x^2 + x - 12 = 0$

$$(x - 3)(x + 4) = 0$$
$$x - 3 = 0 \qquad x + 4 = 0$$
$$x = 3 \qquad x = -4$$

Check: $(3)^2 + 3 - 12 = 0$
$$9 + 3 - 12 = 0$$
$$12 - 12 = 0$$

$$(-4)^2 + (-4) - 12 = 0$$
$$16 - 4 - 12 = 0$$
$$16 - 16 = 0$$

PRACTICE

Solve each quadratic equation.

	a	*b*	*c*
1.	$x^2 + 7x + 12 = 0$	$x^2 + 7x + 6 = 0$	$x^2 + 9x + 20 = 0$
2.	$x^2 - 2x - 8 = 0$	$x^2 - 5x - 6 = 0$	$x^2 - 9x - 10 = 0$
3.	$x^2 - 8x - 33 = 0$	$x^2 - 7x - 44 = 0$	$x^2 - 10x - 39 = 0$
4.	$x^2 - 7x + 6 = 0$	$x^2 - 5x + 4 = 0$	$x^2 - 12x + 20 = 0$

FACTORING AND QUADRATIC EQUATIONS
The Product of Two Binomials with Like Terms

You have been multiplying two binomials in other lessons. These lessons have shown special products. For example, the square of a binomial such as $x - 2$ is a special product, $x^2 - 4x + 4$. You used a special rule. A general method for multiplying any two binomials is the **FOIL** method. The FOIL method shows how to multiply all terms in a certain order.

F	= First terms
O	= Outside terms
I	= Inside terms
L	= Last terms

EXAMPLE

Find: $(2x + 4)(x - 3)$

$$F \qquad L \qquad\qquad F \qquad O \qquad I \qquad L$$

$$(2x + 4)(x - 3) = 2x(x) + 2x(-3) + 4(x) + 4(-3)$$

$$I$$

$$= 2x^2 - 6x + 4x - 12$$

$$O$$

$$= 2x^2 - 2x - 12$$

PRACTICE

Find each product.

	a	*b*
1.	$(x + 2)(2x + 3) =$	$(2x + 1)(x + 2) =$
2.	$(2x + y)(x + 2y) =$	$(2x + 3y)(x + y) =$
3.	$(x + 5y)(2x + y) =$	$(x + 3y)(2x + y) =$
4.	$(x + 3)(2x - 1) =$	$(2x + 3)(x - 1) =$
5.	$(x + 2y)(2x - y) =$	$(2x + y)(x - 2y) =$
6.	$(3x + 1)(x - 2) =$	$(2x - 4y)(x + 3y)$
7.	$(x - 3)(2x - 1) =$	$(x - 4)(2x - 1) =$
8.	$(x - 3y)(2x - y) =$	$(2x - 3)(x - 1) =$
9.	$(2x - y)(x - 2y) =$	$(3x - 3y)(2x - y) =$

Factoring for Two Binomials with Like Terms

The biggest job in factoring trinomials such as $2x^2 + 7x - 4$ lies in finding the proper combination of factors that will give the middle term. Only practice will help you develop this skill. There are however, three important facts to keep in mind when factoring all kinds of trinomials. These facts are listed in the box at the right.

Study the following example.

HINTS FOR FACTORING TRINOMIALS
1. When all terms are added, the terms in both binomials will be added.
2. When only the middle term is subtracted, the terms in both binomials will be subtracted.
3. When the last term is subtracted, the terms in one binomial are added and the terms in the other binomial are subtracted.

EXAMPLE

Factor: $2x^2 + 7x - 4$

Since the last term is subtracted, the terms in one binomial will be added and the terms in the other binomial will be subtracted: List the possible factors of the first and third terms (in pairs).

List possible pairs of binomial factors. Find the middle term for each pair of factors. Keep trying until a pair of factors yields $7x$ as the middle term.

So, $2x^2 + 7x - 4 = (2x - 1)(x + 4)$.

Factors for first term	Factors for third term
$2x^2 = (2x)(x)$	$-4 = (-4)(1)$
	$-4 = (4)(-1)$
	$-4 = (-2)(2)$

Possible factor pairs	Middle term	
$(2x - 4)(x + 1)$	$2x - 4x = -2x$	No
$(2x + 1)(x - 4)$	$-8x + x = -7x$	No
$(2x + 4)(x - 1)$	$-2x + 4x = 2x$	No
$(2x - 1)(x + 4)$	$8x - x = 7x$	Yes

PRACTICE

Factor.

	a	b
1.	$2x^2 + 5x + 2 =$	$3x^2 + 5x + 2 =$
2.	$3x^2 + 7x + 2 =$	$2x^2 + 5x + 3 =$
3.	$2x^2 - 7x + 3 =$	$2x^2 - 9x + 4 =$
4.	$2y^2 - 5y + 2 =$	$3x^2 - 8x + 4 =$
5.	$2x^2 + 3x - 2 =$	$3x^2 + x - 2 =$
6.	$2y^2 - y - 6 =$	$3x^2 - 2x - 8 =$

Use Guess and Check

To solve some problems, you can guess the answer. You can then check to see if the answer is correct, and make another guess if necessary. Your next guess should be better because you will learn from the first guess. Continue to guess and check until you find the correct answer.

Read the problem.

Rhonda has 7 coins with a total value of $0.80. She has no pennies or half-dollars. She has more dimes than nickels. How many quarters, dimes, and nickels does Rhonda have?

Guess and check.

Choose seven coins and find the value. Make sure you choose more dimes than nickels.
(Let Q = quarter, D = dime, and N = nickel.)

	Coins		Value in Cents	
Guess:	Q,Q,D,D,D,D,N	Check:	$2(25) + 4(10) + 5 = 95$	Too high.
Guess:	Q,Q,D,D,D,N,N	Check:	$2(25) + 3(10) + 2(5) = 90$	Too high.
Guess:	Q,D,D,D,D,N,N	Check:	$25 + 4(10) + 2(5) = 75$	Too low.
Guess:	Q,D,D,D,D,D,N	Check:	$25 + 5(10) + 5 = 80$	Correct!

State the answer.

Rhonda has 1 quarter, 5 dimes, and 1 nickel.

Solve. Use the guess-and-check strategy.

1. The product of three whole numbers is 48. The sum of the same three numbers is 12. What are the numbers?

Answer _____

2. Joel has 9 coins with a value of 49¢. He has one quarter. What coins does he have?

Answer _____

3. The product of three whole numbers is 135. The sum of the same three numbers is 17. What are the numbers?

Answer _____

4. The difference between two whole numbers is 10. The product is 1575. What are the two numbers?

Answer _____

Solve. Use the guess-and-check strategy.

5. The square of a certain number is 729. What is the number?

Answer _____

6. The square of a certain number is 2916. What is the number?

Answer _____

7. The cube of a certain number is 13,824. What is the number?

Answer _____

8. The cube of a certain number is 68,921. What is the number?

Answer _____

9. Using each of the digits 2 through 5 only once, write two whole numbers whose product is as large as possible.

Answer _____

10. Using each of the digits 3 through 8 only once, write two whole numbers whose product is as large as possible.

Answer _____

11. The square of a certain whole number is equal to 14 more than 5 times the number. What is the number?

Answer _____

12. The cube of a certain whole number is 48 more than the square of the same number. What is the number?

Answer _____

Solving Quadratic Equations: Type 5

The skill you have acquired in factoring trinomials that are the product of two binomials with a like term can be used to solve quadratic equations where the squared term has a coefficient other than 1. An example is $2x^2 - 10x + 12 = 0$. Notice that the squared term, $2x^2$, has a coefficient of 2.

EXAMPLE

Solve: $2x^2 - 10x + 12 = 0$
$(2x - 4)(x - 3) = 0$
$2x - 4 = 0 \qquad x - 3 = 0$
$2x = 4 \qquad\quad x = 3$
$x = 2$

Check: $2(2)^2 - 10(2) + 12 = 0$
$8 - 20 + 12 = 0$
$-12 + 12 = 0$

$2(3)^2 - 10(3) + 12 = 0$
$18 - 30 + 12 = 0$
$-30 + 30 = 0$

PRACTICE

Solve each quadratic equation.

	a	*b*	*c*
1.	$2x^2 + 5x + 2 = 0$	$2x^2 + 11x + 5 = 0$	$2x^2 + 5x + 3 = 0$
2.	$2x^2 - 5x + 2 = 0$	$2x^2 - 11x + 5 = 0$	$2x^2 - 5x + 3 = 0$
3.	$2x^2 + 3x - 2 = 0$	$2x^2 - 3x - 2 = 0$	$2x^2 + x - 3 = 0$
4.	$3x^2 - 2x - 5 = 0$	$3x^2 + 2x - 5 = 0$	$3x^2 + 14x - 5 = 0$

FACTORING AND QUADRATIC EQUATIONS

Solving Quadratic Equations: Mixed Types

You have seen five general types of products of two binomials.

1. The square of the sum of two terms: $\qquad$ $(x + y)^2 = x^2 + 2xy + y^2$
2. The square of the difference of two terms: $\qquad$ $(x - y)^2 = x^2 - 2xy + y^2$
3. The product of the sum and difference of two terms: $\quad$ $(x + y)(x - y) = x^2 - y^2$
4. The product of two binomials with a common term: $\quad$ $(x + 5)(x + 1) = x^2 + 6x + 5$
5. The product of two binomials with like terms: $\quad$ $(x + 2)(2x + 1) = 2x^2 + 5x + 2$

You have had practice in factoring each type of trinomial. You have also solved quadratic equations involving each type—one at a time. Now you should be able to recognize the different types of trinomials. The equations on this page are mixed to give you an opportunity to improve your skills.

PRACTICE

Solve each quadratic equation.

a	b	c
1. $x^2 - 49 = 0$	$x^2 - 4x + 4 = 0$	$x^2 - 4x - 5 = 0$
2. $x^2 + 10x + 25 = 0$	$x^2 - x - 12 = 0$	$x^2 - 15x + 50 = 0$
3. $x^2 - 2x = -1$ (Hint: Change equation to $x^2 - 2x + 1 = 0$.)	$x^2 - 7x = 30$	$2x^2 + 5x + 3 = 0$
4. $2x^2 + 5x = -2$	$3x^2 + 2x = 5$	$x^2 - 16x = -64$
5. $x^2 - 20x = -75$	$x^2 + 6x + 9 = 0$	$3x^2 - 6x - 9 = 0$

FACTORING AND QUADRATIC EQUATIONS
Writing and Solving Equations

Write an equation and solve.

1. Find the number which when added to the square of the number equals 30.

   Let x = the number,
   x^2 = the square of the number.

   $x^2 + x = 30$
   $x^2 + x - 30 = 0$
   $(x + 6)(x - 5) = 0$
   $x + 6 = 0$ or $x - 5 = 0$
   $x = -6$ or $x = 5$

   Check both solutions in the original problem.

   Answer _____ −6 or 5 _____

2. The product of two consecutive integers is 90. Find the integers.

   Let x = the first integer,
   $x + 1$ = the second integer.

   $(x + 1)(x) = 90$
   $x^2 + x - 90 = 0$
   $(x + 10)(x - 9) = 0$
   $x + 10 = 0$ or $x - 9 = 0$
   $x = -10$ or $x = 9$
   $x + 1 = -9$ $x + 1 = 10$

   Check both solutions in the original problem.

   Answer _−9 and −10, or 9 and 10_

3. Find the number whose square added to itself will give 20.

   Answer _____

4. Find the number which, when subtracted from its square, equals 20.

   Answer _____

5. The product of two consecutive even integers is 80. Find the integers. (Hint: Let x and $x + 2$ be the integers.)

   Answer _____

6. The product of two consecutive odd integers is 99. What are the integers?

   Answer _____

7. The square of a number added to twice the number equals 24. What is the number?

   Answer _____

8. The length of a rectangle is 5 greater than the width. The area is 300 sq m. Find the two dimensions. (Hint: Remember the area equals lw. Therefore $(x)(x + 5) = 300$.)

   Answer _____

9. The length of a rectangle is 20 cm greater than the width. The area is 300 sq cm. Find the two dimensions of the rectangle.

   Answer _____

10. The width of a rectangle is 10 m less than the length. The area of the rectangle is 200 sq m. Find the length and width.

   Answer _____

Completing the Square

One method for solving certain quadratic equations is called **completing the square.** This method works even when the trinomial cannot be factored. It involves changing the equation to make a perfect square trinomial on one side. First, rewrite the equation, if necessary, so that both terms containing variables are on one side of the equal sign and the constant (a number) is on the other. Then add the square of one-half the coefficient of the linear term to both sides of the equation. Note that the coefficient of the squared term must be 1. In the equation $x^2 - 2x - 3 = 0$, the squared term is x^2 and the linear term is $2x$.

EXAMPLE

Solve: $x^2 - 2x - 3 = 0$		**Check:** $(-1)^2 - 2(-1) - 3 = 0$
$x^2 - 2x = 3$	Rearrange terms.	$1 + 2 - 3 = 0$
$x^2 - 2x + 1 = 3 + 1$	Note that $\frac{1}{2}(-2) = -1$ and $(-1)^2 = 1$.	$3 - 3 = 0$
$(x - 1)^2 = 4$	Factor.	$(3)^2 - 2(3) - 3 = 0$
$x - 1 = \pm 2$	Find the square root of both sides.	$9 - 6 - 3 = 0$
$x - 1 = +2 \quad x - 1 = -2$	Solve each equation.	$9 - 9 = 0$
$x = 3 \qquad x = -1$		

PRACTICE

Solve.

	a	b	c
1.	$x^2 - 4x = 3$	$x^2 - 6x = 2$	$x^2 - 12x = -6$
2.	$x^2 + 6x = 4$	$x^2 - 8x = -3$	$x^2 - 4x = 2$
3.	$y^2 + 2y - 8 = 0$	$m^2 - 4m - 32 = 0$	$p^2 - 4p + 1 = 0$
4.	$r^2 + 8r + 14 = 0$	$m^2 = -6m - 7$	$x^2 - 2x - 1 = 0$

The Quadratic Formula

The **quadratic formula** can be used to solve any quadratic equation. It is particularly useful when a quadratic equation cannot be solved by factoring, or when completing the square becomes tedious and time-consuming.

Every quadratic equation can be written in the general form $ax^2 + bx + c = 0$. (Hence, in the equation $x^2 + 6x + 7 = 0$, $a = 1$, $b = 6$, and $c = 7$.) Using this general form and the method of completing the square, solving for x gives this formula:

$$x = \frac{-b \pm \sqrt{b^2 - 4ac}}{2a}$$

Use the quadratic formula by writing each equation in the form $ax^2 + bx + c = 0$. Then substitute for a, b, and c in the formula.

EXAMPLE

Solve: $x^2 - 7x + 6 = 0$

$$ax^2 + bx + c = 0$$

Substitute $a = 1$, $b = -7$ and $c = 6$ in the formula:

$$x = \frac{-b \pm \sqrt{b^2 - 4ac}}{2a}$$

$$x = \frac{-(-7) \pm \sqrt{(-7)^2 - 4(1)(6)}}{2}$$

$$x = \frac{7 \pm \sqrt{49 - 24}}{2}$$

$$x = \frac{7 \pm \sqrt{25}}{2} = \frac{7 \pm 5}{2}$$

$$x = \frac{7 + 5}{2} \qquad x = \frac{7 - 5}{2}$$

$$x = 6 \qquad x = 1$$

Check: $(6)^2 - 7(6) + 6 = 0$

$$36 - 42 + 6 = 0$$

$$-42 + 42 = 0$$

$$(1)^2 - 7(1) + 6 = 0$$

$$1 - 7 + 6 = 0$$

$$-7 + 7 = 0$$

PRACTICE

Use the quadratic formula to solve each quadratic equation.

	a	b	c
1.	$x^2 + 5x + 6 = 0$	$2x^2 + 5x + 2 = 0$	$4x^2 - 9x + 2 = 0$
2.	$2x^2 - 7x + 3 = 0$	$2x^2 - 13x + 6 = 0$	$5x^2 = x + 4$
3.	$2x^2 + x = 1$	$3x^2 = 20 - 7x$	$x^2 + 2x - 15 = 0$

FACTORING AND QUADRATIC EQUATIONS

More Practice with the Quadratic Formula

On the previous page, the exercises could be solved by factoring methods. Some quadratic equations, however, cannot be solved by factoring. The solutions to these equations may be fractions, and may contain square roots.

EXAMPLE

Solve: $2x^2 + x - 2 = 0$
Substitute $a = 2$, $b = 1$, $c = -2$.

$$x = \frac{-b \pm \sqrt{b^2 - 4ac}}{2a}$$

$$x = \frac{-(1) \pm \sqrt{(1)^2 - 4(2)(-2)}}{2(2)}$$

$$x = \frac{-1 \pm \sqrt{1 + 16}}{4}$$

$$x = \frac{-1 + \sqrt{17}}{4} \qquad x = \frac{-1 - \sqrt{17}}{4}$$

PRACTICE

Use the quadratic formula to solve each quadratic equation.

a	b	c
1. $x^2 - 2x - 2 = 0$	$2x^2 - 8x + 3 = 0$	$2x^2 + 3x - 1 = 0$
2. $3x^2 - 4x - 2 = 0$	$6x^2 = 5x + 3$	$5x^2 = 3x + 1$
3. $3x^2 = 5x - 1$	$5x^2 - 3 = 3x$	$2x^2 + 5x = 1$

Select a Strategy

When you read a problem, you may see at once which strategy you will need to use to solve the problem. Sometimes, however, you will need to try two or three strategies before finding one that works. More than one strategy could be used. Some of the strategies are listed in the box at the right.

Problem-Solving Strategies

Make a Table

Make a List

Work Backwards

Find a Pattern

Make a Drawing

Use Guess-and-Check

Use Estimation

Identify Substeps

Use Logic

Read the problem. Select a strategy. Solve.

1. A wall measures 26 feet by 9 feet. It took exactly three cans of paint to cover the wall with one coat of paint. How many square feet of wall were covered with each can of paint?

Strategy _____

Answer _____

2. Sumi took a 7-day vacation. Sumi drove 450 miles the first day, 390 the second day, 330 the third day, and so on. His car averaged 25 miles per gallon of gas. How many gallons of gasoline did he use during the vacation?

Strategy _____

Answer _____

3. A rectangular field with a width of 48 feet has an area of 3456 square feet. Inside the field is a rectangular fenced-in area with length and width that are each one-fourth as long as the corresponding side of the field. What is the area of the fenced-in area?

Strategy _____

Answer _____

4. On her new job, Mona earned $8.40 per hour, which was $3.80 per hour less than twice what she earned at her previous job. What was her hourly wage at her previous job?

Strategy _____

Answer _____

Read the problem. Select a strategy. Solve.

5. Shirley has a nickel, a dime, a quarter, and a half-dollar. How many different values can she make using combinations of one or more of the coins?

Strategy _____

Answer _____

6. Meg weighs 10 pounds more than Mary. Max weighs 10 pounds less than Molly, who weighs 30 pounds more than Mary. Arrange the four in order from lightest to heaviest.

Strategy _____

Answer _____

7. About how many square yards of carpet would be needed for a room that is 14 feet long and 11 feet wide?

Strategy _____

Answer _____

8. The cube of a certain whole number is 100 more than the square of the same number. What is the number?

Strategy _____

Answer _____

9. A farmer wants to divide the plot of land in half with a straight line. How can he do it?

Strategy _____

Answer _____

10. It takes 3 workers 1 hour to pack 6 boxes. At that rate, how long will it take 9 workers to pack 36 boxes?

Strategy _____

Answer _____

Using the Quadratic Formula in Solving Problems

The quadratic formula can be used to solve certain problems.

EXAMPLE

The square of a certain number added to three times the number is equal to 28. What number or numbers satisfy these conditions?

Let x = the number

Then $x^2 + 3x = 28$

Rearrange into $ax^2 + bx + c = 0$
$$x^2 + 3x - 28 = 0$$

Then $a = 1$, $b = 3$, $c = -28$

Substitute into the quadratic formula.
$$x = \frac{-b \pm \sqrt{b^2 - 4ac}}{2a}$$

$$x = \frac{-(3) \pm \sqrt{(3)^2 - 4(1)(-28)}}{2(1)}$$

$$x = \frac{-3 \pm \sqrt{9 + 112}}{2} = \frac{-3 \pm \sqrt{121}}{2} = \frac{-3 \pm 11}{2}$$

$$x = \frac{-3 + 11}{2} = 4 \qquad x = \frac{-3 - 11}{2} = -7$$

Both −7 and 4 satisfy the conditions of the problem.

PRACTICE

First write an equation. Then solve using the quadratic formula. Write the answer.

---

1. One half the square of a number is equal to 16 more than twice the number. What is the number?

   Answer _____

2. Find the two consecutive odd integers whose product is 143.

   Answer _____

---

3. The product of two consecutive odd integers is 323. What are the integers?

   Answer _____

4. Find the number which, when subtracted from its square, equals 72.

   Answer _____

---

5. The length of a rectangle is 10 more than twice the width. The area of the rectangle is 672 square inches. Find the length and width. (Hint: Reject all answers which do not satisfy the conditions of the problem.)

   Answer _____

6. The width of a rectangle is $\frac{1}{2}$ the length minus 11 cm. The area of the rectangle is 700 square centimeters. Find the length and width.

   Answer _____

FACTORING AND QUADRATIC EQUATIONS

Unit 7 Review

Find the product.

a	b	c
1. $(x - y)(x + y) =$	$(4 - 6t)^2 =$	$(2x - y)(x + 4y) =$

Factor.

a	b	c
2. $x^2 + 2xy + y^2 =$	$x^2 - 8xy + 16y^2 =$	$25x^2 - 40x + 16 =$
3. $x^2 - 25 =$	$100 - x^2 =$	$64 - 16x^2 =$
4. $x^2 + 5x + 4 =$	$x^2 - 3x - 4 =$	$3x^2 + x - 2 =$

Solve by factoring.

a	b	c
5. $x^2 + 10x + 25 = 0$	$x^2 + 16x = -64$	$4x^2 + 32x + 64 = 0$
6. $x^2 - 49 = 0$	$4x^2 - 64 = 0$	$x^2 + 5x + 4 = 0$

Solve using the quadratic formula.

a	b	c
7. $2x^2 + 7x + 6 = 0$	$x^2 - 6x = 2$	$x^2 - 8x = -3$

First write an equation. Then solve.

8. The length of a rectangle is 10 inches greater than the width. The area of the rectangle is 75 square inches. Find the dimensions.

Answer _____

9. The product of two consecutive integers is 90. What are the integers?

Answer _____

Cumulative Review

Simplify.

a	b	c
1. $9x^2 + 6x + 4y + x =$	$2a(-12ab - 3ab) =$	$(-23a^2b)(-3ab^2)^2 =$
2. $\dfrac{-90x^2y^3}{-10x^3y^2} =$	$(2a + b)(3a - b) =$	$\left(\dfrac{m}{2} - n\right) + \left(\dfrac{3m}{2} + n\right) =$
3. $\sqrt{16x^2} =$	$\sqrt[3]{64} =$	$\dfrac{6x - 9y}{-3} =$

Solve.

a	b	c
4. $2x^2 = 32$	$x^2 - 25 = 0$	$5x - 1 = 3x + 15$
5. $5a - (a + 6) = 10$	$\dfrac{3r}{100} = \dfrac{9}{10}$	$25m^2 + 10 = 110$

Solve each system of equations.

a	b	c
6. $4x + y = -5$ $4x - y = 9$	$x + y = 1$ $x - 2y = -8$	$3x + 2y = 19$ $2x + 3y = 16$

Graph each equation.

a

7. $2x - y = 0$

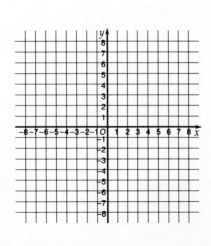

b

$x + y = 3$

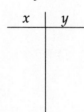

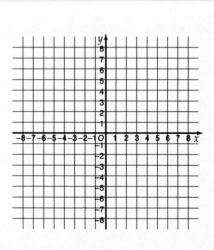

Write an algebraic expression for each verbal expression.

a	*b*
1. the product of *a* and 9 _____	5 decreased by *n* _____

Evaluate each expression if *r* = 8, *s* = 3, and *t* = 6.

a	*b*	*c*	*d*
2. $r + st =$	$\dfrac{rs + t}{s} =$	$t - 2s =$	$r + 5s =$

Solve.

a	*b*	*c*	*d*
3. $n = 2(3 + 6)$	$10k = 200$	$7(5) - 4(3) = b$	$12 + w = 55$

Write the opposite of each integer.

a	*b*	*c*	*d*
4. 7	-16	39	-53

Simplify.

a	*b*	*c*	*d*
5. $7 + (-1) =$	$-8 + 12 =$	$72 - 99 =$	$-5 + (-25) =$
6. $6(-3) =$	$(-3)(-20) =$	$\dfrac{42}{7} =$	$\dfrac{-65}{5} =$
7. $-5x + 2x + (-7x) =$	$30ab - 18ab =$	$3(2.7x) =$	$\dfrac{2.2y}{2} =$
8. $x + 5 + (x - 7) =$	$m + 9 - (3m + 6) =$	$\dfrac{3}{8}(16c - 32) =$	$3r - 2(r + 5) =$

Solve.

---

9. In the formula $A = lw$, find A when l is 10 meters and w is 12 meters.

Answer _____

10. In the formula $A = \pi r^2$, find A when r is 14 inches.

Answer _____

---

11. In the formula $V = lwh$, find w when V is 3000 cubic ft, l is 15 ft, and h is 20 ft.

Answer _____

12. In the formula $D = rt$, find r when D is 500 miles and t is 4 hours.

Answer _____

---

13. In the formula $I = prt$, find I when p is $250, r is $6\frac{1}{2}\%$, and t is 1 year.

Answer _____

14. In the formula $°C = (°F - 32)\frac{5}{9}$, find $°C$ when F is 77°.

Answer _____

Solve.

	a	b	c	d
15.	$16z = 96$	$0.4m = 20$	$x + 2 = -7$	$a - 3 = 45$
16.	$\dfrac{m}{4} = 12$	$\dfrac{3x}{4} = -12$	$2x - 4 = 8$	$3y - 5y = -6$
17.	$4x - 4 = 2x + 8$	$2y + 3 = y + 5$	$6b - 4 = 2(2b + 1)$	$4x - (x + 3) = 12$
18.	$\dfrac{x}{2} + 4 = \dfrac{x}{3} + 5$	$\dfrac{y}{4} + 5 = \dfrac{3y}{2}$	$\dfrac{8}{x} = \dfrac{4}{3}$	$\dfrac{x}{3} = \dfrac{10}{6}$

Write an equation. Solve.

19. Carlos is three times as old as Maria. The sum of their ages is 56 years. How old is each?

Answer _____

20. The sum of three numbers is 180. The second number is twice the first, and the third number is three times the first. Find each number.

Answer _____

---

21. Five times a number increased by 6 is 51. Find the number.

Answer _____

22. The length of a rectangle is twice the width. The perimeter is 120 centimeters. Find the length and width.

Answer _____

174

Simplify.

	a	*b*	*c*
23.	$4 \cdot (-1)^3 =$	$6a^2b(4c) =$	$(7xy^2)(-7x^2y) =$
24.	$(r^3s^5)^2 =$	$\dfrac{5a^6}{a^4} =$	$-\dfrac{30mn^3}{15m^2n} =$
25.	$3a - 2b + (-a + 2b) =$	$(x + y) + (x - y) =$	$-28x^3 - 12y^2 - 7x^3 =$
26.	$\dfrac{2x}{5} \cdot \dfrac{3}{x^2} =$	$\dfrac{x}{y} \div \dfrac{x}{2} =$	$\dfrac{15xy + 25x^2y^2}{10xy} =$
27.	$3(2m + n) =$	$(4x - 3)(x - 2y) =$	$-7c(c^2 - cd^3) =$

Make a table of solutions. Graph the equation.

a

28. $x - y = 4$

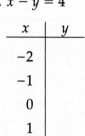

x	y
-2	
-1	
0	
1	
2	

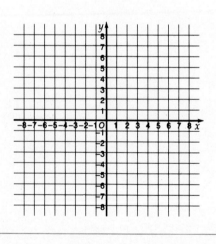

b

$3x + y = 1$

x	y

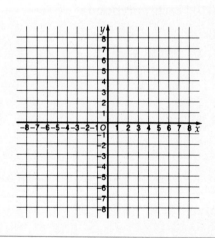

Solve each system of equations.

a	*b*	*c*
29. $x + 2y = 9$ $\quad\; x - \;\; y = 3$	$2x + 3y = 14$ $\quad x + 2y = 18$	$\dfrac{3x}{4} + \dfrac{y}{2} = 5$ $\dfrac{x}{4} - \dfrac{y}{2} = 1$
Ordered pair _____	Ordered pair _____	Ordered pair _____

Simplify.

a	b	c
30. $\sqrt{100} =$	$\sqrt{16x^2y^6} =$	$\sqrt[3]{27a^6} =$
31. $(2x - y)^2 =$	$(3x - 1)(3x + 5) =$	$(x + 5)(2x + 3) =$

Solve.

a	b	c
32. $4x < 28$	$7 - a > -3$	$3y > y - 12$
33. $b^2 = 36$	$3x^3 + 28 = 220$	$\dfrac{x}{3} = \dfrac{10}{6}$

Factor each polynomial.

a	b	c
34. $x^2 + 5x + 4 =$	$4x^2 - 49 =$	$3x^2 + x - 2 =$
35. $x^2 - 6x + 9 =$	$9x^2 + 6x + 1 =$	$25 - 70x + 49x^2 =$

Solve.

a	b	c
36. $x^2 + 49 = -14x$	$16x^2 - 24x + 9 = 0$	$2x^2 + x - 3 = 0$

Solve.

37. The length and the width of a rectangle are in the ratio of 5 to 2 and the area is 1000 sq ft. Find the dimensions.

38. The length of a rectangle is 10 m greater than the width and the area is 600 sq m. Find the two dimensions.

Answer _____

Answer _____

Name _____   Date _____

MASTERY TEST

Write an algebraic expression for each verbal expression.

a	b

1. 7 divided by n _____ r increased by 3 _____

Evaluate each expression if $r = 9$, $s = 4$, and $t = 2$.

a	b	c	d
2. $rs + t =$	$2r + \dfrac{s}{t} =$	$3s - 6t =$	$r - s - t =$

Solve.

a	b	c	d
3. $n = 5(2 + 7)$	$4k = 400$	$8(4) - 2(5) = b$	$11 + w = 38$

Write the opposite of each integer.

a	b	c	d
4. 13	-8	27	-42

Simplify.

a	b	c	d
5. $9 + (-3) =$	$-5 + 13 =$	$24 - 39 =$	$-19 + (-8) =$
6. $5(-7) =$	$(-4)(-14) =$	$\dfrac{35}{5} =$	$\dfrac{-54}{6} =$
7. $-7x + x + (-3x) =$	$49ab - 48ab =$	$4(1.7x) =$	$\dfrac{9.6y}{3} =$
8. $3 + x + (x - 4) =$	$3m + 2 - (m + 4) =$	$\dfrac{4}{5}(15c - 20) =$	$5r - 3(r + 2) =$

Name _____   Date _____

Solve.

9. In the formula $A = lw$, find A when l is 8 inches and w is 14 inches.	10. In the formula $A = \pi r^2$, find A when r is 21 centimeters.
11. In the formula $V = lwh$, find w when V is 6000 cubic feet, l is 20 feet, and h is 30 feet.	12. In the formula $D = rt$, find r when D is 400 miles and t is 8 hours.
13. In the formula $I = prt$, find I when p is \$700, r is $5\frac{1}{2}\%$, and t is 2 years.	14. In the formula $°C = (°F - 32)\frac{5}{9}$, find $°C$ when F is $86°$.

Solve.

	a	b	c	d
15.	$15z = 105$	$0.8m = 24$	$x + 4 = -8$	$a - 6 = 62$
16.	$\frac{m}{9} = 3$	$\frac{2x}{5} = -8$	$3x - 2 = 19$	$2y - 5y = -12$
17.	$5x - 3 = 2x + 9$	$3y + 5 = y + 1$	$8b - 5 = 3(2b + 3)$	$7x - (x + 5) = 13$
18.	$\frac{x}{4} + 4 = \frac{x}{2} + 1$	$\frac{y}{5} + 7 = \frac{2y}{3}$	$\frac{16}{x} = \frac{4}{3}$	$\frac{x}{2} = \frac{21}{6}$

Write an equation. Solve.

19. Conrad is twice as old as Maxine. The sum of their ages is 54 years. How old is each?	20. The sum of three numbers is 160. The second number is three times the first, and the third number is four times the first. Find each number.
Answer _____	Answer _____
21. Four times a number increased by 7 is 43. Find the number.	22. The length of a rectangle is twice the width. The perimeter is 78 centimeters. Find the length and width.
Answer _____	Answer _____

Name _____   Date _____

Simplify.

a	*b*	*c*
23. $7 \cdot (-1)^5 =$	$3x^2y(5z) =$	$(3a^2b)(-2ab^2) =$
24. $(r^4s^2)^3 =$	$\dfrac{4r^5}{r^2} =$	$\dfrac{24c^2d^2}{8c^3d} =$
25. $4a - 4b + (-a + 4b) =$	$(a + b) + (a - b) =$	$-17x^2 - 14y^4 - 20x^2 =$
26. $\dfrac{3m}{4} \cdot \dfrac{3}{m^3} =$	$\dfrac{a}{b} \div \dfrac{a}{3} =$	$\dfrac{10rs + 14r^2s}{2rs} =$
27. $4(7m - n) =$	$(3x + 5)(x - 4y) =$	$-2m(m^3 - mn^2) =$

Make a table of solutions. Graph the equation.

a		*b*	

28. $x - y = 3$

x	y
-2	
-1	
0	
1	
2	

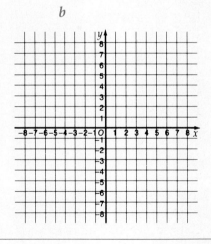

$2x + y = 2$

x	y

Solve each system of equations.

a	*b*	*c*
29. $x + 2y = 13$ $x - y = 1$	$2x + 3y = 7$ $x + 2y = 4$	$\dfrac{3x}{4} + \dfrac{y}{3} = 8$ $\dfrac{x}{4} - \dfrac{y}{3} = 4$

Ordered pair _____   Ordered pair _____   Ordered pair _____

179

Name _____   Date _____

Simplify.

a	*b*	*c*
30. $\sqrt{81} =$	$\sqrt{25x^4y^8} =$	$\sqrt[3]{64a^3} =$
31. $(3x + y)^2 =$	$(2x - 1)(2x + 8) =$	$(x + 3)(2x + 7) =$

Solve.

a	*b*	*c*
32. $3x < 33$	$4 - b > -2$	$4y > y - 15$
33. $r^2 = 16$	$2x^3 + 14 = 700$	$\dfrac{x}{3} = \dfrac{20}{6}$

Factor each polynomial.

a	*b*	*c*
34. $x^2 + 3x + 2 =$	$9x^2 - 1 =$	$3x^2 - 5x - 2 =$
35. $x^2 - 8x + 16 =$	$25x^2 + 10x + 1 =$	$16 - 24x + 9x^2 =$

Solve.

a	*b*	*c*
36. $x^2 + 36 = -12x$	$4x^2 - 20x + 25 = 0$	$2x^2 + 5x - 3 = 0$

Solve.

37. The length and the width of a rectangle are in the ratio of 4 to 3 and the area is 48 square feet. Find the length.

Answer _____

38. The length of a rectangle is 4 meters greater than the width and the area is 60 m². Find the width.

Answer _____

180

WHERE TO GO FOR HELP

The table below lists the problems in the Mastery Test and the pages on which the corresponding skills and concepts are taught and practiced. If you missed one or more problems, find the page number or numbers that correspond to the number of each problem missed. Then turn to these pages, review the teaching, and then practice the skills by doing one or more of the problems. Then correct the problems that you missed on this test.

PROBLEMS	PAGES	PROBLEMS	PAGES	PROBLEMS	PAGES	PROBLEMS	PAGES
1a	13–14	7d	48–49	18c	70	29c	120
1b	13–14	8a	50–51	18d	70	30a	132
2a	15	8b	50–51	19	72–73	30b	132
2b	15	8c	50–51	20	72–73	30c	133
2c	15	8d	50–51	21	72–73	31a	146
2d	15	9	20	22	72–73	31b	158
3a	16	10	29	23a	79	31c	158
3b	17	11	23	23b	82	32a	128
3c	16	12	27	23c	82	32b	127
3d	17	13	24	24a	83	32c	128
4a	36	14	31	24b	84–85	33a	134
4b	36	15a	58	24c	86	33b	135
4c	36	15b	58	25a	87	33c	139
4d	36	15c	56	25b	87	34a	148
5a	37–39	15d	57	25c	89	34b	154
5b	37–39	16a	59	26a	90	34c	159
5c	37–39	16b	61	26b	91	35a	149
5d	37–39	16c	65	26c	93	35b	148
6a	40	16d	62	27a	92	35c	148
6b	40	17a	68	27b	97	36a	163
6c	41	17b	68	27c	92	36b	163
6d	41	17c	71	28a	104	36c	166–167
7a	45–47	17d	71	28b	105	37	1
7b	45–47	18a	69	29a	108–110	38	
7c	48–49	18b	69	29b	111–112		

ANSWER KEY

	a	b		
1.	$6y$	$t + 2$		

	a	b	c	d
2.	20	6	8	10
3.	20	5	10	12
4.	6	-4	31	-56
5.	-7	-8	-6	10
6.	-15	12	4	-3
7.	$-9x$	$12xy$	$4.5x$	$-0.8t$
8.	$6x - 2$	$y - 2$	$9a - 5$	$-b - 24$

9. 125 sq in. **10.** 4 meters
11. 7,539.14 sq cm **12.** 3 inches
13. $7,500 **14.** $168
15. 15°C **16.** 113°F

	a	b	c	d
17.	$x = 30$	$y = 30$	$a = -16$	$b = 29$
18.	$n = 24$	$x = -8$	$n = 11$	$s = 6$
19.	$a = 4$	$b = -10$	$x = 8$	$y = 8$
20.	$x = -18$	$a = -12$	$t = 15$	$s = 3$

21. Jerry is 18 years old. **22.** 1 penny
Lakesha is 54 years old.

23. 5 **24.** Length = $13\frac{1}{2}$ in.
Width = $4\frac{1}{2}$ in.

	a	b	c
25.	72	$6ab^2c$	$-6x^3y^4$
26.	a^3b^6	$2x$	$-\frac{2a^2}{b^2}$
27.	$2a + 2b$	$3a - b$	$7a^2 - 5b^3$
28.	1	$\frac{1}{b}$	$5a + 4$
29.	$6x - 3y$	$2x^2 + 3xy + y^2$	$2a^3 - 6ab$
30.	a		

$$\begin{array}{c|c} x & y \end{array}$$

	a	b	c
31.	(5,1)	(6,4)	(3,1)
32.	(1,1)	(4,2)	(8,2)
33.	9	$4xy^2$	$2x$
34.	$x^2 + 2xy + y^2$	$2x^2 + 7x + 6$	$2x^2 - xy - 3y^2$
35.	$x \leq 7$	$b > 10$	$x < 5$
36.	$s \leq -16$	$a \leq -12$	$y > 2$

	a	b	c
37.	$x = 2$	$x = 3$	$x = 16$

38. Length = 8 in. **39.** $240
Width = 12 in.

	a	b	c
40.	$(x + y)^2$	$(5x - 3)(5x + 3)$	$(2x - 1)(x + 4)$
41.	$(x - 3)^2$	$(3x + 2y)^2$	$(3 + y)^2$
42.	-4	$-2, -\frac{1}{2}$	$6,1$

43. Length = 9 in.
Width = 5 in.

44. 24 and 25, or
-25 and -24

UNIT 1

	a	b
1.	$a \times b = b \times a$	$a - a = 0$
	c	d
	$a + a = 2 \times a$	$0 \times a = 0$

Answers may vary.

	a	b
2.	$1 + 0 = 1$	$3 \times 2 = 2 + 2 + 2$
	$15 + 0 = 15$	$3 \times 5 = 5 + 5 + 5$
	$1.3 + 0 = 1.3$	$3 \times 0.1 = 0.1 + 0.1 + 0.1$
	a	b
3.	$1 + 2 = 3$	$4 \times 1 = 4$
	$8 + 2 = 10$	$4 \times 3 = 12$
	$3.8 + 2 = 5.8$	$4 \times 7 = 28$

	a	b
1.	yz	$e - f$ or $f - e$
2.	$p + q$	$\frac{b}{7}$
3.	$r + 2$	$a - 6$
4.	$\frac{12}{n}$	$3n$
5.	$n - 8$	$n + 1$
6.	$100n$	$20 - n$

Page 14

	a	*b*	*c*	*d*
1.	11	15	80	52
2.	24	21	0	90
3.	39	32	13	6
4.	4	4	5	2
5.	4	8	6	3
6.	16	16	21	18

Page 15

	a	*b*	*c*	*d*
1.	$4a + 7$	$c(c + 3)$	27	27
	$4(9) + 7 = 36 + 7$	$7(7 + 3) = 7(10)$		
	$= 43$	$= 70$		
2.	42	90	90	34
3.	42	42	60	12
4.	6	6	12	6
5.	35	20	750	750
6.	70	5	50	120
7.	10	10	1	25

Page 16

	a	*b*
1.	$2n = 40$	yes

Substitute 10 for n. $2(10) = 40$
$20 \neq 40$

No, 10 is not a solution.

	a	*b*
2.	yes	no
3.	yes	yes
4.	no	yes

	a	*b*	*c*	*d*
5.	9	20	40	67
6.	6	103	66	60
7.	13	8	33	10

Page 17

	a	*b*	*c*	*d*
1.	$b + 9 = 17$	30	5	4

$b + 9 - 9 = 17 - 9$
$b = 8$

The solution is 8.
Check: $8 + 9 = 17$

2.	4	7	16	25
3.	300	11	15	66
4.	9	0	1	12
5.	$\frac{1}{7}$	44	80	505
6.	$\frac{1}{2}$	$1\frac{1}{2}$	$4\frac{1}{3}$	3

Page 18

Variable names may vary.

1. Let p be used as the variable for Randy's hourly rate before his raise.

Hourly rate before raise	Raise per hour	New hourly rate
p +	$0.73 =	$8.45

$p = \$8.45 - \$0.73 = \$7.72$

Page 19

2. $228 + b = 475$
247 boys

3. $3w = 66$
22 kg

4. $5s = 145$
29 student tickets

Variable names may vary.

5. $78 + g = 100$
22 people prefer grape juice

6. $1.8 + m = 4.5$
2.7 miles

7. $5d = 240$
48 km

8. $p + 2.72 = \$36.79$
$34.07

9. $\frac{1}{8}s = 4$
32 students

8. $27 = 1.2w$
22.5 cm

11. $7r = \$44.10$
$6.30 per hour

12. $f + 310 = 624$
314 miles

Page 20

1. $A = lw$
$A = 25(22)$
$A = 550$ sq ft

2. 1500 sq m

3. 240 sq ft

4. 192 sq ft

5. 120 sq ft

6. 360 sq m

7. 375 sq in.

8. 57.12 sq m

Page 21

	a	*b*	*c*
1.	$A = lw$	30 m	60 cm
	$1000 = 20l$		
	$l = 1000 \div 20$		
	$l = 50$ ft		
2.	100 yd	30 ft	20 ft
3.	30 ft	3.5 m	4 mi

Page 22

1. $V = lwh$
$V = 32(30)(9)$
$V = 8640$ cu ft

2. 1296 cu ft

3. 900 cu m

4. 4620 cu in.

5. 128 cu ft

6. 42 cu ft

Page 23

	a	*b*	*c*
1.	$V = lwh$	6 ft	6 yd
	$1800 = 30 \cdot 6 \cdot h$		
	$1800 = 180h$		
	$h = 1800 \div 180$		
	$h = 10$ meters		
2.	9m	10 ft	6 in.
3.	4 ft	10 m	5 yd

Page 24

	a	b	c
1.	$I = prt$	$9	$325
	$I = (\$200)(0.05)(1)$		
	$I = \$10$		
2.	$18	$30	$55
3.	$12.50	$23.63	$4.50
4.	$18.75	$81.25	$172.97

Page 25

	a	b	c
1.	$I = prt$	$400	$1200
	$\$432 = p(0.0625)(3)$		
	$\$432 = 0.1875\,p$		
	$p = 432 \div 0.1875 = \$2304$		
2.	5%	6%	6%
3.	3 years	5 years	2 years

Page 26

1. First, find the number of hours the plane flew. From 2:00 P.M. to 6:00 P.M. is 4 hours.
$D = rt$
$D = 320(4)$
$D = 1280$ miles
2. 2400 mi
3. 2000 mi   **4.** 2120 mi
5. 1600 mi   **6.** 2520 mi

Page 27

1. First, find the number of hours it took the plane to fly from one post to another. From 4:00 A.M. to 6:30 A.M. is 2.5 hours.
$D = rt$
$650 = r(2.5)$
$r = 650 \div 2.5 = 260$ mph
2. 416 mph
3. 400 mph   **4.** 500 mph
5. 5 hr   **6.** 4 hr
7. 6 sec   **8.** 2.5 sec
9. 430 mph   **10.** 55 mph

Page 28

1. $r = \frac{1}{2}d$ **2.** 30 cm
$r = \frac{1}{2}(24)$
$r = 12$ ft
3. 65.94 ft   **4.** 87.92 ft
5. 21.98 ft   **6.** 43.96 in.

Page 29

	a	b
1.	$A = \pi r^2$	63.585 sq cm
	$A = 3.14(4.5^2)$	
	$A = 3.14(20.25)$	
	$A = 63.585$ sq cm	
2.	113.04 sq in.	113.04 sq in.
3.	153.86 sq ft	**4.** 50.24 sq m

Page 30

1. First, find the radius of the standpipe.
$r = \frac{1}{2}d$
$r = \frac{1}{2}(14) = 7$ ft

$V = \pi r^2 h$
$V = 3.14(7^2)(60)$
$V = 3.14(49)(60)$
$V = 9231.6$ cu ft
2. 395.64 cu m
3. 57,697.5 cu ft   **4.** 4 times
5. 6181.875 cu ft   **6.** 197.82 cu in.

Page 31

1. $C = (F - 32) \cdot \frac{5}{9}$ **2.** 113° F
$C = (95 - 32) \cdot \frac{5}{9}$
$C = 63 \cdot \frac{5}{9}$
$C = 35$ or 35° C
3. 20° C   **4.** 59° F
5. 30° C   **6.** 86° F
7. 45° C   **8.** 167° F
9. 25° C   **10.** 140° F

Page 32

1. To use the area formula, $A = lw$, you need to know the length (4.2 cm) and width (4.2 cm). You do not need to know the length of a diagonal (5.9 cm).
$A = lw$
$A = 4.2(4.2)$
$A = 17.64$
Round 17.64 to 18 sq cm.
2. Brad measured a juice box. It was 3.9 cm by 6.3 cm by 10.5 cm ~~and contained 10% apple juice.~~ What was the volume of the box? Round the answer to the nearest whole number.   258 cu cm

Page 33

3. ~~Jackie paid $180 for a train ticket.~~ The train traveled a distance of 240 miles, at an average speed of 60 miles per hour. Without counting stops, how long did the trip take?   4 hours
4. The radius of a circle is 5 inches ~~and the circumference is 31 inches.~~ What is the area of the circle? Round the answer to the nearest whole number.   79 sq in.
5. The high temperature on Monday was 59°F ~~at 4:00 P.M.~~ What was the equivalent Celsius temperature?   15°C
6. The distance from Bob's house to the ocean is 350 miles. ~~The distance from his house to Chicago is 440 miles.~~ Suppose Bob drives to the ocean at an average speed of 50 miles per hour. Without counting stops, how long will the trip take? 7 hours

7. Philip carried meals for 8 people on a circular serving tray. If the diameter of the tray was 72 cm, what was the circumference?   226.08 cm

8. Kasia drove 165 miles in 3 hours and 15 minutes. Altogether, how many minutes was she driving?   195 minutes

9. A gardener planted 40 flower bulbs in a rectangular flower bed. The flower bed is 2 feet wide and $6\frac{1}{2}$ feet long. What is the area of the flower bed?   13 sq ft

10. Pat is reading a recipe for making 24 blueberry muffins. The recipe calls for an oven temperature of 185°C. What is the equivalent Fahrenheit temperature?   365°F

Page 34   Unit 1 Review

	a	b
1.	$b + 9$	$x - 10$
2.	$9k$	$\frac{r}{2}$
3.	$c - 10$	$p + q$

4. Answers may vary.

a	b
$1 \div 1 = 1$	$2 + 1 = 1 + 2$
$12 \div 12 = 1$	$7 + 3 = 3 + 7$
$4.7 \div 4.7 = 1$	$3.6 + 2.5 = 2.5 + 3.6$
c	d
$5 - 5 = 0$	$7 + 2 = 9$
$8 - 5 = 3$	$7 + 5 = 12$
$10.3 - 5 = 5.3$	$7 + 1.7 = 8.7$

	a	b	c	d
5.	84	35	4	7
6.	16	60	50	1
7.	99	9	46	3
8.	5	56	81	$2\frac{1}{2}$

Page 35

9.	6 ft	10.	1.3 m
11.	94.2 in.	12.	53.38 yd
13.	1800 cu m	14.	5 ft
15.	1519.76 sq ft	16.	3077.2 cu cm
17.	$57.75	18.	6 months
19.	6%	20.	45° C

UNIT 2

Page 36

	a	b	c	d
1.	−4	7	21	−45
2.	19	−33	66	0

	a	b	c
3.	+33 or 33	−8	+150 or 150
4.	−10	+6 or 6	+88 or 88
5.	+3500 or 3500	−50	+7 or 7
6.	−4	−30	−9

Page 37

a

1. $3 + 1$
The sum will be positive. Add the absolute values.
$+(3 + 1) = 4$

b

$-2 + (-4)$
The sum will be negative. Add the absolute values.
$-(2 + 4) = -6$

c	d
9	−6

	a	b	c	d
2.	−9	−7	−12	−10
3.	11	−10	−14	−17
4.	19	−15	−27	24
5.	−30	89	−76	−96
6.	18	−13	−15	−21
7.	96	−85	−590	−888

Page 38

a

1. $6 + (-3)$
Subtract the absolute values.
$+(6 - 3) = 3$
The sum will be positive.

b	c	d
−4	−1	5

	a	b	c	d
2.	7	7	1	0
3.	−8	−6	−5	−7
4.	2	12	−11	−13
5.	0	6	6	−8
6.	−4	−3	14	−14
7.	−1	3	0	4
8.	−4	99	−7	75

Page 39

a

1. $5 - (-2)$
The opposite of −2 is 2.
$5 - (-2) = 5 + 2$
$= 7$

b

$-4 - 3$
The opposite of 3 is −3.
$-4 - 3 = -4 + (-3)$
$= -(4 + 3)$
$= -7$

c	d
−6	6

	a	b	c	d
2.	−3	−9	13	16
3.	−9	−5	−21	−25
4.	−10	−22	18	7
5.	−10	19	−8	−6
6.	−10	−43	−48	40
7.	36	42	−42	6
8.	−14	−6	8	−108

Page 40

	a	b	c	d
1.	10	18	-5	6
2.	32	-45	-24	36
3.	35	-48	63	-72
4.	48	91	-115	-64
5.	-6	12	-24	16
6.	-105	216	130	-216

Page 41

	a	b	c	d
1.	$8 \div (-4)$ The quotient will be negative. $-(8 \div 4) = -2$	-7	4	5
2.	5	-7	6	-6
3.	7	-10	11	18
4.	-26	24	12	-10
5.	-14	-18	16	-23
6.	-3	-3	8	-9
7.	-14	-22	18	-17
8.	-18	25	24	25

Page 42

1. The first submarine is at -53 meters. Use the variable d for the depth of the second submarine.

$$d - 15 = -53$$
$$d = -53 + 15$$
$$= -(53 - 15)$$
$$= -38$$

38 m below sea level

2. $-\frac{1}{2}$

3. $69\frac{1}{4}$ per share

4. $102°$ F

Page 43

5. 57 ft below

6. $-1\frac{3}{8}$

7. $-12°$ C

8. 41 ft below sea level

9. $+6\frac{1}{2}$

10. 5560 ft

11. $-8°$ F

12. $45°$ F

Page 44

The following should be circled.

1. -7, 9, $\frac{1}{10}$, 14

2. $5x$, a, $2xy$, $\frac{1}{3}a$, $12z$

3. 5, 4, 1.5, -42, 1250, 1.5, -9, $\frac{2}{3}$

	a	b	c	d	e	f	g	h
4.	$\frac{1}{2}$	$-\frac{3}{4}$	$\frac{1}{5}$	$\frac{3}{2}$	$-\frac{2}{5}$	$\frac{1}{4}$	-1	$\frac{3}{5}$

Page 45

	a	b	c	d
1.	$3y + 4y$ $= (3 + 4)y$ $= 7y$	$11n$	$18m$	$25yz$
2.	$6x$	$3a$	$7st$	$4m$
3.	$80y$	$28b$	$29r + 15s$	$30mn$
4.	$-5x$	$-10t$	$-10cd$	$-12v$
5.	$5ab$	$-2t$	$4rs$	$-31y$
6.	a	$\frac{2}{3}n$	x	$1\frac{1}{2}d$
7.	$1.8b$	$4y$	$0.8k + 0.2y$	$0.12t$
8.	$9a$	$14xy$	$18m$	$10h$

Page 46

	a	b	c	d
1.	$7y - 5y$ $= (7 - 5)y$ $= 2y$	a	$7rt$	$12w$
2.	$-2h$	$-3yz$	$-7f$	$-9mn$
3.	$-9x$	$-12g$	$-14z$	$-59b$
4.	$5n$	$3p$	$-4k$	$-10r$
5.	$2t$	$-6m$	$-11a$	$-27xy$
6.	$4ab$	$4k$	$-t$	$-5x$
7.	$\frac{1}{2}t$	$\frac{1}{5}x$	$\frac{1}{3}h$	b
8.	$0.2n$	$0.5a$	$0.7k$	$1.8st$

Page 47

	a	b	c
1.	$5a + 4a - 2a$ $= (5 + 4 - 2)a$ $= (9 - 2)a$ $= 7a$	$4g$	$-x$
2.	$3y$	$2m$	0
3.	$3a + 3b$	$4s + 12t$	$6ab - 11ac$
4.	$8m - 2r$	$-13k + 11$	$5x + 2$
5.	$23xy - 18$	$-8f + 10$	$rs + st$
6.	$-7g + 3$	$e + ef + 5f$	$-13x$
7.	$15bc - 3bd + 19$	$-105p$	$75r - 89$

Page 48

	a	b	c	d
1.	$20a$	$30b$	$54m$	$21a$
2.	$21xy$	$36mn$	$12rs$	$64ab$
3.	$20x$	$-28a$	$-27b$	$50c$
4.	$12ab$	$50st$	$36xz$	$-14mnp$
5.	$3y$	$2x$	$5at$	$\frac{25}{2}m$ or $12.5m$
6.	$1.2rs$	$3bc$	$4tv$	$4.2z$
7.	$36bc$	$105rt$	$108xyz$	$-120mn$
8.	$60st$	$-320abc$	$-150dmr$	$384st$
9.	$-285rst$	$-768ef$	$700xyz$	$128rst$

Page 49

	a	b	c	d
1.	$4a$	$5a$	$3x$	$4y$
2.	$4ab$	$4xy$	$2mn$	$7rs$
3.	$10a$	$-9b$	$6c$	$-5x$
4.	$-10a$	$-5b$	$16c$	$-9d$
5.	$-3x$	$-5a$	$-4b$	$-4c$
6.	$-3x$	$-8x$	$-8a$	$-4b$
7.	$0.6z$	$0.7x$	$0.3a$	$0.3n$

Page 50

	a	b	c
1.	$4(-7x + 3y)$	$-8m - 18n$	$-40ab + 56$
	$= 4(-7x) + 4(3y)$		
	$= -28x + 12y$		
2.	$3p - 3q$	$-6x - y + z$	$4r - 5s$
3.	$14y - 3$	$9x - 15$	$x - 2y$
4.	$4a - b$	$7x - 17y$	$11m - 11n$
5.	$5s - t$	$2m - 3n$	$12x - 14y$
6.	$5b + 13$	$11x - 9y$	$-5m + 2n$

Page 51

	a	b	c
1.	$\frac{k}{3} - \frac{4k}{3}$	$-r + s$	0
	$= \frac{1}{3}k - \frac{4}{3}k$		
	$= (\frac{1}{3} - \frac{4}{3})k$		
	$= (-\frac{3}{3})k$		
	$= -1k = -k$		
2.	$-\frac{2a}{15}$	$-\frac{nx}{12}$	$-2p + \frac{1}{4}$
3.	$-2y - \frac{1}{3}$	$4a - 2$	$-6x$
4.	$x + 3y$	$-6a + \frac{b}{2}$	$-a$
5.	$-x - 6$	$4y - 32$	$-7x - 5$

Page 52

1. Answers may vary.
   Round 5.9% to 6%.
   Round $890 to $900
   $I = prt$
   $\quad = (\$900)(0.06)(1)$
   $\quad = \$54$
   The interest is about $54.
2. $300
3. $460
4. 45 sq yd

Page 53

Answers may vary.

5.	36,000 cu cm	6.	20 ft
7.	60 words	8.	16 m
9.	6 hr	10.	2400 m
11.	$-\$400$	12.	$600

Page 54   Unit 2 Review

	a	b	c	d
1.	-8	13	1	-75
2.	-30	21	67	-91
3.	-1	6	25	-4
4.	3	-12	-2	-11
5.	-48	88	-99	-70
6.	6	-12	15	-7
7.	$9k$	$9m$	$-3ab$	$7n$
8.	$4y + 2z$	$b + 4c$	$-7t$	$14jk$
9.	$-64p$	$-72xy$	$-160ac$	$-12ky$
10.	$3x$	$5rs$	$-9y$	$-3.5mn$

	a	b	c
11.	$-k + 2$	$7r - 13$	$21a + b$
12.	$a + b$	$-9x + 15$	$6b + 10$

Page 55   Cumulative Review

	a	b
1.	$n + 10$	$\frac{7}{w}$

	a	b	c	d
2.	45	2	24	0
3.	13	20	10	28
4.	-9	12	-75	-8
5.	26	-77	-9	20
6.	$14a$	$8x + 4y$	$13b$	0
7.	$45a$	$-2rx$	$-8ab$	$0.4t$
8.	$28a + 40$	$-12b + 4c$	$4m - \frac{8n}{5}$	$m - 5$

9. 120 cu ft   10. 3 hours

UNIT 3

Page 56

	a	b	c	d
1.	$x + 2 = 5$	8	4	-11
	$x + 2 + (-2) = 5 + (-2)$			
	$x = 3$			
	The solution is 3.			
	Check: $3 + 2 = 5$			
2.	0	-5	-4	3
3.	-13	-18	-12	2
4.	-9	10	-18	63
5.	-19	14	-19	0

Page 57

	a	b	c	d
1.	$x - 13 = 15$	11	2	6
	$x - 13 + 13 = 15 + 13$			
	$x = 28$			
	The solution is 28.			
	Check: $28 - 13 = 15$			
2.	6		2	13	35
3.	0		2	27	31
4.	-7		0	1	-3

	a	b	c	d
1.	$6x = 36$	-6	-9	$-\frac{10}{3}$ or $-3\frac{1}{3}$

$(\frac{1}{6})6x = (\frac{1}{6})36$

$x = 6$

The solution is 6.

Check: $6(6) = 36$

2.	-8	4	6	-12
3.	2	3	4	-4
4.	2	2	-6	5

	a	b	c	d
1.	$\frac{x}{4} = 8$	-6	10	90

$(4)\frac{x}{4} = (4)8$

$x = 32$

Check: $\frac{32}{4} = 8$

2.	64	-81	18	0
3.	70	-40	-6	1
4.	-15	100	100	0

	a	b	c	d
1.	13	22	10	3
2.	-1	-4	-6	1
3.	-6	3	27	-4
4.	15	-8	-2	12
5.	45	$\frac{4}{3}$ or $1\frac{1}{3}$	20	-1
6.	-24	5	-18	-5
7.	-1	-12	0	12
8.	$-\frac{8}{5}$ or $-1\frac{3}{5}$	-26	-12	108
9.	-46	-7	13	90
10.	-108	-59	$-\frac{1}{4}$	-8

	a	b	c	d
1.	$\frac{2n}{3} = 14$	3	-9	20

$(3)\frac{2n}{3} = 3(14)$

$2n = 42$

$(\frac{1}{2})2n = (\frac{1}{2})42$

$n = 21$

Check: $\frac{2(21)}{3} = 14$

2.	-20	60	16	14
3.	20	30	-16	30
4.	40	-30	10	-72

1.
$$-15c + 10c = 100$$
$$-5c = 100$$
$$(-\tfrac{1}{5})(-5c) = (-\tfrac{1}{5})100$$
$$c = -20$$
Check: $-15(-20) + 10(-20) = 100$
$$300 - 200 = 100$$

b	c	d
6	24	5

	a	b	c	d
2.	20	5	-19	-2
3.	6	-55	23	5
4.	40	13	3	-12

1. Let n = the number

$\frac{3}{4}n = 36$

$(\frac{4}{3})\frac{3}{4}n = (\frac{4}{3})36$

$n = 48$

Check: $\frac{3}{4}(48) = 36$

The solution is 48.

2. $\frac{a}{5} = 14$

70

3. $\frac{x}{3} = 15$

45

4. $5y = 35$

7

5. $\frac{b}{3} = 20$

60

6. $\frac{3}{2}n = 30$

20

1. Let a = Arlo's age

$4a$ = his father's age

$a + 4a = 50$

$5a = 50$

$a = 10$

Arlo is 10.

His father's age is 4(10) or 40.

2. $5y + y = \$7.20$

Julia: \$1.20

Ana: \$6.00

3. $3n + n = \$2.40$

Tom: \$0.60

Tim: \$1.80

4. $2a + a = 42$

sister: 14 years old

Carla: 28 years old

5. $4h + h = \$2000$

Susan: \$400

Bridget: \$1600

6. $d + 2d = 900$

Kansas City to
St. Louis = 300 miles

Kansas City to
Denver = 600 miles

Page 65

	a	b	c	d
1.	$3x - 5 = 16$	-4	4	3

Step 1 $\quad 3x = 16 + 5$

$\qquad\qquad 3x = 21$

Step 2 $\quad x = 21(\frac{1}{3})$

$\qquad\qquad x = 7$

Check: $3(7) - 5 = 16$

$\qquad\quad 21 - 5 = 16$

$\qquad\qquad\quad 16 = 16$

	a	b	c	d
2.	-1	3	4	1
3.	9	4	-2	2
4.	-15	3	-3	2

Page 66

1. $84 **2.** $650

Page 67

3. 18 people **4.** 18 years

5. 92 years **6.** $17,995

7. $180.75 **8.** a $10 bill

Page 68

	a
1.	$8x + 5 = 5x - 10$

$8x + 5 + (-5x) = 5x - 10 + (-5x)$

$\qquad\quad 3x + 5 = -10$

$3x + 5 + (-5) = -10 + (-5)$

$\qquad\qquad 3x = -15$

$\qquad\qquad\; x = -5$

Check: $8(-5) + 5 = 5(-5) - 10$

$\qquad\quad -40 + 5 = -25 - 10$

$\qquad\qquad\quad -35 = -35$

	b	c	d
	4	-1	5

	a	b	c	d
2.	5	0	-4	7
3.	2	-44	1	6
4.	-2	7	4	6

Page 69

	a	b	c
1.	$\frac{3x}{2} + 2 = \frac{x}{4} + 7$	14	10

$(4)(\frac{3x}{2} + 2) = (4)(\frac{x}{4} + 7)$

$\qquad 6x + 8 = x + 28$

$\qquad 6x - x = 28 - 8$

$\qquad\quad 5x = 20$

$\qquad\qquad x = 4$

Check: $\frac{3(4)}{2} + 2 = \frac{4}{4} + 7$

$\qquad\quad 6 + 2 = 1 + 7$

$\qquad\qquad\; 8 = 8$

	a	b	c
2.	-66	-20	8
3.	27	7	-7

Page 70

	a	b	c	d
1.	$\frac{x}{3} = \frac{2}{5}$	$\frac{4}{3}$ or $1\frac{1}{3}$	$\frac{15}{4}$ or $3\frac{3}{4}$	3

$\qquad 5x = 3(2)$

$\qquad 5x = 6$

$\qquad\; x = \frac{6}{5}$, or $1\frac{1}{5}$

Check: $\frac{6}{5}(\frac{1}{3}) = \frac{2}{5}$

$\qquad\qquad \frac{2}{5} = \frac{2}{5}$

	a	b	c	d
2.	2	2	$\frac{21}{20}$ or $1\frac{1}{20}$	$\frac{15}{16}$
3.	$\frac{7}{2}$ or $3\frac{1}{2}$	$\frac{35}{8}$ or $4\frac{3}{8}$	6	4
4.	$\frac{28}{27}$ or $1\frac{1}{27}$	4	5	20

Page 71

	a	b	c
1.	$3(x + 2) = 2(x + 5)$	8	-4

$\qquad 3x + 6 = 2x + 10$

$\qquad 3x - 2x = 10 - 6$

$\qquad\qquad x = 4$

Check: $3(4 + 2) = 2(4 + 5)$

$\qquad\qquad 3(6) = 2(9)$

$\qquad\qquad\; 18 = 18$

	a	b	c
2.	5	4	1
3.	6	-5	4
4.	5	4	7
5.	6	3	-5

Page 72

1. Dick: $0.60 **2.** 4
Tom: $2.50

3. 20 **4.** 8

5. 7 **6.** 30

7. 8 **8.** 50

9. 8 **10.** Frank: 32 years old
brother: 8 years old

Page 73

1. Length = 210 ft **2.** 42 and 43
Width = 70 ft

3. Length = 140 m **4.** 30, 60, and 90
Width = 70 m

5. Length = 40 ft **6.** 30, 120, and 150
Width = 10 ft

7. Length = 50 cm **8.** 13, 14, and 15
Width = 10 cm

Page 74

1. The substep is to find Nina's age. Nikos is 5 years old. He is half as old as Nina, so Nina is 2×5 or 10 years old.
Mrs. Pappos is three times as old as Nina, so Mrs. Pappos is 3×10 or 30 years old.

2. Find amount earned first week.
$216.00
Find amount earned second week.
$280.00
$64.00

Page 75

3. $1\frac{1}{2}$ gal   4. 16

5. 392.5 mi   6. $38.64

7. $0.45   8. 288 sq in.

Page 76   Unit 3 Review

	a	b	c
1.	9	−7	−9
2.	2	7	$\frac{2}{5}$
3.	6	12	20
4.	−1	0	6
5.	$\frac{1}{3}$	2	−3
6.	7	3	3

7. Ted: 8 years old   8. Leslie: $2.50
Henry: 15 years old   Elena: $2.75

Page 77   Cumulative Review

	a	b	c
1.	14	5	16
2.	$a + 8$	$−27a$	$2a + 7b$
3.	18	10	45
4.	3	−72	4
5.	−5	$\frac{6}{5}$ or $1\frac{1}{5}$	4
6.	4	−5	$\frac{7}{3}$ or $2\frac{1}{3}$

7. 9 in.   8. $400
9. 18   10. 20 and 21

UNIT 4

Page 78

	a	b	c
1.	5^2	4^3	y^2
2.	2^4	a^3	g^4
3.	9^3	r^3	p^1
4.	s^5	l^5	15^2
5.	3^3	w^2	5^3

6. 27 cu in.   7. 8 cu in.
8. 216 cu in.   9. 125 cu in.

Page 79

	a	b	c	d
1.	16	9	−4	25
2.	27	−216	−125	8
3.	−64	0	100	81
4.	32	81	256	−243
5.	−1	−1000	−32	256
6.	−1331	10	441	−729
7.	196	−8000	289	0
8.	72	400	−432	512
9.	12,500	2187	−12,348	5
10.	324	3136	576	−32,768

Page 80

1. 243, 729, 2187   2. 96, 192, 384
3. 31, 37, 43   4. 31, 20, 9
5. 56, 28, 14   6. −80, 160, −320

Page 81

7. 764   8. $7.10
9. 1296   10. 1
11. 21 handshakes   12. 243 employees

Page 82

	a	b	c	d
1.	a^8	b^7	c^8	d^{10}
2.	a^4x^2	a^4b^3	m^7n^2	x^7y^4
3.	a^2bc	x^3yz	rs^3t	de^6f
4.	a^4x^3y	a^5b^3c	$c^7d^2e^2$	$b^8d^2f^3$
5.	$7m^5n^4$	$18a^6b^7$	$16b^4cd$	$25x^4y^6$
6.	$−72axy$	$54ab^3c$	$12xy^3z^4$	$−12mr^7s^5$
7.	$48x^5yz$	$50a^6xy$	$−144yz^4$	$75c^6rs$
8.	$30ax^4y^3$	$50abc^4d^2$	$−36ax^4y^2$	$48abc^2d^3$

Page 83

	a	b	c	d
1.	729	256	15,625	46,656
2.	$4a^8$	$81h^{12}$	$16n^{20}$	$125k^{21}$
3.	a^4b^4	s^6t^6	$x^5y^5z^5$	$m^8n^8p^8$
4.	a^8b^2	y^4z^2	m^3n^{12}	$p^{18}q^3$
5.	m^4n^8	$p^{10}q^4$	r^6s^{12}	$x^{16}y^8$
6.	$4c^4d^2e^6$	$16x^6y^4z^2$	$16m^4n^{20}p^{12}$	$125r^{12}s^6t^9$

	a	b	c
7.	a^5b^4	m^8n^3	j^8k^9
8.	$x^{11}y^8$	$m^{11}n^{18}$	$g^{24}h^9$
9.	$9x^6y^{10}$	$49p^{14}q^{24}$	$27x^5y^8$

Page 84

	a	b	c	d	e
1.	1	d^3	b^4	m^5	c^4
2.	x^2	y^2	a^2	m^3	s^3
3.	x	a	c	c^6	1
4.	2	$3a^2$	$5e^5$	9	$2d^3$
5.	2	10	$5b^3$	$2d^2$	$3b$
6.	$2a$	$2y^2$	e^5	d^6	$4f^6$

Page 85

	a	b	c	d	e
1.	$\frac{1}{x}$	$\frac{1}{y^2}$	$\frac{1}{a^3}$	$\frac{1}{b}$	$\frac{1}{s}$
2.	$\frac{1}{x^2}$	$\frac{1}{a}$	$\frac{1}{y^3}$	$\frac{1}{b}$	$\frac{1}{d^2}$
3.	$\frac{−1}{y}$	$\frac{−1}{x}$	$\frac{−1}{z^2}$	$−\frac{1}{r^2}$	$−\frac{1}{d^3}$
4.	$\frac{3}{c^2}$	$\frac{3}{x^2}$	$\frac{9}{b}$	$−\frac{3}{r}$	$\frac{6}{e^4}$
5.	$\frac{2}{x}$	$\frac{3}{y}$	$\frac{6}{a^4}$	$\frac{5}{b^4}$	$\frac{3}{z}$
6.	$−\frac{3}{a}$	$−\frac{4}{b}$	$−\frac{9}{x}$	$−\frac{9}{r^2}$	$\frac{2}{z}$

Page 86

	a	*b*	*c*	*d*	*e*
1.	$\frac{x^3y^2}{x^2y^2}$	$\frac{b}{a}$	$\frac{a^2}{b^2}$	$\frac{x^2y^2}{z}$	$\frac{yz^2}{x}$

$= x^{3-2}y^{2-2}$
$= x^1y^0$
$= x$

	a	*b*	*c*	*d*	*e*
2.	$\frac{3y^2}{x}$	$\frac{4y^3}{x}$	$\frac{1}{2a}$	$\frac{5a^2}{c^2}$	$\frac{a^2}{4bc^3}$
3.	$-\frac{3x}{y}$	$-\frac{x}{2y}$	$-\frac{4x}{y}$	$-\frac{2y}{x}$	$-\frac{y^2}{3x}$
4.	$-\frac{b}{5a^2}$	$\frac{-3y}{x}$	$\frac{-4y^2}{x^2}$	$-\frac{a}{5b}$	$\frac{6z^2}{x^2}$
5.	$\frac{3}{xy}$	$\frac{z}{6x}$	$\frac{x^2}{2y}$	$\frac{2b}{a}$	$\frac{5b^2}{a}$
6.	$\frac{2a}{3y}$	$\frac{8y}{5x^2}$	$\frac{2b}{3a}$	$\frac{2c^2}{3a^2}$	$\frac{7a}{6bc^2}$

Page 87

a

1. $(4a - 2b) + (4a + 2b)$
$= (4a + 4a) + (-2b + 2b)$
$= 8a + 0$
$= 8a$

b   *c*
$6x$ $10m - 14n$

	a	*b*	*c*
2.	$8a + 4b$	$7x + y$	$3m - 7n$
3.	$-10a$	$13r - 2s$	$3m + 2n$
4.	$2r + 6st$	$3b - 4cd$	$-12xy - 16z$
5.	$8x - y$	$28p - 33q$	$10ab - 15yz$
6.	0	0	$2cd + 2d$
7.	$2xyz$	$7ab + 5abc$	$5rst + 7t$
8.	$10ab - 2abc$	$11xy - 11x$	$14y - 2yz$

Page 88

	a	*b*	*c*
1.	$(x + y) - (x - y)$	$-a + 5b$	$m + 11n$

$= x + y + (-x + y)$
$= (x - x) + (y + y)$
$= 0 + 2y$
$= 2y$

	a	*b*	*c*
2.	$-2y$	$-3a - 3b$	$4m - 3n$
3.	$2x - 2y$	$4b - 3c$	$-5r + s$
4.	$b - 5cd$	$3m + 7np$	$3rs - 7t$
5.	$-3x + 6yz$	0	$-8rs - 10t$
6.	$9x - yz$	$9x + 2wy$	$-3mn$
7.	-9	0	$2rs - 2t$
8.	$9z + -9xyz$	$abc - 2c$	$2rs - 2rst$

Page 89

	a	*b*
1.	$4x^3 + 3y^2 + 3x^3 + 4y2$	$8a^2 + 9b^2$

$= (4x^3 + 3x^3) + (3y^2 + 4y^2)$
$= 7x^3 + 7y^2$

	a	*b*
2.	$8m^2 - 6n^2 + n$	$2x^2 - 2y$
3.	$2b^2 + 2b$	$3m^2 + 4n^4$
4.	$10x^3 - y^2$	$8a^3 + b^2$
5.	$-m$	$-8x^2 + 2y^3$
6.	$-8a^3 - 4a^2 + 4a$	$-3b^3 + 4b^2 + b$
7.	$-8x^4 - 2x^2 - 3$	$2b^2 + 1$
8.	$-6x^4 - 2x^3 + 3x^2$	$-16m + 6m^2$

c

1. $5b^2 + 12c^2$
2. $3a^2 - 3b$
3. $x^2 - 3y$
4. $9b^3 - 6b^2$
5. $11y^2$
6. $-6m^2 - 6m$
7. $-3x^2 - x + 6$
8. $12a^4$

Page 90

	a	*b*	*c*
1.	$\frac{p}{q} \cdot \frac{q}{p}$	$\frac{x}{9y}$	$\frac{30y}{b}$

$= \frac{1\,p}{1\,q} \cdot \frac{q\,1}{p\,1} = 1$

	a	*b*	*c*
2.	$\frac{ax}{2}$	$\frac{a}{x^3}$	$\frac{72a^2}{b}$
3.	$-8bx^4$	$\frac{-18a}{5}$	$-6b$
4.	$\frac{x^3}{4a^2}$	$6a^2x^2$	$\frac{x}{4a}$
5.	$2b$	$\frac{z^2}{6}$	$-\frac{1}{p}$
6.	1	$2x + 2y$	$\frac{-1}{2x}$

Page 91

	a	*b*	*c*
1.	$\frac{x^2}{a} \div \frac{x^4}{a^2}$	$\frac{1}{a^2x^2}$	ax^3

$= \frac{1\,x^2}{1\,a} \cdot \frac{a^2\,a}{x^4\,x^2} = \frac{a}{x^2}$

	a	*b*	*c*
2.	$\frac{5x}{2y}$	$\frac{4xy}{3ab}$	$\frac{x}{y}$
3.	$\frac{xy}{18}$	$\frac{ab}{12x}$	$\frac{3x^2y^2}{ab}$
4.	$\frac{2x}{3}$	$\frac{3ab}{4}$	$\frac{ab}{4}$
5.	$\frac{-3a^3}{5}$	$\frac{-3x}{2}$	$\frac{-4y}{3}$
6.	$36a^2$	$\frac{15x^2y}{2}$	$28a^3b^2$
7.	a	$\frac{2}{a}$	$2x$

Page 92

	a	b
1.	$x(x + y) = (x \cdot x) + (x \cdot y)$ $= x^2 + xy$	$2xy + y^2$

	a	b
2.	$2x^2 + 2xy$	$6x^2 + 9xy$
3.	$-4ab - 2b^2$	$-6ab - 2b^2$
4.	$4x^3 + 4xy$	$4b^3 - 2a^2b$
5.	$6x^2 - 10xy - 4xz$	$4xy - 6y^2 + 8yz$
6.	$16a^2b - 20b^3 - 12bc^2$	$-14ab + 6b^5 + 2b$
7.	$10x^2y - 4xy^2 + 6xyz$	$x^2z + xyz - xz^2$
8.	$-5x^2yz + 3xy^2z - 4xyz^2$	$2a^3bc + 2ab^3c + 2abc^3$

c
1. $x^4 + 2x^3y$
2. $12a^4 - 6a^3b$
3. $12ab^3 - 9b^4$
4. $15c^5 + 20c^2$
5. $15ab^2 + 12b^3 + 6b^2c$
6. $12c^4 + 9c^3 - 6c^2$
7. $8a^2b^2 + 8ab^3 + 8ab^2$
8. $-4x^2y^3z - 4xy^3z^2$

Page 93

	a	b
1.	$\dfrac{a^2 + a}{a}$ $= \dfrac{a^2}{a} + \dfrac{a}{a} = a^{2-1} + a^{1-1}$ $= a + a^0$ $= a + 1$	$3xy + 2z$
2.	$2b + 3c + 4d$	$9x + 12y + 8z$
3.	$-2a^2 + 5a + 1$	$3x^2 - 4x - 6$
4.	$-3x^2 - 5x - 7$	$-3a^2 - 4ay - 5y^2$
5.	$4x^2 + 3x + 5$	$2a^3 + 3a^2 + 2a$
6.	$2x + 6 - 4y$	$5x^2 - 4xy + 6y^2$

c
1. $4y + 3z$
2. $ay + 2y^2 + 3y^3$
3. $-5x^2 - 4x + 3$
4. $-2x^2 - 3xy - 4y$
5. $4x^2 + 2xy + 3y^2$
6. $3c + 4cd - 2d^2$

Page 94
1. Farmer: Diane
   Lawyer: Felicia
   Teacher: Ella

Page 95
2. Bowling: Kelly
   Swimming: Jan
   Basketball: Laura

3. White: Norman
   Green: Penny
   Yellow: Manuel
   Blue: Oliver

4. Silver: 816ZPN
   Black: GX2378
   Tan: MDY340
   Red: AB764

5. Son: Bill
   Father: Carl
   Brother: Dean
   Grandfather: Allan

Page 96

a
1. $7mn - 14mp - 21mq$
Since 7 and m are factors of each term, the common monomial factor is $7m$.
Divide by $7m$.
$$\frac{7mn - 14mp - 21mq}{7m} = n - 2p - 3q$$
$$7mn - 14mp - 21mq = 7m(n - 2p - 3q)$$

b
$5x(x^2 - 2x + 3)$

	a	b
2.	$4a(x + 2y - 3z)$	$6ab(a^2 - 2ab + 3b^2)$
3.	$2x(5x^2 + 4x - 1)$	$3(3a^2b^2 + 2ab + 5)$
4.	$4xy(2x + 1 - 3y)$	$2x(5x^2 - 6x - 3)$
5.	$5ab(4a^2 - 3ab + 2b^2)$	$4xy^2(4y - 3x + 5xy)$
6.	$3a^2(1 - 5ay + 6a^2y^2)$	$5ab(4b^2 - 3ab - 5a^2)$
7.	$-4a(3a^2 - 2ab + 4b^3)$	$-3(3x^2 - 2xy + 6y^2)$

Page 97

a
1. $(a + b)(a + b)$
   $= a(a + b) + b(a + b)$
   $= a^2 + ab + ba + b^2$
   $= a^2 + 2ab + b^2$
2. $9a^2 - 12ab + 4b^2$
3. $-3x^2 + 10xy + 8y^2$
4. $-y^2 + 4z^2$
5. $x^2y^2 + 2xyz + z^2$
6. $x^3y^2 + x^2yz - xyz - z^2$
7. $a^2 + 2ab + b^2 + ac + bc$

b
1. $a^2 + 4ab + 4b^2$
2. $-6x^2 - 5xy + 6y^2$
3. $-a^2 + 4ab - 4b^2$
4. $3a^2 + 5ab - 12b^2$
5. $8a^2b^2 - 10abc + 3c^2$
6. $12x^4y^5 - 3x^2y^4 + 4x^3y^4 - xy^3$
7. $2x^3 - x^2 + x + 2x^2y - xy + y$

c
1. $4x^2 + 4xy + y^2$
2. $-2c^2 - 3cd + 2d^2$
3. $x^2 - 4y^2$
4. $-36x^2 + 18xy - 2y^2$
5. $a^2b^2 - c^2$
6. $-6a^2bc + 8abc + 3ad - 4d$
7. $4x^3 - 6x^2y + xy^2 + y^3$

Page 98

	a	*b*	*c*

1.
$$\begin{array}{r} a + 2b \\ a + 2b\ \overline{\smash{\big)}\ a^2 + 4ab + 4b^2} \\ \underline{a^2 + 2ab} \\ 2ab + 4b^2 \\ \underline{2ab + 4b^2} \\ 0 \end{array}$$
  $x - y$ $a - 2b$

2. $2x + 3y$ $3x - 2y$ $5a + 2b$
3. $x + 2$ $x - 3$ $x + 1$

Page 99

a

1. $6b^3 - 8b^2 + 12b$
2. $x^3 - x^2 - x + 10$
3. $-4x^2 + 13x$
4. $3x^2 - 3y^2 + 6yz - 3z^2$
5. $x + 4$
6. 3
7. $5 + x$

b   *c*

1. $12x^3y - 6x^2y^2 - 9xy^3$ $40x^2 + 12x^2y^2$
2. $4a^3 - 7ab^2 + 3b^3$ $6x^4 - 7x^3 + x$
3. $6x^3 - 15x^2 + 12x - 2$ $-6a^2 + 4a$
4. $36x^2y^2 + 54x^2y - 6xy^2 - 9xy$ $-28b^3 - 3b^2$
5. $2x + 1$ $y - 2$
6. $18y - 6x - 6x^2$ $y + xy - x^2y$
7. $4 + 2x$ $2 + 3x$

Page 100   Unit 4 Review

	a	*b*	*c*
1.	25	-729	900
2.	c^3d^3	$25x^6y^6$	$x^3y^9z^{12}$
3.	m^6	$\dfrac{3}{xy}$	$-\dfrac{2a^2}{3c^2}$
4.	$6xy + 2x$	$-2b - 6$	$-6m^3 - 15m^2 + 5m$
5.	$\dfrac{b}{a}$	x^2yz	$-\dfrac{3x^3}{5}$
6.	$x - 1$	$3xy - 2z$	$4a^3 - 3a - 1$
7.	$x^2 - xy$	$4x^2y^2 - 6y$	$6a^3b + 6ab^3$
8.	$a^2 - b^2$	$4a^2b^2 - c^2$	$a^3b + ab^3 + 3ab$ $- a^2b - b^3 - 3b$
9.	$x - 2$	$x + 2y$	$2x - 3y$

Page 101   Cumulative Review

	a	*b*	*c*
1.	27	-5	2
2.	44	4	-1
3.	24	$1\frac{1}{2}$ or $\frac{3}{2}$	6
4.	5	-16	-24

5. 14 $5rs^2$ $a - \dfrac{1}{2}$
6. $5a^3b^8c^3$ $3x$ $\dfrac{1}{9}$
7. -16 $16a^4x^2$ $12a^2 + 2ab - 2b^2$
8. $-27a^2$ $12x^2 + 10y^3z^6 - 5$ $x + 3$
9. 92, 93, and 94   10. 75.36 ft

UNIT 5

Page 102

	a	*b*	*c*
1.	(0,5)	(1,7)	(2,6.5)
2.	(2,0)	(0,2)	$(-2,4)$
3.	$(0,-1)$	$(-1,0)$	$(1,-2)$

Page 103

	a	*b*	*c*	*d*	*e*
1.	$(2,-2)$	$(-6,-7)$	$(-2,7)$	$(-4,0)$	$(8,-6)$
2.	$(7,0)$	$(0,-5)$	$(-4,-2)$	$(3,7)$	$(0,2)$

3.

4.

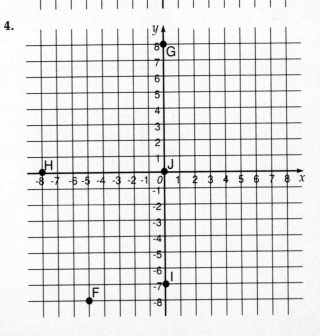

1.

x	y
−4	6
0	3
4	0
8	−3

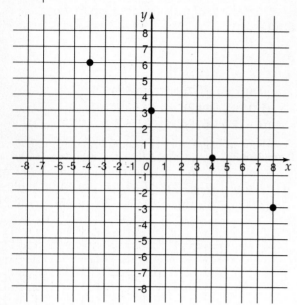

3.

x	y
0	6
2	0
1	3
3	−3

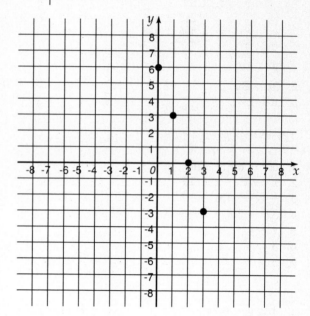

2.

x	y
−5	−6
0	−3
5	0

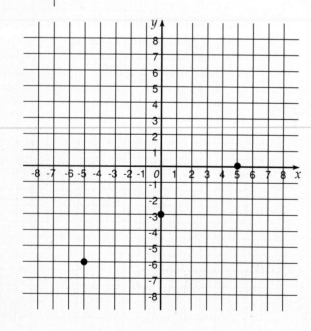

Page 105

Answers may vary.

1.

x	y
1	0
0	−4
−1	−8

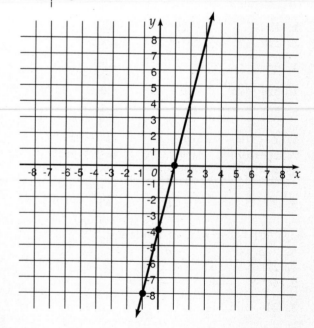

2.

x	y
3	0
0	2
−3	4

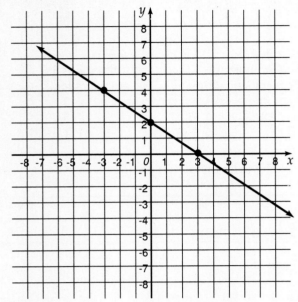

3.

x	y
0	−8
−1	−7
−2	−6

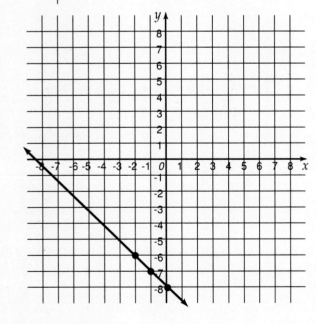

1.

A	B	
6	4	6 + 4 = 10
5	5	5 + 5 = 10
4	6	4 + 6 = 10

There are 3 different ways that a sum of 10 can turn up.

2. 2

3. Number the catchers 1, 2, 3, and 4.
Number the pitchers 1, 2, 3, 4, and 5.

Catcher	Pitcher	Catcher	Pitcher
1	1	3	1
1	2	3	2
1	3	3	3
1	4	3	4
1	5	3	5
2	1	4	1
2	2	4	2
2	3	4	3
2	4	4	4
2	5	4	5

There are 20 different combinations of catcher and pitcher.

3. 20   **4.** 10
5. 8   **6.** 12
7. 16   **8.** 12

1. Add.

$$a + b = 15$$
$$\underline{a - b = 5}$$
$$2a = 20$$
$$a = 10$$

Subtract.

$$\overset{a}{a + b = 15}$$
$$\underline{a - b = 5}$$
$$2b = 10$$
$$b = 5$$

Check: Substitute into the original equations.
$$a + b = 15 \qquad a - b = 5$$
$$10 + 5 = 15 \qquad 10 - 5 = 5$$
The solution to the system of equations is (10,5).

$$\overset{b}{(9,4)} \quad \overset{c}{(10,4)}$$

2. $\overset{a}{(5,1)}$ $\overset{b}{(5,2)}$ $\overset{c}{(15,10)}$

	a	b	c
1.	(12,5)	(22,5)	(30,21)
2.	(22,15)	(36,19)	(16,7)
3.	(20,15)	(30,15)	(20,5)
4.	(21,12)	(25,18)	(10,8)

a

1. Add. $2a + 3b = 28$ Subtract. $2a + 3b = 28$

   $\underline{2a - 3b = \ \ 4}$ $\underline{2a - 3b = \ \ 4}$

   $\quad 4a \qquad = 32$ $6b = 24$

   $\qquad\qquad a = 8$ $b = 4$

   Check: Substitute into the original equations.

   $\qquad\qquad 2a + 3b = 28 \qquad 2a - 3b = 4$

   $\qquad\quad 2(8) + 3(4) = 28 \quad 2(8) - 3(4) = 4$

   $\qquad\qquad\ 16 + 12 = 28 \qquad 16 - 12 = 4$

   The solution is (8,4).

b	*c*
(4,1)	(3,2)

a	*b*	*c*
2. | (2,4) | (5,6) | (3,8) |
3. | (4,9) | (7,5) | (6,5) |

a

1. Step 1   Step 2

   Multiply by 5.   Subtract.

   $5(a + 3b) = 5(15)$ $5a + 2b = 23$

   $5a + 15b = 75$ $\underline{5a + 15b = 75}$

   $\qquad\qquad\qquad\qquad -13b = -52$

   $\qquad\qquad\qquad\qquad\quad b = 4$

   Step 3

   Substitute.

   $\ a + 3b = 15$

   $a + 3(4) = 15$

   $\qquad\quad a = 3$

   Check: Substitute into the original equations.

   $\qquad\qquad 5a + 2b = 23 \qquad a + 3b = 15$

   $\qquad\quad 5(3) + 2(4) = 23 \quad 3 + 3(4) = 15$

   $\qquad\qquad 15 + 8 = 23 \qquad 3 + 12 = 15$

   $\qquad\qquad\qquad 23 = 23 \qquad\qquad 15 = 15$

   The solution is (3,4).

b	*c*
(4,5)	(5,1)

	a	*b*	*c*
1.	(2,2)	(2,6)	(3,1)
2.	(2,4)	(1,3)	(2,5)
3.	(3,2)	(1,5)	(7,2)

a

1. Step 1   Step 2

   Multiply the first   Multiply the second

   equation by 2.   equation by 5.

   $2(5a - 2b) = 2(3)$ $5(2a + 5b) = 5(7)$

   $\ 10a - 4b = 6$ $\ 10a + 25b = 35$

   Step 3   Step 4

   Subtract the   Substitute $b = 1$

   new equations.   in any equation.

   $10a - 4b = 6$ $5a - 2(1) = 3$

   $\underline{10a + 25b = 35}$ $\qquad 5a = 5$

   $\quad -29b = -29$ $\qquad\ a = 1$

   $\qquad\ b = 1$

   The solution is (1,1).

b	*c*
(4,2)	(5,2)

	a	*b*	*c*
2. | (3,2) | (2,3) | (5,3) |

a

1. $\qquad\qquad 12x - 4y = 48$

   $12x - 12x - 4y = 48 - 12x$

   $\qquad\qquad -4y = 48 - 12x$

   $\qquad -\tfrac{1}{4}(-4y) = -\tfrac{1}{4}(48 - 12x)$

   $\qquad\qquad\qquad y = -12 + 3x,$ or

   $\qquad\qquad\qquad y = 3x - 12$

b	*c*
$y = 5 - 3x$	$y = 15 - \tfrac{3}{4}x$

	a	*b*	*c*
2.	$y = \tfrac{1}{2}x + 4$	$y = -\tfrac{1}{3}x + 2$	$y = -2x - \tfrac{1}{2}$
3.	$x = 3y - 1$	$x = 2y - 4$	$x = -\tfrac{1}{3}y + 3$
4.	$x = \tfrac{2}{3}y + 1$	$x = y + 10$	$x = 4 - \tfrac{4}{7}y$

Page 115

a

1. **Step 1**
Solve for x in terms of y.

$$x + 4y = 12$$
$$x + 4y - 4y = 12 - 4y$$
$$x = 12 - 4y$$

Step 2
Substitute $12 - 4y$ for x in the second equation.

$$2x - y = 6$$
$$2(12 - 4y) - y = 6$$
$$24 - 8y - y = 6$$
$$-9y = -18$$
$$y = 2$$

Step 3
Substitute 2 for y in either equation.
$$x + 4y = 12$$
$$x + 4(2) = 12$$
$$x + 8 = 12$$
$$x = 4$$

Check: $x + 4y = 12$ $2x - y = 6$
$4 + 4(2) = 12$ $2(4) - 2 = 6$
$4 + 8 = 12$ $8 - 2 = 6$
The solution is (4,2).

b	*c*
(6,5)	(3,2)

	a	*b*	*c*
2.	(3,2)	(4,2)	(3,1)

Page 116

	a	*b*	*c*
1.	(5,2)	(4,2)	(5,2)
2.	(5,1)	(3,2)	(4,3)
3.	(4,5)	(4,7)	(4,3)

Page 117

	a	*b*	*c*
1.	(2,4)	(2,2)	(6,−6)
2.	(4,1)	(2,2)	(4,9)
3.	(1,5)	(6,7)	(5,3)

Page 118
1. Let x = the first number.
Let y = the second number.
Then, $x + y = 15$
    $2x - y = 6$

Add. $x + y = 15$ Substitute. $x + y = 15$
    $2x - y = 6$ $7 + y = 15$
    $3x = 21$ $y = 8$
    $x = 7$

Check: $x + y = 15$ $2x - y = 6$
    $7 + 8 = 15$ $2(7) - 8 = 6$
        $14 - 8 = 6$
The two numbers are 7 and 8.

2. (14,4)   **3.** (4,3)   **4.** (2,3)

Page 119

1. (4,3)	**2.** (5,3)	**3.** (5,2)	**4.** (4,5)
5. (4,7)	**6.** (6,5)	**7.** (5,4)	

8. Length = 4 units.
Width = 3 units.

Page 120

a

1. **Step 1**
Add.
$$\tfrac{1}{2}m + n = 3$$
$$\tfrac{1}{2}m - n = 1$$
$$1m = 4$$
$$m = 4$$

Step 2
Subtract.
$$\tfrac{1}{2}m + n = 3$$
$$\tfrac{1}{2}m - n = 1$$
$$2n = 2$$
$$n = 1$$

Check: Substitute the values of a and b into the original equations.

$\tfrac{1}{2}m + n = 3$ $\tfrac{1}{2}m - n = 1$
$\tfrac{1}{2}(4) + 1 = 3$ $\tfrac{1}{2}(4) - 1 = 1$
$2 + 1 = 3$ $2 - 1 = 1$
The solution is (4,1).

b	*c*
(8,2)	(4,3)

	a	*b*	*c*
2.	(10,5)	(6,−4)	(12,2)

Page 121
1. Let x = the first number.
Let y = the second number.

Then, $\tfrac{1}{2}x + y = 4$
    $\tfrac{1}{2}x - y = 0$

Add. $\tfrac{1}{2}x + y = 4$ Subtract. $\tfrac{1}{2}x + y = 4$
    $\tfrac{1}{2}x - y = 0$ $\tfrac{1}{2}x - y = 0$
    $1x = 4$ $2y = 4$
    $x = 4$ $y = 2$

Check: $\tfrac{1}{2}x + y = 4$ $\tfrac{1}{2}x - y = 0$
    $\tfrac{1}{2}(4) + 2 = 4$ $\tfrac{1}{2}(4) - 2 = 0$
    $2 + 2 = 4$ $2 - 2 = 0$
The two numbers are 4 and 2.

2. (6,5)	**3.** (20,5)	**4.** (6,5)	
5. (6,2)	**6.** (4,3)		

Let x = one number
Let y = the other number.
Then, $2x - y = 2$
$x + y = 7$

$2x - y = 2$

x	y
1	0
3	4
5	8

$x + y = 7$

x	y
1	6
3	4
5	2

The point of intersection has coordinates (3,4).
So, $x = 3$ and $y = 4$. The numbers are 3 and 4.

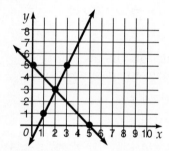

Page 123

2. 2 and 3

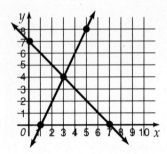

3. Length = 9 cm
Width = 2 cm

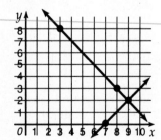

4. Length = 6 in.
Width = 3 in.

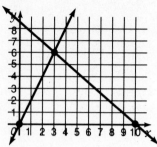

5. 3 lb of cashews
7 lb of peanuts

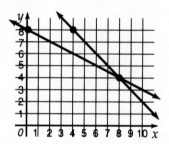

6. 8 lb of pretzels
4 lb of cereal

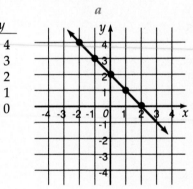

Page 124   Unit 5 Review

1.

x	y
−2	4
−1	3
0	2
1	1
2	0

a

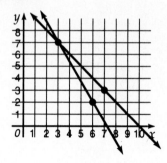

198

Answers may vary.

x	y
0	−3
3	0
4	1
−1	−4

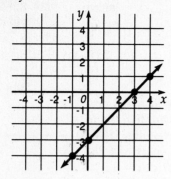

	a	b	c
2.	(7,5)	(9,1)	(3,2)
3.	(6,5)	(16,4)	(−1,3)
4.	(6,5)	**5.** (6,2)	

Page 125 Cumulative Review

	a	b	c
1.	−4	−51	−48
2.	$22a + 24b$	r	$2a^2b + 10$
3.	$−16x^4$	$10rt^3 − 1$	$18x^2 − 15x − 12$
4.	90	−7	$y = 3 − \frac{3}{2}x$
5.	(2,3)	(20,5)	(3,−3)
6.	$\frac{1}{2}$ or 6 months	**7.** 6782 cu m	

UNIT 6

Page 126

	a	b	c
1.	<	<	>
2.	>	<	>
3.	<	>	>
4.	<	=	>
5.	False	False	True
6.	True	True	False
7.	True	True	False

Page 127

	a	b	c
1.	$x > 22$	$x ≤ 15$	$x < 20$
2.	$x ≤ 1$	$x > 15$	$x ≥ −4$
3.	$x ≥ 6$	$x > −24$	$x > −8$
4.	$x < −4$	$x < 31$	$x ≤ −16$
5.	$x < −4$	$x > 2$	$x ≤ −4$
6.	$x ≤ 1$	$x > −6$	$x ≤ −34$

Page 128

	a	b	c
1.	$x > 10$	$x ≤ −12$	$x ≤ −12$
2.	$x < 2$	$x ≤ −5$	$x ≥ 3$
3.	$x ≥ 2$	$x > 4$	$x < −3$
4.	$x > 6$	$x > −1$	$x ≥ 20$
5.	$x < \frac{4}{5}$	$x ≥ −\frac{1}{2}$	$x > −2$

Page 129

1. Let x = the jockey's weight

$\frac{1}{8}x$ = the combined weight of the equipment

The jockey's weight plus the equipment is less than 130 pounds.

$$x + \frac{1}{8}x < 130$$
$$1\frac{1}{8}x < 130$$
$$\frac{9}{8}x < 130$$
$$\frac{8}{9}(\frac{9}{8}x) < \frac{8}{9}(130)$$
$$x < 115\frac{5}{9} \text{ lb}$$

The maximum the jockey can weigh is $115\frac{5}{9}$ pounds.

2. $4800   **3.** 60   **4.** 11

Page 130

1.

Number	Factors	Number	Factors
1	1	11	1,11
2	1,2	12	1,2,3,4,6,12
3	1,3	13	1,13
4	1,2,4	14	1,2,7,14
5	1,5	15	1,3,5,15
6	1,2,3,6	16	1,2,4,8,16
7	1,7	17	1,17
8	1,2,4,8	18	1,2,3,6,9,18
9	1,3,9	19	1,19
10	1,2,5,10	20	1,2,4,5,10,20

2. 1,4,9,16   **3.** 6,8,10,14,15

Page 131

4. June   **5.** after seventh meeting
6. eighth year   **7.** April
8. 256 pieces   **9.** house number is 567

Page 132

	a	b	c	d	e
1.	11	7	12	5	13
2.	15	9	4	18	14
3.	a	a^2	x^3	y^4	b^2
4.	ab	x^2y^2	xy^2	abc	x^2bc^2
5.	$3a$	$4b^2$	$6ab$	$8xy^2$	$9ab^2c^4$
6.	$13x^5y^2$	$17x^6$	$18b^2c^3$	$20ab^3$	$10x^2yz^3$

Page 133

	a	b	c	d	e
1.	3	4	8	1	16
2.	y	y^2	b^3	c^4	z^5
3.	$2y$	$6x^2$	$11z^3$	$20a$	$16b^4$
4.	$7ab$	$9x^2y^5$	$2c^4d^3$	$6xy^2$	$15z^9$
5.	$8abc^2$	$10xy^2z^3$	$13r^3s^3$	$18t^{10}$	$5x^5y^5$

Page 134

1. $2x^2 = 200$ Check: $2(10)^2 = 200$
$\dfrac{2x^2}{2} = \dfrac{200}{2}$ $2(10)(10) = 200$
         $2(100) = 200$
$x^2 = 100$

Find the square root $2(-10)^2 = 200$
of both sides. $2(-10)(-10) = 200$

$x = \pm 10$ $2(100) = 200$

	b	c	d	
	± 5	± 7	± 4	

	a	b	c	d
2.	± 5	± 6	± 8	± 10
3.	± 3	± 5	± 5	± 2

	a	b	c
4.	± 2	± 3	± 4

Page 135

1. $3x^3 = 24$ Check: $3(2)^3 = 24$
$\dfrac{3x^3}{3} = \dfrac{24}{3}$ $3(2)(2)(2) = 24$
         $3(8) = 24$
$x^3 = 8$
$x = 2$

	b	c	d
	5	6	9

	a	b	c	d
2.	3	2	4	10
3.	5	7	4	6

	a	b	c
4.	2	4	6

Page 136

1. Let x = width.   Since $A = 288$ sq cm
   $2x$ = length $2x^2 = 288$
         $x^2 = 144$
         $x = \pm 12$
Then $A = (2x)x$ Check:
   $A = 2x^2$ $(2x)x = 288$
      $(24)(12) = 288$

Length = 24 cm
Width = 12 cm
The negative value of $x = -12$ is not a solution since dimensions cannot be negative.

2. Length = 32 in.
Width = 4 in.

3. Length = 20 m   **4.** Length = 114 in.
Width = 5 m   Width = 19 in.

5. Length = 25 cm   **6.** Length = 114 ft
Width = 5 cm   Width = 38 ft

Page 137

1. Let x = width.   Since $V = 512$ cu cm
   $2x$ = length $8x^3 = 512$
   $4x$ = height $x^3 = 64$
         $x = 4$
Then $V = 2x(x)(4x)$ Check:
   $= 8x^3$ $2x(x)(4x) = 512$
      $8(4)(16) = 512$

Width = 4 cm
Length = 8 cm
Height = 16 cm

2. Length = 6 m
Width = 3 m
Height = 9 m

3. Length = 8 m   **4.** Length = 5 cm
Width = 4 m   Width = 5 cm
Height = 12 m   Height = 5 cm

5. Length = 3 ft   **6.** Length = 8 m
Width = 3 ft   Width = 6 m
Height = 15 ft   Height = 12 m

Page 138

	a	b
1.	1:16 or $\frac{1}{16}$	1:12 or $\frac{1}{12}$
2.	1:1000 or $\frac{1}{1000}$	1:5280 or $\frac{1}{5280}$
3.	1:10 or $\frac{1}{10}$	100:1 or $\frac{100}{1}$

4. $\frac{16}{15}$ or 16:15   **5.** $\frac{6}{5}$ or 6:5

6. Length = 21 ft   **7.** Length = 100 m
Width = 14 ft   Width = 70 m

Page 139

	a
1.	$\dfrac{x}{4} = \dfrac{5}{10}$ Check: $\dfrac{2}{4} = \dfrac{5}{10}$

$10x = 4(5)$ $\dfrac{1}{2} = \dfrac{1}{2}$
$10x = 20$
$x = 2$

	b	c	d
	4	3	16

	a	b	c	d
2.	12	16	14	15

3. \$12.60   **4.** $26\frac{2}{3}$ mi

Page 140

1. Length = 35 cm   **2.** Length = 24 in.
Width = 15 cm   Width = 6 in.

3. Length = 12 ft   **4.** Length = 20 ft
Width = 8 ft   Width = 10 ft

5. \$118.25   **6.** \$145.60
7. \$25,000   **8.** \$67.79

Page 141

1. $\dfrac{AB}{DE} = \dfrac{BC}{EF}$

$\dfrac{10}{6} = \dfrac{15}{EF}$

10EF = 90

EF = 9 ft

2. 12 ft   3. 25 ft   4. 32 ft

Page 142

1.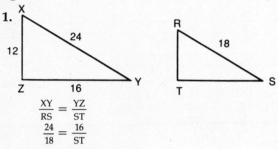

$\dfrac{XY}{RS} = \dfrac{YZ}{ST}$

$\dfrac{24}{18} = \dfrac{16}{ST}$

24 ST = 288

ST = 12 in.

2.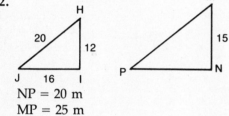

NP = 20 m

MP = 25 m

Page 143

3.

47 m

4.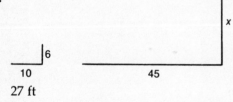

27 ft

5.

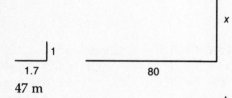

75 ft

6.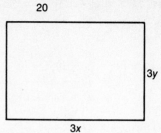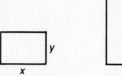

The area of larger rectangle is 9 times greater than the area of the smaller rectangle.

Page 144   Unit 6 Review

	a	b	c
1.	>	<	=
2.	$x < 26$	$y \geq 5$	$m \geq 6$
3.	±5	±3	2
4.	6	27	2

	a	b	c	d
5.	7	3	$5xy^2$	6

6. Length = 30 cm   7. Length = 12 cm
   Width = 15 cm   Width = 4 cm
                      Height = 12 cm

8. Length = 40 in.   9. $468.75
   Width = 30 in.

10. 15 m   11. 20 ft

Page 145   Cumulative Review

	a	b	c
1.	38	$115xy$	$16c^2d^6$
2.	$\dfrac{-2m^2}{n}$	$9y$	$\dfrac{r^2s^3}{2}$
3.	1	ab^3	$a + b$
4.	4	$k \geq 6$	$x \geq -3$
5.	(5, 1)	(10, −1)	(3, 8)

6. A (1,1)   7. Length = 20 cm
   B (−2, −3)   Width = 12 cm
   C (6, −1)
   D (0, 7)
   E (−7, 0)
   F (−3, 3)
   G (4, −8)

1. $(a + b)^2 = (a + b)(a + b)$
 $ = a(a) + a(b) + a(b) + b(b)$
 $ = a^2 + 2ab + b^2$

 b
 $b^2 + 2ab + a^2$

	a	b
2.	$m^2 + 2mn + n^2$	$r^2 + 2rs + s^2$
3.	$b^2 + 2bc + c^2$	$c^2 + 2cd + d^2$
4.	$4a^2 + 4ab + b^2$	$x^2 + 4xy + 4y^2$
5.	$4a^2 + 8ab + 4b^2$	$4y^2 + 4yz + z^2$
6.	$x^2 + 6xy + 9y^2$	$9x^2 + 6xy + y^2$
7.	$4x^2 + 12xy + 9y^2$	$9x^2 + 12xy + 4y^2$
8.	$9x^2 + 30x + 25$	$25x^2 + 30x + 9$
9.	$m^2 + 8m + 16$	$16 + 8m + m^2$
10.	$4x^2 + 12x + 9$	$16a^2 + 24a + 9$

1. $(x - 4)^2 = (x - 4)(x - 4)$
 $ = x(x) - 4(x) - 4(x) + 16$
 $ = x^2 - 8x + 16$

 b
 $x^2 - 6x + 9$

	a	b
2.	$x^2 - 10x + 25$	$x^2 - 16x + 64$
3.	$25 - 10x + x^2$	$49 - 14x + x^2$
4.	$a^2 - 24a + 144$	$a^2 - 20a + 100$
5.	$c^2 - 4cd + 4d^2$	$x^2 - 6xy + 9y^2$
6.	$x^2 - 12xy + 36y^2$	$x^2 - 20xy + 100y^2$
7.	$x^2 - 10xy + 25y^2$	$x^2 - 18xy + 81y^2$
8.	$9 - 12x + 4x^2$	$25 - 40x + 16x^2$
9.	$49 - 28x + 4x^2$	$100 - 60x + 9x^2$
10.	$9x^2 - 12xy + 4y^2$	$25x^2 - 40xy + 16y^2$

1. $a^2 + 2ay + y^2 = (a + y)(a + y)$
 $ = (a + y)^2$

 b
 $(m + n)^2$

	a	b
2.	$(c + d)^2$	$(r + s)^2$
3.	$(x + 2y)^2$	$(2x + y)^2$
4.	$(m + 3n)^2$	$(r + 7t)^2$
5.	$(x + 4y)^2$	$(x + 4)^2$
6.	$(7y + 4)^2$	$(x + 5y)^2$
7.	$(3 + y)^2$	$(z + 3)^2$
8.	$(2 + x)^2$	$(x + 3y)^2$
9.	$(8 + x)^2$	$(7 + x)^2$
10.	$(3x + 2y)^2$	$(2x + 4y)^2$
11.	$(9 + 2x)^2$	$(8x + 1)^2$
12.	$(10 + x)^2$	$(6x + 2)^2$

1. $x^2 - 2xy + y^2 = (x - y)(x - y)$
 $ = (x - y)^2$

 b
 $(c - d)^2$

	a	b
2.	$(b - d)^2$	$(m - n)^2$
3.	$(r - s)^2$	$(y - z)^2$
4.	$(x - 2)^2$	$(a - 3)^2$
5.	$(a - 4)^2$	$(x - 6)^2$
6.	$(x - 8)^2$	$(x - 7)^2$
7.	$(x - 3y)^2$	$(x - 4y)^2$
8.	$(x - 6y)^2$	$(x - 8y)^2$
9.	$(x - 5y)^2$	$(x - 7y)^2$
10.	$(x - 9y)^2$	$(x - 11y)^2$
11.	$(3x - 2)^2$	$(4x - 2)^2$
12.	$(6x - 3)^2$	$(7x - 3)^2$

 a
1. $x^2 + 4x + 4 = 0$ Check:
 $(x + 2)(x + 2) = 0$ $(-2)^2 + 4(-2) = 0$
 $ x + 2 = 0$ $4 - 8 + 4 = 0$
 $ x = -2$ $-4 + 4 = 0$

	b	c	
	$x = -3$	$x = -4$	

	a	b	c
2.	$x = -7$	$x = -\frac{2}{3}$	$x = -\frac{3}{4}$
3.	$x = -\frac{3}{2}$	$x = -2$	$x = -3$

 a
1. $x^2 - 4x + 4 = 0$ Check:
 $(x - 2)(x - 2) = 0$ $(2)^2 - 4(2) + 4 = 0$
 $ x - 2 = 0$ $4 - 8 + 4 = 0$
 $ x = 2$ $-4 + 4 = 0$

	b	c	
	3	4	

	a	b	c
2.	5	4	6
3.	2	$\frac{1}{4}$	$\frac{2}{3}$

a

1. $(x + 3)(x + 3) = x(x) + 3(x) + (-3)(x) + (-3)(3)$
$= x^2 + 3x - 3x - 9$
$= x^2 - 9$

b

$x^2 - 64$

	a	*b*
2.	$x^2 - 36$	$x^2 - 49$
3.	$a^2 - b^2$	$y^2 - z^2$
4.	$25 - x^2$	$36 - b^2$
5.	$4x^2 - 9$	$9m^2 - 25$
6.	$64x^2 - 4$	$36x^2 - 25$
7.	$25 - 9x^2$	$49 - 36x^2$
8.	$9 - 49y^2$	$81 - 25a^2$
9.	$9x^2 - 16y^2$	$16m^2 - 36n^2$

	a	*b*
1.	$(x)(x) = x^2$	$x^2 + 8x + 12$
	$(5) + (4) = 9, 9 \cdot x = 9x$	
	$(5)(4) = 20$	
	$x^2 + 9x + 20$	
2.	$x^2 + 4x + 3$	$x^2 + 7x + 12$
3.	$x^2 + 9x + 14$	$x^2 + 10x + 24$
4.	$x^2 + 11x + 10$	$x^2 + 13x + 42$
5.	$x^2 + 3x - 4$	$x^2 - x - 6$
6.	$x^2 + 6x - 16$	$x^2 + 5x - 14$
7.	$x^2 - 5x - 14$	$x^2 - 9x - 10$
8.	$x^2 - 6x + 5$	$x^2 - 10x + 21$
9.	$x^2 - 9x + 20$	$x^2 - 8x + 15$

a

1. $x^2 - y^2$
(1) x is the square root of x^2
y is the square root of y^2
(2) $x + y =$ sum of two square roots
(3) $x - y =$ difference
So, $(x + y)(x - y)$ are the factors
Check: $(x + y)(x - y) = x^2 + xy - xy - y^2$
$= x^2 - y^2$

b

$(x + 6)(x - 6)$

	a	*b*
2.	$(a + b)(a - b)$	$(a + 9)(a - 9)$
3.	$(m + n)(m - n)$	$(m + 3)(m - 3)$
4.	$(x + 10)(x - 10)$	$(x + 11)(x - 11)$
5.	$(5 + a)(5 - a)$	$(8 + a)(8 - a)$
6.	$(15 + x)(15 - x)$	$(30 + z)(30 - z)$
7.	$(2x + 7)(2x - 7)$	$(6x + 8)(6x - 8)$
8.	$(5a + 4)(5a - 4)$	$(7a + 2)(7a - 2)$
9.	$(10x + 3)(10x - 3)$	$(12x + 10)(12x - 10)$
10.	$(5x + 5y)(5x - 5y)$	$(4x + 9y)(4x - 9y)$

a

1. $x^2 + 8x + 15$
(1) $x =$ square root of first term
(2) (3)(5)   These are factors of the third
(−3)(−5)   term. In this example, both
(1)(15)   factors must be positive or
(−1)(−15)   both must be negative since the
third term (+15) is positive.
(3) $3 + 5 = 8$ Two factors are added to find the
coefficient of the middle term.
So, $(x + 3)(x + 5)$ are the two binomial factors.
Check: $(x + 3)(x + 5) = x(x) + 3(x) + 5(x) + 3(5)$
$= x^2 + 3x + 5x + 15$
$= x^2 + 8x + 15$

b

$(x + 2)(x + 3)$

	a	*b*
2.	$(x + 2)(x + 1)$	$(x + 2)(x + 6)$
3.	$(x + 2)(x + 5)$	$(x + 1)(x + 8)$
4.	$(x + 6)(x - 2)$	$(x + 10)(x - 2)$
5.	$(x - 2)(x + 4)$	$(x + 8)(x - 3)$
6.	$(x - 6)(x + 2)$	$(x - 10)(x + 2)$
7.	$(x - 10)(x + 1)$	$(x - 12)(x + 2)$
8.	$(x - 3)(x - 4)$	$(x - 4)(x - 5)$

a

1. $a^2 - 49 = 0$
$(a - 7)(a + 7) = 0$
$a - 7 = 0 \qquad a + 7 = 0$
$a = 7 \qquad\quad a = -7$
$a = \pm 7$
Check: $(7)^2 - 49 = 0 \qquad (-7)^2 - 49 = 0$
$49 - 49 = 0 \qquad\quad 49 - 49 = 0$

b	*c*	
± 8	± 9	

	a	*b*	*c*
2.	± 12	± 20	± 4
3.	$\pm \frac{5}{2}$	$\pm \frac{5}{2}$	$\pm \frac{2}{3}$
4.	± 3	± 2	± 2

Page 157

a

1. $x^2 + 7x + 12 = 0$
$(x + 4)(x + 3) = 0$
$x + 4 = 0 \quad x + 3 = 0$
$x = -4 \quad\quad x = -3$
$-4, -3$
Check: $(-4)^2 + 7(-4) + 12 = 0$
$16 - 28 + 12 = 0$
$-12 + 12 = 0$

$(-3)^2 + 7(-3) + 12 = 0$
$9 - 21 + 12 = 0$
$-12 + 12 = 0$

	b	*c*
	$-6, -1$	$-4, -5$

	a	*b*	*c*
2.	$-2, 4$	$6, -1$	$10, -1$
3.	$11, -3$	$-4, 11$	$-3, 13$
4.	$1, 6$	$1, 4$	$2, 10$

Page 158

a

1.
$\quad\quad\quad\quad\quad F \quad O \quad I \quad L$
$(x + 2)(2x + 3) = x(2x) + 3x + 2(2x) + 2(3)$
$= 2x^2 + 3x + 4x + 6$
$= 2x^2 + 7x + 6$

b
$2x^2 + 5x + 2$

	a	*b*
2.	$2x^2 + 5xy + 2y^2$	$2x^2 + 5xy + 3y^2$
3.	$2x^2 + 11xy + 5y^2$	$2x^2 + 7xy + 3y^2$
4.	$2x^2 + 5x - 3$	$2x^2 + x - 3$
5.	$2x^2 + 3xy - 2y^2$	$2x^2 - 3xy - 2y^2$
6.	$3x^2 - 5x - 2$	$2x^2 + 2xy - 12y^2$
7.	$2x^2 - 7x + 3$	$2x^2 - 9x + 4$
8.	$2x^2 - 7xy + 3y^2$	$2x^2 - 5x + 3$
9.	$2x^2 - 5xy + 2y^2$	$6x^2 - 9xy + 3y^2$

Page 159

a

1. $2x^2 + 5x + 2$

Factors for first term   Factors for third term
$2x^2 = (2x)(x)$ $2 = (2)(1)$
$\quad\quad\quad\quad\quad\quad\quad\quad 2 = (-2)(-1)$

Possible factor pairs   Middle term
$(2x + 2)(x + 1)$ $2x + 2x = 4x$ No
$(2x + 1)(x + 2)$ $4x + x = 5x$ Yes
$2x^2 + 5x + 2 = (2x + 1)(x + 2)$

b
$(3x + 2)(x + 1)$

	a	*b*
2.	$(3x + 1)(x + 2)$	$(2x + 3)(x + 1)$
3.	$(2x - 1)(x - 3)$	$(2x - 1)(x - 4)$
4.	$(2y - 1)(y - 2)$	$(3x - 2)(x - 2)$
5.	$(2x - 1)(x + 2)$	$(3x - 2)(x + 1)$
6.	$(2y + 3)(y - 2)$	$(3x + 4)(x - 2)$

Page 160

1.

	Numbers	Sum	
Guess:	2, 2, 12	$2 + 2 + 12 = 16$	Too high
Guess:	2, 3, 8	$2 + 3 + 8 = 13$	Too high
Guess:	2, 4, 6	$2 + 4 + 6 = 12$	Correct!

The numbers are 2, 4, and 6.
2. 1 quarter, 4 nickels, and 4 pennies
3. 3, 5, 9   **4.** 35 and 45

Page 161

5. 27   **6.** 54   **7.** 24   **8.** 41   **9.** 43, 52
10. 853, 764   **11.** 7   **12.** 4

Page 162

a

1.
$\quad\quad\quad 2x^2 + 5x + 2 = 0$
$(2x + 1)(x + 2) = 0$
$2x + 1 = 0 \quad x + 2 = 0$
$2x = -1 \quad\quad x = -2$
$x = -\frac{1}{2}$

Check: $2(-\frac{1}{2})^2 + 5(-\frac{1}{2}) + 2 = 0$
$2(\frac{1}{4}) - 2\frac{1}{2} + 2 = 0$
$\frac{1}{2} - 2\frac{1}{2} + 2 = 0$
$-2 + 2 = 0$

$2(-2)^2 + 5(-2) + 2 = 0$
$2(4) - 10 + 2 = 0$
$8 - 10 + 2 = 0$
$-2 + 2 = 0$

	b	*c*
	$-\frac{1}{2}, -5$	$-1, -\frac{3}{2}$

	a	*b*	*c*
2.	$2, \frac{1}{2}$	$\frac{1}{2}, 5$	$\frac{3}{2}, 1$
3.	$\frac{1}{2}, -2$	$-\frac{1}{2}, 2$	$1, -\frac{3}{2}$
4.	$-1, \frac{5}{3}$	$1, -\frac{5}{3}$	$-5, \frac{1}{3}$

Page 163

	a	*b*	*c*
1.	±7	2	$5, -1$
2.	-5	$-3, 4$	$5, 10$
3.	1	$-3, 10$	$-1, -\frac{3}{2}$
4.	$-2, -\frac{1}{2}$	$1, -\frac{5}{3}$	8
5.	5, 15	-3	$-1, 3$

Page 164

1. -6 or 5
2. $-10, -9$ or $9, 10$
3. 4 or -5
4. 5 or -4
5. $-10, -8$ or $8, 10$
6. $9, 11$ or $-9, -11$
7. 4 or -6
8. 15 m, 20 m
9. 10 cm, 30 cm
10. 10 m, 20 m

Page 165

a

1. $x^2 - 4x = 3$

$x^2 - 4x + 4 = 3 + 4$ Note that $\frac{1}{2}(-4) = -2$ and $(-2)^2 = 4$.

$(x - 2)^2 = 7$ Factor.

$x - 2 = \pm\sqrt{7}$ Find the square root of both sides.

Solve each equation.

$x - 2 = \sqrt{7}$ $\qquad$ $x - 2 = -\sqrt{7}$
$x = 2 + \sqrt{7}$ $\qquad$ $x = 2 - \sqrt{7}$

$2 \pm \sqrt{7}$

b $\qquad$ **c**

$3 \pm \sqrt{11}$ $\qquad$ $6 \pm \sqrt{30}$

	a	**b**	**c**
2.	$-3 \pm \sqrt{13}$	$4 \pm \sqrt{13}$	$2 \pm \sqrt{6}$
3.	$-4, 2$	$-4, 8$	$2 \pm \sqrt{3}$
4.	$-4 \pm \sqrt{2}$	$-3 \pm \sqrt{2}$	$1 \pm \sqrt{2}$

Page 166

a

1. $x^2 + 5x + 6 = 0$ $\qquad$ $a = 1, b = 5, c = 6$

$x = \dfrac{-b \pm \sqrt{b^2 - 4ac}}{2a}$

$x = \dfrac{-5 \pm \sqrt{(5)^2 - 4(1)(6)}}{2(1)}$

$x = \dfrac{-5 \pm \sqrt{25 - 24}}{2(1)}$

$x = \dfrac{-5 \pm \sqrt{1}}{2} = \dfrac{-5 \pm 1}{2}$

$x = \dfrac{-5 + 1}{2}$ $\qquad$ $x = \dfrac{-5 - 1}{2}$

$x = -2$ $\qquad$ $x = -3$

Check: $(-2)^2 + 5(-2) + 6 = 0$
$\qquad$ $4 - 10 + 6 = 0$
$\qquad$ $-6 + 6 = 0$
$\qquad$ $(-3)^2 + 5(-3) + 6 = 0$
$\qquad$ $9 - 15 + 6 = 0$
$\qquad$ $-6 + 6 = 0$

b $\qquad$ **c**

$-\frac{1}{2}, -2$ $\qquad$ $\frac{1}{4}, 2$

	a	**b**	**c**
2.	$\frac{1}{2}, 3$	$\frac{1}{2}, 6$	$-\frac{4}{5}, 1$
3.	$\frac{1}{2}, -1$	$\frac{5}{3}, -4$	$-5, 3$

Page 167

a

1. $x^2 - 2x - 2 = 0$ $\qquad$ $a = 1, b = -2, c = -2$

$x = \dfrac{-b \pm \sqrt{b^2 - 4ac}}{2a}$

$x = \dfrac{-(-2) \pm \sqrt{(-2)^2 - 4(1)(-2)}}{2(1)}$

$x = \dfrac{2 \pm \sqrt{4 + 8}}{2}$

$x = \dfrac{2 \pm \sqrt{12}}{2}$

$x = \dfrac{2 \pm \sqrt{4 \times 3}}{2}$

$x = \dfrac{2 \pm 2\sqrt{3}}{2} = \dfrac{2}{2} \pm \dfrac{2\sqrt{3}}{2}$

$x = 1 \pm \sqrt{3}$

b $\qquad$ **c**

$\dfrac{4 \pm \sqrt{10}}{2}$ $\qquad$ $\dfrac{-3 \pm \sqrt{17}}{4}$

	a	**b**	**c**
2.	$\dfrac{2 \pm \sqrt{10}}{3}$	$\dfrac{5 \pm \sqrt{97}}{12}$	$\dfrac{3 \pm \sqrt{29}}{10}$
3.	$\dfrac{5 \pm \sqrt{13}}{6}$	$\dfrac{3 \pm \sqrt{69}}{10}$	$\dfrac{-5 \pm \sqrt{33}}{4}$

Page 168

Strategies selected may vary.

1. Use logic.
   78 sq ft
2. Find a pattern
   75.6 gal
3. Make a drawing
   216 sq ft
4. Work backward
   $6.10

Page 169

5. Make a table
   15
6. Use logic
   Mary, Meg, Max, Molly
7. Estimation
   17 sq yd
8. Guess and check
   5
9. Make a drawing
10. Find a pattern
    2 hours

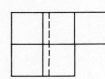

Page 170

1. Let $x =$ the number

   Then $\frac{1}{2}x^2 = 2x + 16$

   Rearrange into $ax^2 + bx + c = 0$

   $$\frac{1}{2}x^2 - 2x - 16 = 0$$

   Then $a = \frac{1}{2}$, $b = -2$, $c = -16$

   Substitute into the quadratic formula.

   $$x = \frac{-b \pm \sqrt{b^2 - 4ac}}{2a}$$

   $$x = \frac{-(-2) \pm \sqrt{(-2)^2 - 4(\frac{1}{2})(-16)}}{2(\frac{1}{2})}$$

   $$x = \frac{2 \pm \sqrt{4 + 32}}{1}$$

   $x = 2 \pm \sqrt{36} = 2 \pm 6$
   $x = 2 + 6 \qquad x = 2 - 6$
   $x = 8 \qquad\quad x = -4$

   Check: $\frac{1}{2}(8)^2 = 2(8) + 16 \quad \frac{1}{2}(-4)^2 = 2(-4) + 16$

   $\qquad \frac{1}{2}(64) = 16 + 16 \quad \frac{1}{2}(16) = -8 + 16$

   $\qquad\qquad 32 = 16 + 16 \qquad\qquad 8 = 8$

   Both 8 and -4 satisfy the conditions of the problem.

2. $x(x + 2) = 143$
   11, 13 or $-13, -11$

3. $x(x + 2) = 323$
   17, 19 or $-19, -17$

4. $x^2 - x = 72$
   -8 or 9

5. $w(2w + 10) = 672$
   Length = 42 in.
   Width = 16 in.

6. $l(\frac{1}{2}l - 11) = 700$
   Length = 50 cm
   Width = 14 cm

Page 171   Unit 7 Review

	a	b
1.	$x^2 - y^2$	$16 - 48t + 36t^2$
2.	$(x + y)^2$	$(x - 4y)^2$
3.	$(x - 5)(x + 5)$	$(10 - x)(10 + x)$
4.	$(x + 1)(x + 4)$	$(x - 4)(x + 1)$
5.	-5	-8
6.	± 7	± 4
7.	$-2, -\frac{3}{2}$	$3 \pm \sqrt{11}$

c

1. $2x^2 + 7xy - 4y^2$
2. $(5x - 4)^2$
3. $(8 - 4x)(8 + 4x)$
4. $(3x - 2)(x + 1)$
5. -4
6. $-1, -4$
7. $4 \pm \sqrt{13}$
8. $w(w + 10) = 75$
   Length = 15 in.
   Width = 5 in.
9. $x(x + 1) = 90$
   $-10, -9$ or 9, 10

	a	b	c
1.	$9x^2 + 7x + 4y$	$-30a^2b$	$-207a^4b^5$
2.	$\frac{9y}{x}$	$6a^2 + ab - b^2$	$2m$
3.	$4x$	4	$-2x + 3y$
4.	± 4	± 5	8
5.	4	30	± 2
6.	$(\frac{1}{2}, -7)$	$(-2, 3)$	$(5, 2)$

7.

a

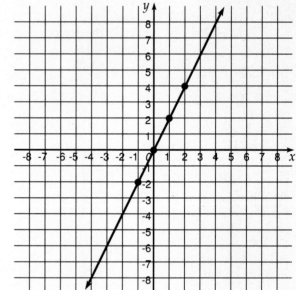

b

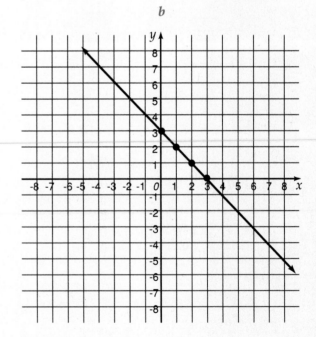

FINAL REVIEW

Page 173

	a	b
1.	9a	5 − n

	a	b	c	d
2.	26	10	0	23
3.	18	20	23	43
4.	−7	16	−39	53
5.	6	4	−27	−30
6.	−18	60	6	−13
7.	−10x	12ab	8.1x	1.1y
8.	2x − 2	−2m + 3	6c − 12	r − 10

Page 174

9. 120 sq m
10. 615.44 sq in.
11. 10 ft
12. 125 mph
13. $16.25
14. 25° C

	a	b	c	d
15.	6	50	−9	48
16.	48	−16	6	3
17.	6	2	3	5
18.	6	4	6	5

19. 14 yr, 42 yr
20. 30, 60, 90
21. 9
22. Length = 40 cm
    Width = 20 cm

Page 175

	a	b
23.	−4	$24a^2bc$
24.	r^6s^{10}	$5a^2$
25.	$2a$	$2x$
26.	$\frac{6}{5x}$	$\frac{2}{y}$
27.	$6m + 3n$	$4x^2 − 8xy − 3x + 6y$

	c
23.	$−49x^3y^3$
24.	$−\frac{2n^2}{m}$
25.	$−35x^3 − 12y^2$
26.	$\frac{3 + 5xy}{2}$
27.	$−7c^3 + 7c^2d^3$

28.

a

x	y
−2	−6
−1	−5
0	−4
1	−3
2	−2

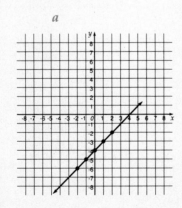

b

Answers may vary.

x	y
−2	7
−1	4
0	1
1	−2
2	−5

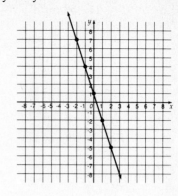

	a	b	c
29.	(5, 2)	(−26, 22)	(6, 1)

Page 176

	a	b
30.	10	$4xy^3$
31.	$4x^2 − 4xy + y^2$	$9x^2 + 12x − 5$
32.	$x < 7$	$a < 10$
33.	±6	4
34.	$(x + 4)(x + 1)$	$(2x + 7)(2x − 7)$
35.	$(x − 3)^2$	$(3x + 1)^2$
36.	−7	$\frac{3}{4}$

	c
30.	$3a^2$
31.	$2x^2 + 13x + 15$
32.	$y > −6$
33.	5
34.	$(3x − 2)(x + 1)$
35.	$(5 − 7x)^2$
36.	$−\frac{3}{2}, 1$

37. Length = 50 ft
    Width = 20 ft
38. Length = 30 m
    Width = 20m

MASTERY TEST

Page 177

	a	b
1.	$\frac{7}{n}$	r + 3

	a	b	c	d
2.	38	20	0	3
3.	45	100	22	27
4.	−13	8	−27	42
5.	6	8	−15	−27
6.	−35	56	7	−9
7.	−9x	ab	6.8x	3.2y
8.	2x − 1	2m − 2	12c − 16	2r − 6

9. 112 sq in.   10. 1384.74 sq cm
11. 10 ft   12. 50 mph
13. $77   14. 30°

	a	b	c	d
15.	7	30	−12	68
16.	27	−20	7	4
17.	4	−2	7	3
18.	12	15	12	7

19. 36, 18   20. 20, 60, 80
21. 9   22. 26 cm, 13 cm

	a	b	c
23.	−7	$15x^2yz$	$-6a^3b^3$
24.	$r^{12}s^6$	$4r^3$	$\frac{-3d}{c}$
25.	$3a$	$2a$	$-37x^2 - 14y^4$

	a	b
26.	$\frac{9}{4m^2}$	$\frac{3}{b}$
27.	$28m - 4n$	$3x^2 + 5x - 12xy - 20y$

c
26. $5 + 7r$
27. $-2m^4 + 2m^2n^2$
28.

x	y
−2	−5
−1	−4
0	−3
1	−2
2	−1
3	0

a
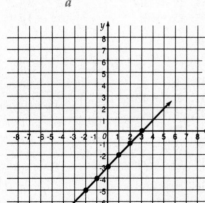

b
x	y
2	−2
1	0
0	2
−1	4
−2	6

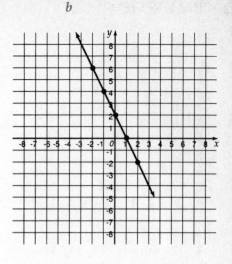

	a	b	c
29.	(5, 4)	(2, 1)	(12, −3)

	a	b
30.	9	$5x^2y^4$
31.	$9x^2 + 6xy + y^2$	$4x^2 + 14x - 8$
32.	$x < 11$	$b < 6$
33.	±4	7
34.	$(x + 1)(x + 2)$	$(3x - 1)(3x + 1)$
35.	$(x - 4)^2$	$(5x + 1)^2$
36.	−6	$2\frac{1}{2}$

c
30. $4a$
31. $2x^2 + 13x + 21$
32. $y > -5$
33. 10
34. $(3x + 1)(x - 2)$
35. $(4 - 3x)^2$
36. $\frac{1}{2}$, −3
37. 8 feet   38. 6 meters